The Art of Carl Fabergé

by the same author

✳

EIGHTEENTH CENTURY GOLD BOXES OF EUROPE

I. Coronation Presentation Box in red gold enamelled translucent chartreuse yellow on sun-ray and wave-patterned grounds, with green gold carved husk borders, the lid mounted with a diamond set trellis with opaque black enamelled Romanoff double-headed eagles and the Imperial cypher of Nicholas II in diamonds against a sun-ray background enamelled opalescent oyster. This sumptuous box was given by the Tsarina to her husband on Easter Day 1897, the day she received the Coronation Egg

Signed: A.H.   Gold mark: crossed anchors $3\frac{5}{8}'' \times 2\frac{9}{16}'' \times \frac{15}{16}''$

In a private collection in the United States

THE ART OF
CARL FABERGÉ

by

A. Kenneth Snowman

FABER AND FABER LIMITED

24 Russell Square

London

First published 1953
by Faber and Faber Limited
24 Russell Square London WC1
Second impression 1955
Revised and enlarged edition 1962
Third edition 1964
Reprinted 1968
Printed in Great Britain by
R. MacLehose and Company Limited
The University Press Glasgow

SBN 571 05113 8

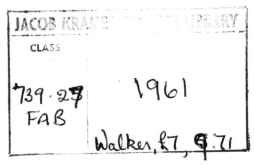
© *A. Kenneth Snowman 1962*

FOR SALLIE
AND NICHOLAS

Foreword

It is a special pleasure for me to introduce and bless this book, which I know is the result of the most careful and tireless research. My late father was celebrated for his minute attention to detail and thorough knowledge of the subject in hand, and I feel for this reason he would have approved of the method adopted by my friend Kenneth Snowman in his analysis.

We live at such a feverish pace in our modern world that we sometimes forget that not so long ago craftsmen were still able to work unhurriedly and with a real love of creation. It is important that we should be reminded that we are in danger of losing a heritage of incalculable value. As more is done for the comfort of man, so he seems to become more and more incapable of doing anything for himself.

Our world is spinning round too quickly to allow us to think clearly, let alone to create things of eternal beauty.

I well remember the mounting excitement which spread imperceptibly throughout the St. Petersburg workshop as each year the Easter Eggs for presentation to the two Tsarinas gradually took shape and neared completion. It is, therefore, particularly gratifying for me to turn the pages of the illustrated catalogue of these Eggs, which is contained in this book.

In all, I am delighted to salute a fitting monument to the achievement of my dear father.

Eugène Fabergé

PARIS, *May* 1952

Contents

Illustrations

COLOUR PLATES

Illustrations

Illustrations

MONOCHROME PLATES

Illustrations

Illustrations

15

Illustrations

Illustrations

Illustrations

18

Illustrations

Acknowledgments

I wish to record my sincere gratitude to His late Majesty King George VI and Her Majesty the Queen Mother for graciously allowing me such ready access to the unique and splendid collection of Fabergé objects at Sandringham; no study of this goldsmith's work could be regarded as truly representative which neglected to show characteristic examples from the collection that started as Queen Alexandra's own. I should like to express my grateful thanks to Her Majesty the Queen for permission to reproduce these pieces.

I am deeply indebted to Her late Majesty Queen Mary, who not only graciously consented to permit items from her own exquisite collection to be included in this work, but made a personal selection. Queen Mary was acknowledged to be the most discriminating and imaginative of connoisseurs whose knowledge of and feeling for Fabergé's work was quite unrivalled, and the beautiful objects from Marlborough House included here, demonstrate the justice of this recognition most eloquently.

The French egg in the Royal Collection at Rosenberg is reproduced by kind permission of His Majesty the King of Denmark, and the nephrite bowl supported by Brahmin figures by permission of His Majesty the King of Siam.

I wish to thank Her Royal Highness the Duchess of Kent for so readily allowing me to include a photograph of her interesting cigarette-case. As a result of the great kindness of Her late Imperial Highness the Grand Duchess Xenia, I am able to reproduce a picture of the Imperial Egg from her collection. His Grace the Duke of Devonshire has kindly allowed me to include his lovely box with painted panels of Chatsworth.

A special note of gratitude is due to Sir Harold and Lady Zia Wernher for granting me the freedom of their beautiful collection at Luton Hoo, the first, and so far the only, museum in this country where the art of Fabergé is represented.

Acknowledgments

I extend my sincere thanks to all the collectors of Fabergé objects who have allowed me to reproduce photographs of their treasures; without their generosity this book could never have become a reality.

Throughout the preparation of my manuscript, I had the unique advantage of numerous detailed conversations with Fabergé's eldest son Eugène on every aspect of his father's art, and it is a particular pleasure for me to acknowledge my sincere gratitude to him.

Before his death in 1951, M. Agathon Fabergé wrote to me by letter from Finland, saying that it would have been difficult for him to have added anything at all to what his brother had already told me. The late M. Alexander Fabergé, however, Carl's third son, was able to tell me a great deal that was helpful, especially in connection with the technical side of enamelling. I should like especially to express my sincere thanks to the late Mr. H. C. Bainbridge whose generous and valuable advice and friendly interest were forthcoming at all times.

My search for relevant material in museums and libraries in this country and abroad was always made easier by the helpful co-operation of those in charge; I want especially to acknowledge the assistance accorded to me by the British Museum, the Victoria and Albert Museum, the Wallace Collection, the Geological Museum and the Laboratory of the Diamond, Pearl and Precious Stone Trade section of the London Chamber of Commerce, the New South Wales Museum of Technology, the Virginia Museum of Fine Arts, and the Walters Art Gallery, Baltimore; the Cabinet des Estampes of the Bibliothèque Nationale, the Musée des Arts Décoratifs in Paris and the Musée Lambinet in Versailles. For valuable technical or historical advice or for material assistance in research, I want to record my thanks to the late Baroness Buxhoeveden; The late Marquess of Carisbrooke; the late Prince Vladimir Galitzine; Lady (David) Kelly; Sir William Seeds, K.C.M.G.; Prince Youssoupoff; the late Madame E. Balletta; the late Mr. S. M. Benjamin; Mr. Hans Beran; Mr. Gudmund Boesen; Mr. Henrik C. Bolin; Mr. J. S. Callam; M. Charles Theodore Fabergé; M. Leon Grinberg; Mr. Victor Hammer; the late Mr. W. Hanneford Smith; Mr. Simon Harcourt-Smith; Mr. Bertram Hill, Mr. Henry Hill and Mr. Sidney Hill; the late Mr. H. de Koningh; Mr. Jack Linsky; the late Major Alfred A. Longden; Mr. E. Moghilevkine, A.R.S.M.; Miss June Nakamura; Sir John and Lady Nicholls; M. Paul Nicoulin; M. Victor Nikolaef; Mr. George Pimenov, Mr. Alfred Pocock,

Acknowledgments

Mr. A. Poklewski-Koziell, Madame Betsy Popoff, Mr. W. F. Ramsden, Mr. Marvin C. Ross; Mr. Alexander Schaffer; Mr. Sacheverell Sitwell; the late Captain Harold Spink; M. George Stein; Mrs. E. Tomlin; Mr. Fred Uhlman; Mr. Horace Wallick; Mr. Erhard Warnecke; the late Mr. Harry Wartski; Mr. R. Webster and the late Mr. K. W. Woollcombe-Boyce.

The following Business Houses have supplied me with much valuable material: 'A la Vieille Russie' of New York, Messrs. Berry-Hill of London and New York, the Hammer Galleries of New York, Messrs. Spink and Son Ltd. of London, and Messrs. Wartski of London and Llandudno. Mr. Herbert Tillander, the well-known Crown Jeweller of Helsingfors, and his chief designer, Oskar Pihl Jr., have helped me a very great deal in my search for accurate details regarding Fabergé's craftsmen.

Professor Alfred Chapuis has kindly allowed me to use four photographs from his scholarly work 'Les Automates' published in 1949 by Editions du Griffon in Neuchatel.

The two illustrations of His Majesty King George VI's cigarette-cases shown on Pl. 199 were first reproduced in Mr. Bainbridge's splendid Monograph on the Life and Work of Fabergé and are here included by permission of His late Majesty, and of Messrs. B. T. Batsford Ltd., the publishers of the work. My thanks are due to the indefatigable Miss White of *The Antique Collector* for allowing me to use material from an article I contributed in 1945. The editor of the *Connoisseur*, Mr. Guy Ramsey, has also accorded me the same favour in regard to a contribution in June 1955.

A book of this type stands or falls by the quality of the photographs reproduced, and in this respect I have been handsomely served by Messrs. A. C. Cooper Ltd. and The Fine Art Engravers Ltd., with a special note of thanks to Mr. Jack Philpin, whose unerring taste and unflagging energy have contributed so much. The extra plates for this edition have necessitated further colour photography, and the work has been carried out with great care and, I think, success by J. J. O. Webb, F.R.P.S. in London and James Dull of Messrs. Taylor and Dull in New York. I should like to thank Mr. Morley Kennerley, Mr. Frank Herrmann and Mr. M. Shaw of Messrs. Faber and Faber Ltd. for their understanding and seemingly inexhaustible patience.

A debt of gratitude is owing to the late Morris Wartski, my grandfather, who together with my father, Alderman Emanuel Snowman, O.B.E., J.P., had the imagination and vision to make possible the early trips to Russia

Acknowledgments

resulting in so many priceless examples of Fabergé's work, including many of the Imperial Eggs, being brought to this country.

Finally, a word of sincere thanks to my wife, whose knowledge of Russian, coupled with her inexhaustible capacity for continental travel, has helped me so much in my search for clues along a trail growing fainter every day.

A. K. S.

II. Imperial Presentation Box in dull yellow gold set with brilliant diamonds with floral and foliate motifs in dull red and green golds, the lid enamelled opalescent rose against an engraved radiating wave-patterned background with the Imperial cypher of Nicholas II applied to an opalescent oyster-enamelled sun-ray plaque

Signed: H.W.   Gold Mark: crossed anchors $3\frac{11}{16}'' \times 2\frac{1}{2}'' \times \frac{13}{16}''$

In a private collection in England

Preface to the Second Edition

In 1953, the year of her Coronation, Her Majesty the Queen, with customary generosity, allowed the incomparable Sandringham collection of Fabergé animals, flowers and miscellaneous objects, including the Colonnade Egg, to be exhibited publicly for the first time, and the catalogue compiled by Messrs. Wartski, who had the privilege of holding the exhibition, contained illustrations of items not previously shown or reproduced, together with others in the collection of Her Majesty Queen Elizabeth the Queen Mother, and these also are now included here. One of the most enchanting of the Easter Eggs, given in 1914 to the Empress, a gossamer mosaic of coloured gems and diamonds, is now shown in colour as a result, again, of the kindness of Her Majesty the Queen.

One man more than any other has helped me in my research, but it is above all with the sadness of losing a sincere and genial friend, that I have to record the passing in his eighty-seventh year of Fabergé's eldest son Eugène.

When the material for the original edition of this book was delivered some years ago, I realized too well that a very important part of the task I had undertaken had not been accomplished. The Imperial Easter Eggs which form part of the collection in the Kremlin Armoury in Moscow were only represented by either poor photographs taken before the Revolution in which, for example, yellow registered as black, or by inadequate drawings reconstructed from the combined testimony of friends who had actually seen these extraordinary objects. I am now able to include new photographs of the Eggs specially taken for me by the authorities at the Armoury Museum. Several of these Eggs are dated and I have been able to correct the sequence where necessary in the light of this new welcome information. Thanks are due also to Dr. and Mrs. W. S. Hunter of San Francisco for the snapshots taken inside the Armoury.

During my travels in the Soviet Union I was able to obtain photographs of the famous replicas which Fabergé made in diamonds of the Imperial Regalia, and which were put on permanent exhibition in Leningrad at the Hermitage by the Tsar during the goldsmith's lifetime.

Mr. Loevinson-Lessing, a monument of good nature and scholarship, has also sent me, from the Hermitage, photographs of Fabergé drawings and other subjects which I very much wanted to include.

I am particularly grateful to be able, for the first time, to show many examples in colour from what is undoubtedly the most beautiful and extensive private Fabergé collection in the United States.

The famous Balletta collection is now worthily represented: this lovely actress, an object of the twin devotions of both the Grand Duke Alexander and his nephew Nicholas II himself, received a number of charming Fabergé articles as a result of this Imperial concurrence.

A number of objects of special importance which appeared originally in monochrome I am now able to reproduce in colour, giving a far more vivid impression of their natural appearance—several of the Imperial Eggs, further examples from Sir William Seeds's marvellous posse of Russian types, the sensational carving of the gipsy which Eugène Fabergé told me was considered their masterpiece in this genre, and the superb purpurine cat smouldering with a new haughtiness.

As the office blocks rise like huge dead crossword puzzles, and standards of individual craftsmanship fall, the consumer who still has eyes in his head will naturally tend to cherish in a special way any objects which show some evidence of human endeavour—things unavailable in super-markets and chain stores.

It is hardly surprising, then, that articles which have successfully run the critical gauntlet imposed by the stern uncompromising eye of Carl Fabergé should be sought today with all the desperate energy of a rescue operation.

Introduction

So much has been written about the work of Carl Fabergé in newspaper and magazine articles, some of it adulatory, some disparaging, some wildly ecstatic, and some unequivocally hostile, that a sober evaluation of his achievement may serve a useful purpose, as a guide for collectors and connoisseurs on the one hand, and on the other as an act of justice to one of the finest goldsmiths and jewellers of all times.

This achievement can be broadly divided under two main heads. In the first place, it was given to Fabergé to understand, master, and in many cases perfect the complicated techniques of his craft, to gather together the threads of the accumulated experience of generations of craftsmen in every corner of the world. From these many sources he gradually evolved his own personal and recognizable style which therefore is, in a sense, a summing up of those earlier styles.

Once armed with this technical proficiency, Carl Fabergé and his younger brother Agathon were in a position to make their second positive contribution to the decorative art of their country. This contribution turned out to be one of the most astonishing revolutions in the history of fashion.

They decreed, and the entire court and those on its fringe meekly obeyed this decree, that in the matter of objects of *virtu* and jewels generally, the emphasis previously placed squarely on sheer value should be shifted, without compromise, on to craftsmanship. In other words, the sincerity of a gift was to be measured rather by the amount of imagination shown than by a noisy demonstration of wealth. To appreciate fully just how remarkable was this change of heart, it must be remembered that Russia at the turn of the century, living on the dwindling capital of a glittering past, was very near cultural bankruptcy, while the administration was committing moral suicide by its unbridled corruption.

The arts that delight the eye, as opposed to those that charm the ear or stir the imagination, were never particularly strong in Russia, and it is not for nothing that even a passing reference to *les arts décoratifs* of that country, especially in the nineteenth century, inevitably strikes a chill in the heart of any amateur of the beautiful.

In comparing Tsarist Russia with what we know of its Soviet counterpart, we are inclined to overstate the brilliance of the epoch that is past; the legend has grown, distance lending its traditional enchantment, that life at Court, for example, was rather like being present on the stage during a non-stop gala performance of 'Aurora's Wedding'. The testimony of those who actually remember things as they were, contradicts this picture, however, and we are left with the impression that life as lived in the various Royal Residences must have been a great deal more humdrum than is popularly believed.

Apart from the attractions of the Imperial Ballet and one or two theatre groups, the House of Fabergé must have stood out of the surrounding shadows like a beacon in a dark night; indeed, from the point of view of the Imperial Family itself, the combined duties of State affairs and the ceremonial demands of the Church must have made its existence little short of a fundamental necessity.

How eagerly the Tsar and his entourage, and in fact anyone with enough roubles to spare, must have sought out and vied for the possession of each new golden treasure or jewelled confection produced by Monsieur Fabergé!

Creative patronage, as exemplified by the Medici or the Electors of Saxony, however, was a far cry from the purely customer-shopkeeper attitude which prevailed at this time. With a few notable exceptions, such as one or two of the Grand Dukes and a number of private families, the only part the eventual owner of the object had to play was to make his selection and settle the bill. It is precisely the difficulty encountered nowadays in fulfilling the last part of this contract that is responsible for the near extinction of first-class goldsmiths, lapidaries and, above all, enamellers.

The call today is for quick and cheap production and it is no wonder that the articles which emerge from this demand lack for the most part any genuine character whatever. A modern cigarette-case, with all its 'clean lines', is usually one soulless piece of machinery emitted from a larger and more complicated— but equally soulless—piece of machinery.

Fabergé's good fortune, and for that matter ours, was that he was born into an age which was still able to afford him—he could experiment with his materials without always having to keep a weather eye on the clock to see if he was up to schedule. He extracted the best service from modern machinery without ever allowing it to enslave his inspiration. In short, he proved himself at all times equal to the golden opportunities that were offered and brought about a renaissance in his craft.

To call Fabergé the last of the great goldsmiths, as many have done, is possibly to strike too pessimistic a note, but it must be admitted that the advent of a rival to that proud title, considered from the viewpoint of our own troubled times, does not appear to be imminent.

CHAPTER I

The House of Fabergé

In 1685 the Fabergés, natives of Picardy, in common with many other Huguenot families, found it increasingly difficult to lead a tolerable life in their own country. The Revocation of the Edict of Nantes was the signal for hundreds of thousands of Protestants to take flight, moving doggedly over Europe as refugees seeking shelter in more sympathetic lands.

The adventures that befell them during their one and a half centuries' wandering are not recorded. Although it has proved impossible up to the present to confirm or refute it, a tradition persists that a goldsmith from Würtemberg named Farberger or Farbiger, working in Russia under the patronage of Catherine the Great, was in fact an ancestor of the Fabergés of St. Petersburg. Whether or not this is true, there is ample evidence of the vital part that the early German craftsmen played in moulding the style of the modern goldsmith.

All that can be set down with any precision is that before they made their appearance in St. Petersburg in 1842, the Fabergés had changed their name at least twice, once to Fabri or Favri in order to facilitate their exit from France, and again at Schwedt-on-Oder, near Stettin, this time to Fabrier; from thence they must have proceeded, whether directly or circuitously cannot be said, to the Baltic States, where Peter Fabergé, the grandfather of Carl, felt himself sufficiently free to revert to the family name, and become a Russian subject.

It was at Pernau, modern Estonia, that Gustav, Carl Fabergé's father, was born on 30th February, 1814.

We do not know exactly when he removed to St. Petersburg; we only know that, having been apprenticed to Andreas Ferdinand Spiegel, he worked with the celebrated firm of Keibel before opening up in business on his own account in 1842 as goldsmith and jeweller in a small basement in Bolshaya Morskaya Street. His wife was Charlotte Jungstedt, daughter of Carl Jungstedt, a painter of Danish origin. This was the modest beginning of a concern which was to bring about an artistic revolution affecting every branch of the jeweller's art.

The principal figure in this revolution, Peter Carl Fabergé, was born on the 30th May, 1846.

Ever since the Court removed from Moscow to St. Petersburg early in the eighteenth century, a traditionally generous welcome awaited any foreign craftsman of talent, were he French, German or Scandinavian. For about fifty years two Englishmen, Nichols and Plincke, ran a particularly successful business known as 'The English Shop' which they were able to stock from their own silver workshops which Plincke had had the foresight to set up in 1815. This shop was the favourite of the Court until it finally closed its doors in 1870. The next firm to receive as much of the imperial patronage as this was Fabergé's, and by one of those odd historical coincidences, it was in precisely that same year that young Carl took over control of the business.

Gustav Fabergé must have done well in his affairs, because he was able to send his son to one of the best and most fashionable schools in St. Petersburg, the Gymnasium Svetaya Anna, an institution run on rigidly German lines. Gustav himself retired in 1860 to Dresden, the Florence of the Elbe, leaving his business under the charge of his manager Zaiontchkovsky.

Peter Hiskias Pendin, a Finn from St. Michel, and in effect Gustav's partner, friend and general aide-de-camp in his early beginnings, took Carl under his wing, and made himself responsible for his thorough training as a jeweller and goldsmith. He was a genial character with a large and generous view of life, in the tradition of Mishka, the lovable bear in the stories of Chemnitzer and Krylov. He obviously took great pleasure in guiding his friend's son along the paths of fine craftsmanship, exploring the various technical processes, and passing on all the special knowledge he himself had laboriously acquired during his life at the bench. Later, when Fabergé was in a position to do so, he was not slow in rendering a similar service to his first teacher; he it was who made it possible for Pendin's son to study medicine and gain all the diplomas necessary for his profession, becoming eventually the Fabergés' family doctor.

It was the opinion of Eugène, the eldest son of Carl Fabergé, that it would be difficult to exaggerate the importance of Pendin's influence on his father's career, coming, as it did, at the most impressionable period of his life. It may be that his interest in articulated toys, awakened by his frequent visits to the

1. Peter Carl Fabergé sorting a parcel of loose stones. Photographed by Hugo Oeberg, one of his designers in St. Petersburg

2. Gustav Petrovitch Fabergé and his wife, parents of Carl Fabergé, photographed in Dresden

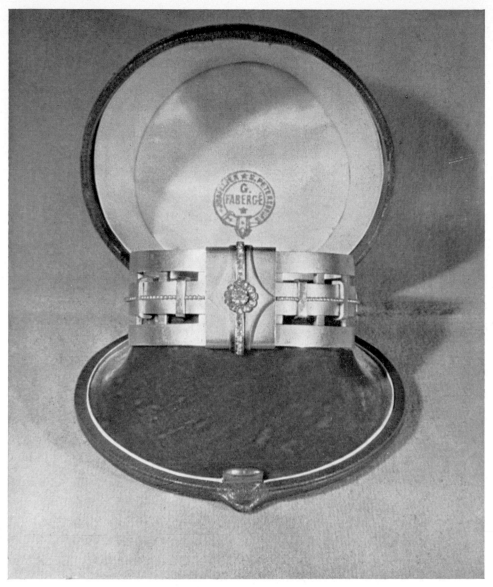

3. Gold Bangle set with brilliant and rose diamonds by Fabergé's father, Gustav, fitted in the original leather case with named lid lining $1\frac{1}{8}'' \times 2\frac{5}{8}''$

4. One of the original stick-on labels used by the firm of Gustav Fabergé

Photograph by permission of Mrs. J. M. Kingsmill

5. Fabergé modelled by Joseph Limburg of Berlin, in 1903. Formerly in the possession of Eugène Fabergé

6. Madame Augusta Fabergé, the gold-smith's wife, photographed in St. Petersburg at the age of 42

7. A corner of Fabergé's apartment in Morskaya Street, over the shop. Part of his collection of *netsuké* is displayed in a show-case. The family stock-pot on the right was brought over from France by the Fabergés. The plaster figure by Limburg on the mantelpiece portrays the monk Don Ugo, and the picture hanging over the sofa where Carl took his siesta, shows Gustav Fabergé as a boy with his parents

8. Fabergé's shop in Morskaya Street, St. Petersburg

9. Compare the busy commercial aspect of the Moscow shop, shown here, with the quiet and exclusive House in St. Petersburg

10. Fabergé's younger brother and partner Agathon, photographed in Dresden, 1892

11. Fabergé's eldest son, Eugène, photographed about 1915

12. François Birbaum, Fabergé's chief designer, photographed in Switzerland, 1935

13. Andrea Marchetti, manager of the Moscow shop. Photographed about 1905

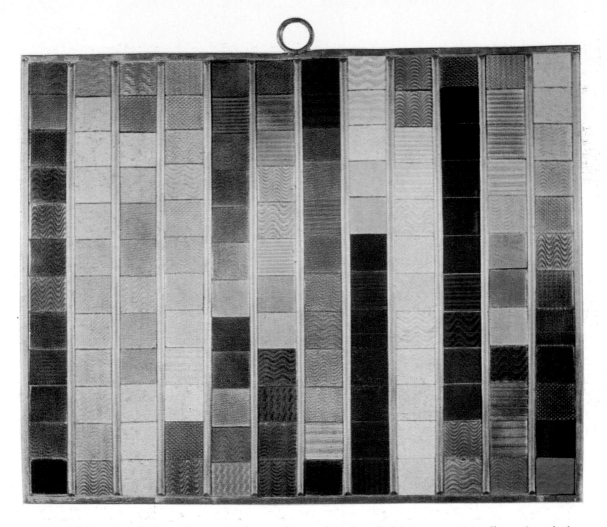

III. One of the original charts showing colours of enamels and *guilloché* patterns on small numbered silver squares. It can be seen hanging in the studio on plate 20
Reproduced with the permission of the late Eugène Fabergé $9\frac{3}{4}'' \times 12\frac{1}{4}''$

14. The reverse side of the colour chart, illustrated opposite, showing the numbers engraved on the back of each square

15

16. Allan Bowe, Fabergé's partner, who was born in Springbok Fontaine, South Africa, photographed about 1900

17. The notice which appeared in the Moscow-German newspaper (Pl. 15 above), announcing the opening of a new shop by Fabergé and Allan Bowe on February 1st, 1887

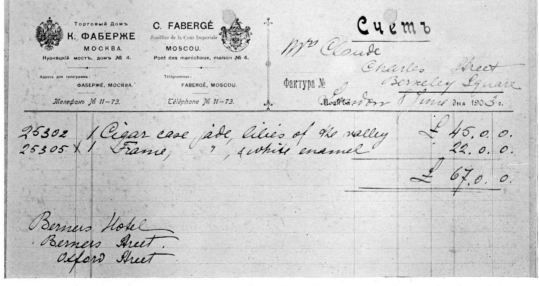

18. An original Moscow invoice made out by Allan Bowe for the London branch

19. The interior of the St. Petersburg shop

20. The studio where most of the twenty-five or so designers worked. Alexander Fabergé is seen on the extreme left, Eugène stands at the back of the room, Oscar May is seated in front of him, Ivan Lieberg sits in the foreground, and Alexander Ivashov stands in front of the library. At the back of the studio, a number of the original wax models used for the animal carvings are seen. This photograph was taken by Nicholas Fabergé

21 and 22. The cover of the catalogue issued by the Moscow house in 1899; it is printed in green with Fabergé's name in red, the words Diamonds, Gold and Silver, in white, gold and silver respectively. The title page reads 'C. Fabergé, supplier to the Court, Gold, Diamonds, and Silverware. Moscow. Kuznetski Most. (Blacksmith's Bridge). House No. 4 of the Merchants' Society'

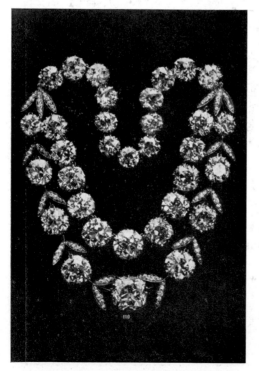

23 and 24. An impressive item always available in stock, reproduced pale blue to indicate the purity of the stones. The following details are given on the facing page: 'A diamond *rivière*, photographed from nature, reproduced life size. The necklace is composed of thirty-three important diamonds of superb quality and of the first water. Price—50,000 roubles. The same size, but in second grade diamonds, Price—30,000 roubles.' The equivalent prices would be £5,000 and £3,000

25 and 26. Two views of the workshop in Moscow, under the control of Mitkievitch, seen standing in the top picture. Original Fabergé photographs

27. The silver workshop under the control of Michael Tchepournov in Moscow. Original Fabergé photograph

29.

28.   30.

28. Alfred Pocock's dismantled studio in Blomfield Road, Venice in London, in 1914. 29. George Stein, who made the coach contained in the Coronation Egg, (Col. Pl. LXXIII), photographed in France after the 1917 revolution. 30. Miniature of Catherine the Great painted by Horace Wallick, an Englishman living in St. Petersburg, from Levitsky's portrait. On the evidence of this work, Wallick was appointed a miniaturist to the House. *In the possession of the artist.* $1\frac{7}{8}'' \times 2\frac{5}{16}''$

IV. Presentation Box in engraved yellow gold with red and green gold carved mounts, enamelled translucent yellow and opalescent white and set with the crowned cypher of Nicholas II in brilliant diamonds with a diamond border surrounded by four Imperial double-headed eagles enamelled opaque black

Signed: M.II.   *In the Collection of Sir William Seeds, K.C.M.G.* $3\frac{3}{16}''$ square, $1''$ depth

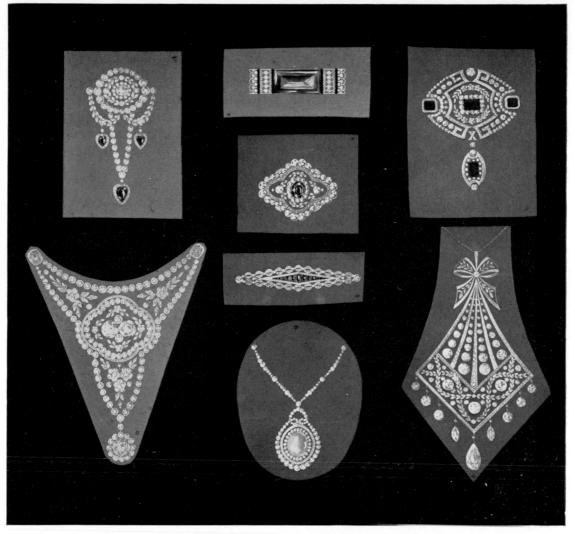

31. Original Fabergé jewellery designs from Holmström's workshop painted in natural colours on celluloid panels and reproduced just under half size.

Left column, top: Cabochon ruby and diamond brooch-pendant. *Below:* Diamond *jabot.*★

Centre column, top: Aquamarine, *calibré* ruby and diamond bar-brooch. *Below:* Ruby and diamond panel-brooch. *Below:* *Pavé* set sapphire and diamond bar-brooch. *Below:* Mecca stone and diamond pendant.★

Right column, top: Emerald and diamond brooch-pendant.★ *Below:* Diamond *corsage* ornament.

Designs marked ★ are by Alma Pihl, the others by Alina Zwerschinskaya.
Reproduced with the permission of Herbert Tillander, Esq.

32. Inside the Moscow shop: from left to right, the various members of the staff shown are Charles Bowe and Oswald Davies (with a selection of the delightful miniature Easter Eggs for which the House was renowned), Nicholas Hobé, Otto Jarke, Lemkuhl, George Piggott, Theodore Juvé and Oliver

33. The silver department of the Moscow shop. Andrea Marchetti is seen at the scales

34, 35, 36. Original Fabergé silver designs from the Hermitage Collection, Leningrad

37, 38. Further Fabergé silver designs from the Hermitage Collection, Leningrad

V. Presentation snuff-box in *quatre-couleur* gold enamelled translucent emerald green on a wave-patterned ground, the sides bordered with opaque white enamel and the lid with enamelled opalescent beads and cabochon rubies, decorated with *ciselé* gold foliate swags and a Louis XVI painted enamel miniature within a rose diamond frame with diamond bow-knots and coloured gold roses

Signed: H.W. Gold mark: 72 $3'' \times 2\frac{5}{16}'' \times 1\frac{3}{16}''$

In the Collection of Charles Clore, Esq.

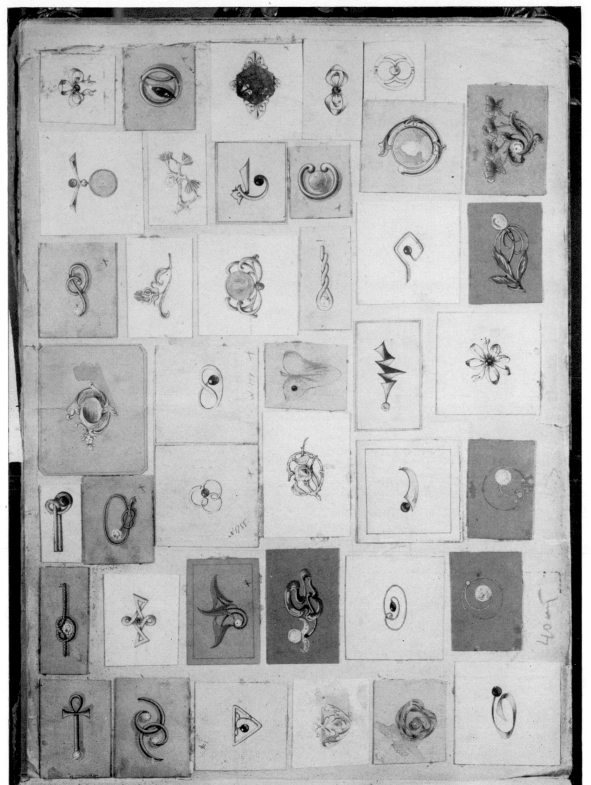

39. A page from an album of original Fabergé jewellery designs probably used in Moscow

40. Pair of engraved red gold taper-sticks, enamelled translucent royal blue and yellow, the Rothschild racing colours, with carved green gold mounts and rock crystal drip-plates

Signed: H.W.   *In the Wernher Collection, Luton Hoo*   Height: $2\frac{3}{4}''$

41. Engraved silver cigarette-box similarly enamelled with polished red and dull green gold carved mounts; the bottom of this fine box is also enamelled in stripes

Signed: H.W.   *In a private collection in England* $5\frac{5}{16}'' \times 4\frac{1}{16}'' \times 2''$

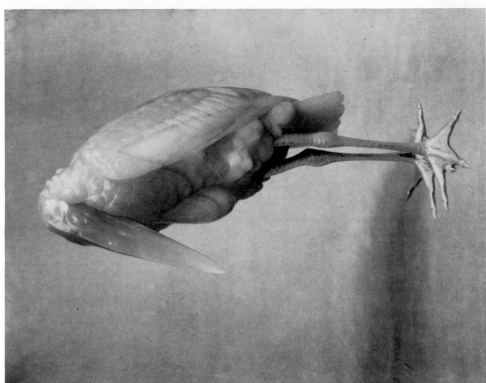

43. Maribou in varicoloured agate of chestnut and grey-blue with gold legs and half-closed eyes in gold. Traditionally believed to be a cartoon figure of Edward VII   Height: 7½"

In the Collection of Dr. J. G. Wurfbain

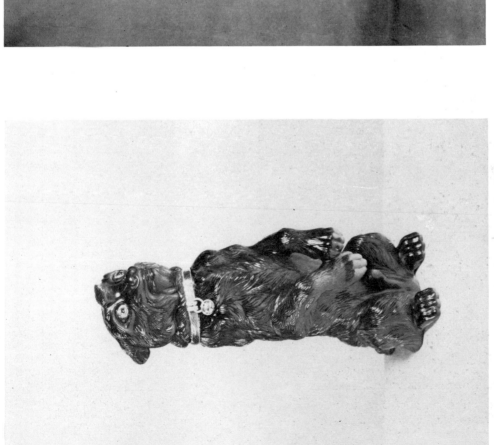

42. A carving of a dog in obsidian with gold collar enamelled translucent ruby red with gold bell and pink diamond eyes.   Height: 6¾"

Originally owned by Madame Balletta

In a private collection in the United States

44 and 45. A postcard sent by Fabergé from Frankfurt to Andrea Marchetti in Italy in 1919: A translation will be found in Appendix D

46. Carl Fabergé photographed at Pully, near Lausanne, in July 1920, two months before his death

VI. Cigarette-case in pink and green ribbed gold with cabochon sapphire thumb-piece
Signed: A★H
$3\frac{3}{4}'' \times 2\frac{5}{8}'' \times \frac{11}{16}''$

VII. Engraved silver powder box enamelled translucent pink, with two small compartments
and a mirror in the lid: decorated with mounts and swags in four colours of gold and three
rose diamond thumb-pieces
Signed: H.W.   *Both in the Collection of Max Harari, Esq.* $4'' \times 2\frac{1}{2}'' \times \frac{11}{16}''$

VIII. Gold musical box presented to the Prince and Princess Youssoupoff on their twenty-fifth
wedding anniversary
In a private collection in the United States
Full description in Appendix D

47. Gold box in the French classic manner, enamelled translucent grey, with green and red gold mounts. Miniature of Catherine the Great, signed by Zehngraf, set in lid within a pearl border. Signed: M.Π. *In a private collection in England.* Diameter: $2\frac{5}{8}''$

48. Moss-agate Easter Egg in Renaissance style, gold mounted and enamelled translucent strawberry and emerald green and opaque white, and set with rose diamonds
Signed: M.Π.   Gold Mark: 72   Height: $3\frac{7}{8}''$
In the Collection of Stavros S. Niarchos

49. Silver seal in the German manner with four caryatids, arm-in-arm, supporting a nephrite ball. Carved silver acanthus leaves decorate the red gold base, which is set with a cornelian. The seal is decorated with two rings of rose diamonds within red gold bands. A very early Fabergé object.   Signed: M.Π.   Height: $2\frac{11}{16}''$
In the Wernher Collection, Luton Hoo

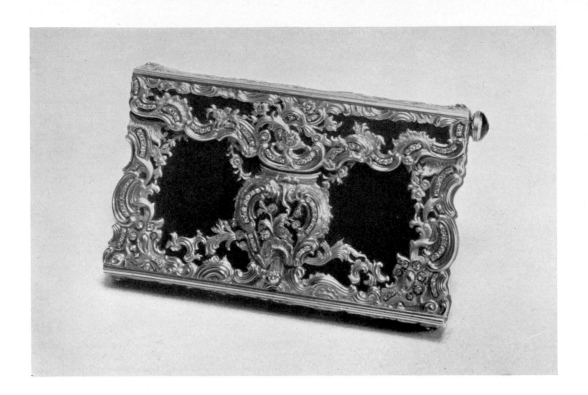

50 and 51. Green jasper notecase elaborately decorated with yellow gold scroll mounts set with rose diamonds in the Louis XV style. Fitted with two yellow silk pockets, a notebook and a gold interchangeable pen and pencil with a jasper cameo of a warrior set in the top

Signed: M.II.   Gold marks: 72 and crossed anchors $4\frac{3}{8}'' \times 2\frac{3}{4}'' \times \frac{5}{8}''$

In the Wernher Collection, Luton Hoo

IX. Snuff-box in engraved red gold enamelled translucent green, decorated with opalescent beads and borders of translucent green and strawberry enamel. The lid is set with an allegorical scene painted in *grisaille* enamels on a panel rimmed with rose diamonds. This box is a pastiche based on the French snuff-box shown on plate 52; they were both originally in the Hermitage Collection

Signed: M.II.   Gold marks: 72 and crossed anchors $3\frac{1}{4}'' \times 2\frac{9}{16}'' \times 1\frac{5}{16}''$

In a private collection in the United States

52. Compare this Louis XVI French snuff-box with the box on Colour Plate IX. Fuller description in Appendix D
In a private collection in the United States

53. Cigarette-case with match compartment and tinder attachment in yellow gold made up of the original two main *repoussé* panels of a Louis XV card case

Signed: M.Π.   Gold mark: 72 and crossed anchors $3\frac{7}{8}'' \times 2\frac{3}{4}'' \times \frac{3}{4}''$
In the Collection of Her Royal Highness the Duchess of Kent

54. This drinking-horn from the Green Vaults Collection might well have inspired the Fabergé match-stand reproduced below; it was made in Dresden by Valentin Grefner in 1580

55. A fantastic creature in a fine-grain sandstone with silver mounts and carbuncle eyes. Designed as a holder for matches to be struck on the stone, this curiosity by Fabergé appears to have strayed from Hieronymus Bosch's 'Garden of Delights'

Signed: I.P.   Silver mark: crossed anchors   Length: 5½″. Height: 3″

In a private collection in England

X. Clock in red gold and nephrite decorated with translucent pink enamel panels painted with
dark violet tree motifs on sun-ray backgrounds. The dial is set within an opaque white enamel
bezel mounted with rose diamond ties in the form of a life-belt. This clock was designed for
use aboard the Royal Yacht.

Signed: M.II.   Gold mark: crossed anchors   Height: 5¼″

In the Collection of Dr. and Mrs. Leonard Slotover

Green Vaults Museum in Dresden, received practical encouragement from Pendin who had been originally trained as an optician. This does not appear too extravagant a surmise when it is remembered that some of the most skilful makers of these mechanical wonders—the great nineteenth-century Swiss craftsman Emil Wick is only one outstanding example—were themselves trained in the first place as opticians.

Eugène told a story about old Pendin which illustrates very well the particular rough charm that endeared him to the Fabergés; it concerns the wife of a well-to-do merchant who had selected for herself a pair of pendant ear-rings, and after a few days' careful thought, returned them to Pendin saying that while she very much regretted not having them, she really thought she was now too old for such frivolous appendages. Pendin, clearly a salesman of no mean order, persuaded her to keep them by his outraged *cri de coeur*: 'But my dear lady, just imagine what you will look like without ear-rings—like a cow without a bell!'

Gustav Fabergé had not himself founded a successful business without acquiring a lively appreciation of the difficulties and hazards involved in the process. He, of all people, had grasped the importance of a thorough commercial training, and he determined that his son should not neglect this side of his education. He arranged for him to attend the local Handelsschule at Dresden, where he was himself resident, and where he could conveniently keep a paternal eye on his progress.

Carl Fabergé was confirmed there in the Kreuzkirche when he was fifteen, in the year 1861. The next we hear of the student Fabergé is at Frankfort-on-Main, where he served his apprenticeship with the goldsmith Friedmann, whose House was renowned throughout Germany; it was in Frankfort that young Fabergé acquired a taste for and a certain skill in the art of fencing.

Fabergé visited England about this time to learn the language, residing in a guest house for some months where his flair for organization was soon recognized and rewarded by the special responsibility of carving the joint on Sundays, and being allowed to prepare the salads according to his own private prescription. Italy was not left out of this Grand Tour, which was undertaken with his friend Jules Butz, the son of Alexander Franz Butz, the St. Petersburg jeweller, and the work of the Florentine enamellers and goldsmiths in particular made a lasting impression on his imagination.

It was wise of Gustav to have saved Paris for the final stage of his son's training, for there he must have had his eyes opened to a conception of style and elegance not approached in either Russia or Germany. He was studying at Schloss's Commercial College, but it is certain that this did not prevent his haunting the Louvre and the numerous smaller collections, as well as the Palace at Versailles, that sumptuous flowering of the Baroque, committing to memory all the while the treasures that most attracted him.

In our examination of the various influences to which Fabergé was subject, it will be seen, time and again, that it is above all to the French that he is most deeply indebted for the successful expression of his own inspiration.

When he eventually returned to St. Petersburg, he brought back with him a genuine feeling and love for the most splendid achievements of the European decorative artists, from their early beginnings to his own day.

In the year 1870, when he was only twenty-four years old, trained and confident, he took over complete control of the family business. As if to mark the inauguration of a new era for the House of Fabergé, larger premises were taken on the opposite side of the street, this time on the ground floor.

The various changes of address, and the most noteworthy honours gained as the success and fame of the House grew, together with other relevant points of interest, are recorded in a chronological chart set out at the end of this essay.

Fabergé married Augusta Julia Jacobs in 1872; she was the daughter of Gottlieb Jacobs, Chief Manager of the Imperial Furniture Workshops, who came from Riga—of Swedish stock. 1874 saw the arrival of his first child, Eugène, and two years later, Agathon was born; Alexander and Nicholas followed in 1877 and 1884 respectively.

As the head of a thriving and fashionable jewellery business, Fabergé now found himself ideally placed to carry out the ambitious projects that had crystallized in his imagination since his return from Europe.

The major decision to switch more and more from the production of conventional articles of jewellery, which had been the financial mainstay of the House up till then, to the designing of decorative objects composed of materials of considerable beauty, but no great intrinsic value, was probably not taken until Fabergé had really found his feet in the business, and not before he had had the opportunity of discussing so fundamental a question of policy with his father and his young brother Agathon. This was, after all, by far the most important decision of Fabergé's life and he realized very well the full implications involved.

XI. A toadstool naturalistically carved in various shades of agate growing from a mound of unpolished material set with brilliant diamonds. The cap removes to reveal a gold lined inkwell. This must be one of the most sensational exercises in lapidary work undertaken by Fabergé—a terrifying foretaste of Disneyland

Signed: M.II.   Height: 4″

In a private collection in England

XII. *Left*, Box in tawny aventurine in the Louis XV style with red gold scroll mounts and set with rose diamonds and olivines

Signed: M.II. $3\frac{3}{8}'' \times 2\frac{9}{16}'' \times 1\frac{7}{8}''$

Gold mark: crossed anchors

Right, Round hinged box in red gold with green gold carved mounts, the sides striped with translucent green and opaque white enamel, the lid and base set with rhodonite panels

Signed: Fabergé   Gold mark: 72   This box also bears the English control mark   Diameter: $2\frac{1}{2}''$. Height: $1\frac{7}{16}''$

From the Collection of Her late Majesty Queen Mary

On the face of it, selling these *objets d'art* did not appear as profitable or, for that matter, as reliable an occupation as the disposal of costly diamond jewels had been.

Perhaps in order to gauge the public's reaction to this turnabout, the House of Fabergé, for the first time in its history, put examples of its work on exhibition—the occasion was the Pan-Russian Exhibition of 1882 which was held in Moscow. The newly-made objects of fantasy displayed were, in effect, on trial; needless to say they acquitted themselves with honour and were awarded the Gold Medal.

Agathon, sixteen years younger than Carl, was already showing unmistakable evidence of a rare talent as an artist and designer, and despite the considerable difference in their years, had become, even while still a student in Dresden, his brother's most valued adviser in artistic matters. He actually joined the firm in 1882 when he was twenty. This lends a certain colour to Eugène Fabergé's view that the original idea that an Easter Egg containing a surprise be made for presentation to the Tsarina was discussed in the year 1883, for it is known that the design for this first Easter Egg, which probably followed a year later, was the joint work of the two brothers; it seems reasonable to assume that Agathon must have been actually working with his brother for some little time before this first Egg was made.

Eugène Fabergé added an extremely valuable fresh clue to the purely circumstantial evidence we had on this subject; when confronted by the photograph of this first Easter Egg, which he recognized and authenticated at once, and when further, the lack of identifying marks was commented upon his reaction was that he had always understood it to have been made in either Holmström's or Kollin's workshops, and that the more he thought about it the surer he became that this was indeed the case—especially as Perchin, the workmaster responsible for all the other Eggs up to the time of his death in 1903, was not established with Fabergé until 1886.

It seems, therefore, that the year 1884 may be taken as a reasonably accurate approximation of the date of the first Egg. Alexander III granted the firm his Royal Warrant, according to Eugène, after the delivery of either the first or the second Easter Egg.

The prestige of the House grew very considerably in the following years as a direct result of this new programme, and in 1900 at the Exposition Internationale Universelle in Paris, Fabergé exhibited for the world to see, for the first time, all the Imperial Eggs he had made, together with a representative selection of his other wares (see Appendix A, Page 138).

The effect on the craftsmen of Europe was electric. Fabergé was unanimously proclaimed *Maître* and decorated with the Légion d'Honneur.

As a result of this remarkable demonstration, the name of the Russian goldsmith became internationally known and respected. From then on, it is a story of unbroken success and expanding interests. Besides delivering annually Surprise Easter Eggs for the Tsar to give to the Tsarina and the Dowager Empress, Fabergé was required to produce a gift for Edward VII to present to Queen Alexandra, the sister of Marie Feodorovna, on her birthday each year.

One of the most elaborate commissions he carried out for the King of England took the form of a series of carvings in various stones of colour depicting many of the domestic animals at Sandringham. A group of artists was set to work making the wax models, which were sent to Russia and there carved from the stone.

Among the many influential patrons of the House, apart from the Grand Dukes, mention should be made of the Youssoupoff, Kelch and Nobel families for whom, in addition to many of his most beautiful pieces, Fabergé made a number of Easter Eggs quite as original and lovely as the Imperial ones.

In England, the Russian goldsmith had many followers; one of the most enthusiastic of these was Leopold de Rothschild who acquired the engaging habit of presenting his friends with specially ordered objects vividly enamelled with dark blue and yellow stripes—his racing colours. 'Something from Fabergé's' became the fashionable solution to the perennial problem of how an anniversary, birthday or other happy event should be commemorated.

To the world, Carl Fabergé himself presented a matter-of-fact and urbane personality, the prototype of the diligent craftsman unruffled by the activities of the outside world; this, however, was only a part of the truth, for under this smooth exterior a sparkling and extremely dry sense of humour lay concealed. This accorded well with his own personal tastes—Eugène, remembering his father's distrust of the medical profession, recalled how he used to declare that the only doctor in whom he had any faith at all was a good *Berncasteler Doktor*—his favourite dry white Moselle.

There was, in him, nothing of the calculating or rapacious, and the men in his employ, from the merest boy who swept out the shops to the most experienced designer, were each individually responsive to this generosity of spirit.

His flair for selecting the most suitable material for a particular *objet de luxe* was translated exactly into human terms when it came to employing a craftsman to carry out a specific job for him. As we shall see in a subsequent chapter, he held firmly in his hand the reins of many differing manners, enabling him by judicious selection to form his own personal style, so he was able, through the sheer magnetism of his own personality, to combine and give special meaning to the diverse human elements in his workshops; the particular nationality of the craftsmen from Russia, Finland, Sweden, Germany and so on, became a matter of secondary consideration—the important point was that they became, at once, Fabergé craftsmen. Another characteristic which no doubt endeared him even more to his workpeople was that once he had decided to take on a new man, that man became right away a trusted recruit, and bore his share, however modest, of both the privileges and responsibilities of the House. Altogether, a total of about five hundred people were employed in the various Fabergé establishments.

He was especially fond of young children, and it was with mixed feelings of wonder and anxiety that grown-up customers in the shop would watch him settle their offspring on the floor with a number of his exquisite, but not unbreakable, animal carvings.

Fabergé must undoubtedly have made a number of pieces himself during the time he was apprenticed, and possibly later as well, but examples of these are unfortunately not now to be found; generally speaking, however, he confined his attention to designing and guiding the object through its various processes, watching and checking it at every stage of its creation.

Sacheverell Sitwell has likened Fabergé to Diaghilev, the inspired genius of the *Ballets Russes,* pointing out that, like the great impresario, he 'directed and animated his craftsmen, and imbued their works with his own personality'.

Mr. A. Poklewski-Koziell, whose father Mr. Stanislas Poklewski-Koziell was one of the most enthusiastic of Fabergé's regular patrons, describes how he used to enjoy his visits to the wonderful shop, and how much he admired the old gentleman's double-pointed white beard which gave him the appearance of a benevolent Father Christmas. Carl Fabergé himself had his own private office in a strategic position off the main show-room, whence he was able to observe the comings and goings of his various clients without himself being seen; he was thus free to choose for himself whether or not to emerge from his arcana and talk to a particular visitor. It will be seen from even this circumstance that Carl Gustavovitch was not really quite as simple as he would have had people believe. All his life he was an inveterate traveller and was never without his passport enabling him to leave the country if necessary at a moment's notice. It may be said finally that he was a man of rare sensibility, wide vision and dry humour; a man of great generosity and few words.

Then came 1914 and the outbreak of the First World War; this was disenchantment indeed. At the first harsh stab of reality from the outside world, the fairyland of Fabergé melted away—the spell was shattered. The Revolution, when it broke, finally put the shutters up, but the *coup de grâce* had already been dealt. The workshops were given over more and more to the manufacture of small arms and medical supplies, and hundreds of workers were taken on for this purpose in St. Petersburg and Moscow, increasing the normal Fabergé personnel to something like eight hundred. Even the craftsmen engaged in making the Imperial Easter Eggs were required to base their composition on a suitably warlike theme. The designers of Morskaya Street, unequipped as they were for such commissions, floundering in unfamiliar waters, quickly succumbed; just how aesthetically disastrous was this inevitable surrender to circumstances can be all too easily assessed by an examination of the banal and tasteless Red Cross Eggs of 1916. It is perhaps not altogether in the nature of a kindness to Fabergé's memory that I feel obliged to reproduce photographs of the Gunmetal Egg supported on miniature artillery shells. The dream world of fantasy which had appeared so natural until that moment, the wonderful enamel follies with their coloured jewels and their gold swags and ties, all vanished in a moment.

This was the striking of the midnight hour for the House of Fabergé, and the knell having once sounded, the dawn of the following day was to find no time or place for the particular brand of magic that it had distilled so successfully over the years.

When the Communists took over control of private business houses, Fabergé himself is said to have asked with a characteristic absence of ceremony for ten minutes' grace 'to put on my hat and coat'.

He died in Lausanne in 1920, an exile both from his country and his work.

CHAPTER II

Artist or Craftsman

The nature of art, its purpose and its demands, are questions which have exercised the minds of some of the wisest philosophers throughout the world since the dawn of time.

It is not intended here to enter this particularly contentious arena for very long, but it is necessary to have by us a serviceable formula of some sort to help us through the critical estimate we are attempting.

To that end, let us then agree that that man is an artist who, making use, consciously or unconsciously, of his past experiences, is able to express successfully, in some recognizable and permanent form, whatever hopes, convictions, fears, likes and dislikes and so on he may have.

Accepting this as our working definition, it is clear that while Goya, painter of 'The Last Communion of San José of Calasanz' comes well within its scope, Jean Henri Riesener, designer of beautiful furniture, does not; by the same token, neither does Fabergé.

It would be idle, as well as plainly unjust to the Russian goldsmith, to claim that he and his numerous craftsmen ever intended anything more aesthetically profound than the graceful giving of pleasure to others. Not, I think, an unworthy ideal, and certainly one which we, in our own day of rapidly declining standards of taste, can ill afford to despise.

Fabergé was, in the fullest sense, an applied artist, in the same way as we describe the designers of Sèvres porcelain or the weavers of oriental rugs as applied artists.

On certain occasions, it may be said that he touched the fringe of fine art; an obvious example is the astonishing procession of Easter Eggs made year by year for Alexander III and Nicholas II. Many of these Imperial gifts, completely non-functional objects of fantasy for the most part, are the worthy successors, in a direct line of descent, of the masterpieces of the Renaissance goldsmiths. The animals carved from stone, even the very slightest examples, must also be regarded as objects of pure art, each one existing as the individual work of a particular sculptor.

To point the distinction between fine art and the applied or decorative arts where Fabergé is concerned, the following instance is relevant.

Collectors of Fabergé objects are frequently irritated by loosely expressed comparisons with the work of Benvenuto Cellini—journalists never tire of expatiating at length on 'The Modern Cellini' or 'The Cellini of the North' and so on. Their irritation is justified in that Fabergé, as we have seen, lays claim to the title of an applied artist, and as such, performs certain decorative functions for which he is specially equipped both by technical proficiency and by his own personal taste, whereas the maker of the magnificent Perseus statue in Florence is, in the main, a creative artist, making objects with his own hands in his studio or at his bench with a small group of assistants, sometimes triumphantly successful, and at others surprisingly unsuccessful. The uncomfortable suspended action of the two large figures in the celebrated Kunsthistorisches Museum salt cellar provides ample evidence of at least one splendid catastrophe.

Considered technically, however, and leaving aside any purely aesthetic question, Cellini, as a goldsmith, was a child compared with Fabergé, who had at his disposal the most elaborate processes and the most highly skilled experts to put them into practice.

Fabergé was completely free in his medium; whether dealing with golds of colour, translucent or mat enamels, precious or semi-precious stones, he was able to execute technically whatever his imagination proposed, be it always understood that the intuitive feeling and respect he had for his materials would prevent his undertaking any project which would in any way abuse them.

This feeling is essential to a decorative artist, whereas a purely creative artist of sufficient genius and with a sufficiently burning obsession or message has sometimes got very near a perfect expression armed with only the most rudimentary equipment of his craft.

There are certain examples of Fabergé's work which do not have the same appeal for us today that they must have had at the time they were originally made; but even these pieces, over-loaded with decoration as they are, are never in any way shoddy or carelessly made. A glance through the illustrated work of Chippendale, the Adam brothers, or any other first-class decorator will reveal, to say the least, ample parallels.

56. Diamond rose brooch, a replica by Fabergé of an antique, beautifully set with white stones for the leaves and carefully graded champagne diamonds for the flower, mounted in pale gold. The total weight of diamonds is not less than 100 carats, and the height is $4\frac{1}{2}''$

57. Made hurriedly for the Tsarina in 1898 for the famous 'Bal de Costumes Russes' at the Winter Palace, this sumptuous necklace in emeralds, diamonds and pearls was made up of some of the finest gems in the Imperial reserve, and was a tremendous success. The emeralds from the Urals are set in gold, and the diamonds (Brazilian) in silver. The overall length is $11\frac{3}{8}''$

Both these items from the Russian Imperial Treasure are in the Kremlin

58. "Tiffany glass" jar set with pearls
In the Collection of Robert Strauss, Esq.

59. Grey-blue enamelled strut clock
In the Wernher Collection, Luton Hoo

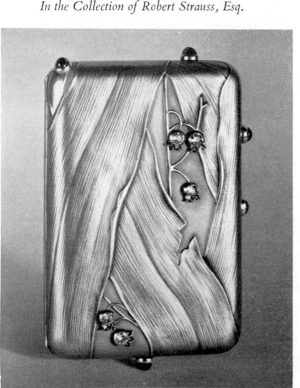

60. Green gold *minaudière* in an 'Art Nouveau' design
In the Collection of Lady Cox

61. Crimson frame with portrait of Nicholas I
In the Wernher Collection, Luton Hoo

Fuller descriptions in Appendix D

62. Coronation drinking-vessel and cover in the seventeenth-century Russian style, in topaz–quartz and set in an elaborate gold base decorated with a varicoloured *champ-levé* enamel scroll design, set with rubies and rose diamonds, punctuated at intervals by six large emeralds, the whole supported on three ball feet. The quartz and gold cover, reminiscent of seventeenth-century Russian headgear, is set with emeralds, rubies and rose diamonds to match the base, and is surmounted by a large emerald bead finial

Signed: M.Π.   *In the Collection of Alexander Schaffer, Esq.*   Height: 8½″

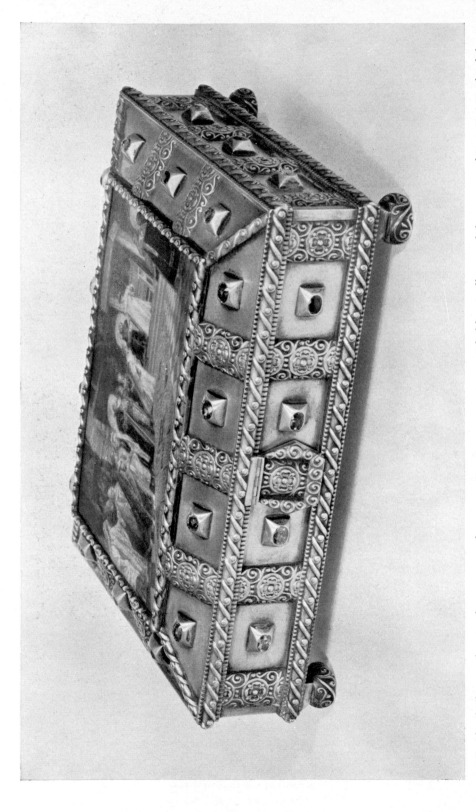

63. Oxidised silver casket in the seventeenth-century Russian manner, set with blue, yellow and brown sapphires. Set in the lid, an enamelled miniature copy by Haritonov of Constantine Makovsky's masterpiece in the Tretiakov Gallery in Moscow, depicting the traditional selection of a Bride for the Tsar during the sixteenth century. One of the pieces made during the 1913 Romanov Tercentenary celebrations
Signed: K. ФАБЕРЖЕ
$7\frac{7}{8}'' \times 5\frac{7}{8}'' \times 2\frac{5}{8}''$
In the Collection of M. Kennedy Leigh, Esq.

XIII. Group of four small boxes
In a private collection in England
Full description in Appendix D

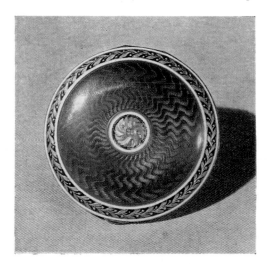

XIV. Powder box enamelled translucent deep magenta on a *moiré* ground with borders of opaque white and carved leaf and berry motifs heightened with black enamel

Signed: H.W.   Diameter: $2\frac{1}{16}''$

In the Collection of Mrs. Emanuel Snowman

XV. Siberian nephrite cup with a gold handle enamelled *champlevé* in translucent strawberry on a *guilloché* background and set with rose diamonds. This was a favourite design of Erik Kollin; another example is illustrated on Colour Plate XXX

Height: $1\frac{5}{8}''$

In the author's collection

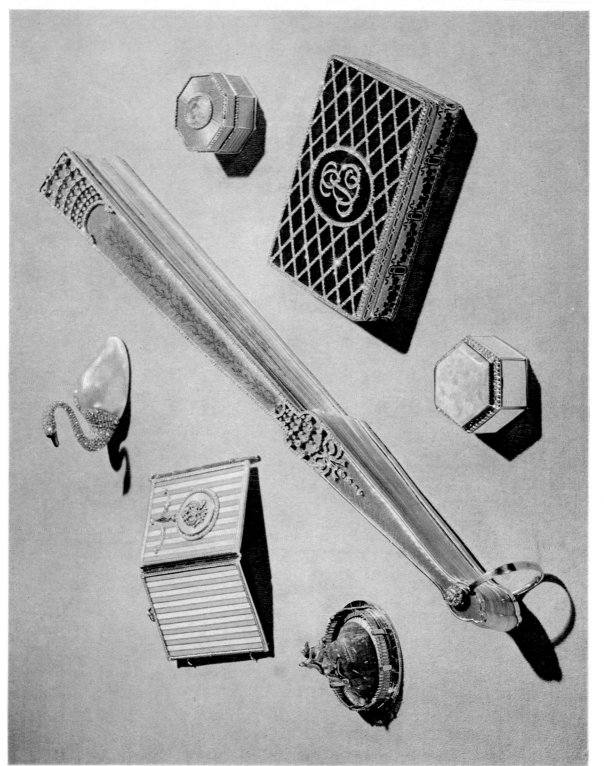

XVI. Group of objects from the collection formed by Madame Elisabeth Balletta of the Imperial Michel Theatre

In a private collection in the United States

Full description in Appendix D

65. Silver-gilt lyre clock in the classical manner by Fabergé, mounted on a pale coffee-coloured agate base, and set with rose diamonds and a tallow glass   Height: 7⅞"

Signed: M.Π.   Silver mark: crossed anchors

In the Collection of Messrs. Wartski

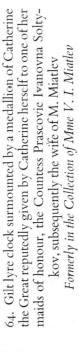

64. Gilt lyre clock surmounted by a medallion of Catherine the Great reputedly given by Catherine herself to one of her maids of honour, the Countess Prascovie Ivanovna Soltry-kov, subsequently the wife of M. Miatlev

Formerly in the Collection of Mme V. I. Miatlev

66. Antique Chinese carved box in mutton-fat jade, converted by Fabergé into a powder compact with red gold bezel decorated with translucent emerald green leaves and opalescent beads, the red gold interior fitted with two airtight compartments

Signed: H.W.   *In the Collection of Messrs. Wartski*   Diameter: $2\frac{3}{4}''$

67 and 68. Nephrite scent bottle in the Chinese style, carved as a mask, and set with rose diamonds in red gold mounts and a pearl

Signed: H.W.   *In a private collection in the United States*   Height: $2\frac{3}{4}''$

69 and 70. Carved smoky topaz shell box mounted in gold and enamelled translucent pale green on an engraved ground, with a gold leaf *paillon* and rose-diamond thumb-piece

Signed: К.Ф.   *From the Collection of the late Lady F. N. Peel* $1\frac{7}{8}''$ across

71 and 72. Circular Chinese porcelain bowl and dish in peacock blue (Ch'ien Lung) supported on specially designed dull silver-gilt carved stands by Fabergé.

Both signed: I.P.   An Imperial double-headed Eagle is engraved on each stand

Diameter of bowl: 9¼″; Height: 3⅜″; Diameter of dish: 11⅜″; Height: 4″

In a private collection in England

73, 74, 75. Triptych ikon in the Byzantine style
In the Collection of Alexander Schaffer, Esq.
Fuller description in Appendix D

Artist or Craftsman

From the most elaborate Easter gift for the Empress down to the most modest parasol-top, Fabergé never for one moment betrayed his trust by varying the excellence of his craftsmanship, and it is this steadfast loyalty to his own high standards that must be accounted one of his most satisfying qualities.

CHAPTER III

Formative Influences

If the knowledge of the sources of an artist's inspiration affects our enjoyment of the final work at all, it is to increase rather than lessen that enjoyment; by comparing the one with the other, we are often able to assess more precisely the nature of the artist's worth.

Our respect for Shakespeare the artist is not in any way minimized by the discovery that he culled his plots from the works of historians, biographers, other playwrights and novelists—on the contrary, a reading of Kyd's excellent *Spanish Tragedy* merely emphasizes the overwhelming genius of the author of *Hamlet*.

No work of art drops from the skies ready made; the legend of Pallas Athene's unconventional birth is clearly no more than a legend.

Originality for its own sake is a quality in art that is too often overrated. No one would claim that Liszt was a more important composer than Mozart, although no one could deny that Liszt introduced many more musical innovations and novelties than Mozart.

Fabergé, recognizing that art is a slow and gradual process of growth—a handing on of a precious heritage from one generation to another, knew that there could be no art *in vacuo*; consequently he was not blind to the work of earlier craftsmen in his own field; in fact there is convincing evidence that he was, on the contrary, a fascinated and intelligent student, able to refine and adapt what he discovered, for his personal expression.

Whatever he borrowed, and his taste was universal and catholic, he made his own; Fabergé never lost his identity; indeed, superb craftsman that he was, he endowed every piece with the unmistakable mark of his own personality, very often ennobling it beyond recognition.

The effect on Carl, and even more on his younger brother Agathon, of their research and deep interest in the origins of their craft, was to be dynamic.

Formative Influences

As more facts are unearthed about the early beginnings of the Fabergé brothers, the clearer it becomes that the sixteenth- and seventeenth-century goldsmiths working in Germany and the Low Countries for the Elector of Saxony, influenced their work in no small measure. This influence is clearly seen in some of the Imperial Easter Eggs (Pls. 346 and 360).

Although it has been generally believed that Carl Fabergé was trained almost exclusively in Paris, it now turns out, not altogether surprisingly, that he, and more especially his brother Agathon, spent some of the most precious formative years of study in Dresden, where the famous Grüne Gewölbe (Green Vaults) Museum proved an irresistible attraction.

As is generally the case with any artist, the early work of the Fabergés was unashamedly derivative, and besides the influence exerted by the German goldsmiths it is not difficult to discern even more affinities with French work, especially of the eighteenth and nineteenth centuries; indeed to the end of his days Fabergé delighted in producing pastiches in the French manner. His snuff-boxes and cases and *carnets* in the style of Louis XV and Louis XVI are of a beauty and distinction that match the originals.

It is true to say of the pastiches that, however literally these are transcribed, they retain their right to be accounted Fabergé objects. It is sometimes difficult to define precisely what it is that makes them so individual. One of the distinguishing characteristics of the Russian pieces seems to be the invariable use of a rather thicker gauge of metal for such details as carved mounts; thicker, be it understood, than would ordinarily have been used by the French goldsmiths, even allowing for the gradual wearing down of the metal of those objects, brought about by the perennial thumbing and stroking of their previous owners.

On the plane of the fine arts, it is interesting to observe how, without changing a single factual circumstance, without altering the position of a single muscle, Rubens painted, with obvious reverence, his version of one of the ageing Titian's most sublime masterpieces, the beautiful 'Fall of Man'. The Titian and the Rubens are hung quite near one another in the Prado, and I, for one, should not like to have to say which I considered the more marvellous canvas—the typical Titian or the equally typical Rubens.

In other words, it is impossible, even if he were so minded, for an artist to suppress his own personality; it appears just as impossible for a decorative artist of the calibre of Fabergé, a man with a vision and an artistic discipline of his own, merely to surrender slavishly to another style. It is the indefinable stamp of his own strong personality that, in the last analysis, differentiates the Fabergé pastiche from the original.

Besides producing French pastiches, Fabergé occasionally turned his attention to the Italian Renaissance, and his exercises in this manner are usually very successful. The small moss-agate Egg on Pl. 48 is decorated with opaque white as well as red and green translucent enamels, and is an exceptionally pleasing object. The agate is carved to such an unbelievably thin shell that the light passes easily through its surface, allowing the moss design to be clearly seen. The early Imperial Easter Egg made for Alexander III in the form of a monstrance (Pl. 317) is perhaps Fabergé's most faithful tribute to the goldsmiths of the Italian Renaissance, although the Egg for 1894 (Col. Pl. LXXII) is also strikingly reminiscent of Florentine craftsmanship at its most splendid.

Now and again one comes across a piece by Fabergé which has a distinctly Greek flavour; these are not common, however, and usually take the form of bowls or *tazze*. The famous gold replicas made at the suggestion of Count Stroganov of the ancient Greek ornaments known as the Scythian Treasure discovered during the excavations conducted at Kerch in the Crimea, are still on exhibition in the Hermitage Museum.

When Fabergé submitted the finished replicas together with the originals to Alexander III, the Tsar was quite unable to distinguish between the two sets, and decided on the spot that his work should be exhibited in the Hermitage beside the originals as an example of fine craftsmanship.

Always looking for new horizons, he even turned his attention to English pottery; I remember my surprise when I came upon a Royal Doulton vase which had been mounted on a three-legged silver stand by the Moscow branch of the firm.

Elements sometimes to be found in earlier Fabergé pieces have been variously described as late Victorianism, Edwardianism and 'Art Nouveau'. Fabergé was certainly one of the first exponents and indeed pioneers of the 'Art Nouveau' movement, which clutched at the artistic vitals of Europe in the Nineties, and for that very reason was happily in a position to purge his system of its baleful influence at a time when it was enjoying its widest popularity. The other terms are not really to be trusted in our analysis of the many sources of Fabergé's inspirations, and even 'Art Nouveau' is only partially applicable.

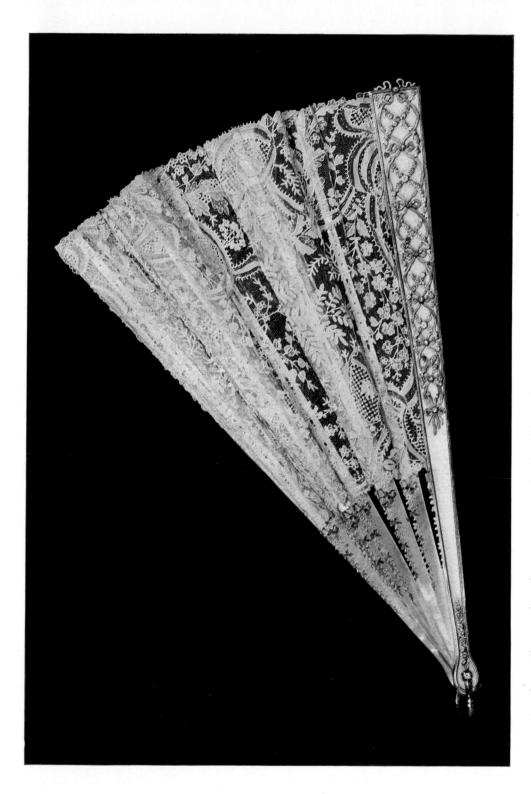

XVII. Brussels needlepoint lace fan with engraved red gold sticks, enamelled opalescent white, with loops of flowers chiselled in *quatre-couleur* gold intertwined with engraved gold ribbons and bows enamelled translucent pale blue and set with rose diamonds. The pinion is set with brilliant diamonds, and the mother of pearl blades are inlaid with pierced *quatre-couleur* gold sprays of flowers
Gold mark: crossed anchors   Length: 13¾″
Signed: M.II.

In a private collection in the United States

XIX. Triangular frame in varicoloured golds set with six cabochon rubies, ivory backed and containing a miniature painting of the Tsarina within a border of rose diamonds   Height: 5"

Signed: К. ФАБЕРЖЕ

In the Collection of Mrs. India Minshall

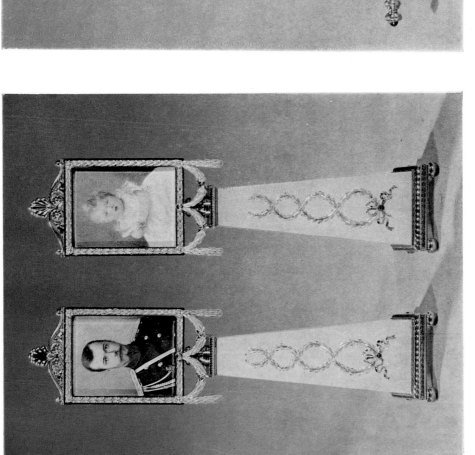
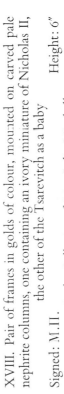

XVIII. Pair of frames in golds of colour, mounted on carved pale nephrite columns, one containing an ivory miniature of Nicholas II, the other of the Tsarevitch as a baby   Height: 6"

Signed: M.Π.

In the Collection of Mrs. India Minshall

Formative Influences

As well as the deliberate employment of unnatural forms, and the wanton interference with the sweep of a graceful line, giving the impression that determined philistine teeth have been nibbling away at the design, 'Art Nouveau' came to imply the deliberate use of the wrong materials for the particular job in hand, outsize Brazil-nuts doing service for the heads of ridiculous woodpeckers on ash-trays, human hair being twisted and turned to represent willow trees in pictures, and so on. Fabergé respected his materials far too much ever to have been guilty of such shifts and contortions.

His use of pearls and rose diamonds to render lilies of the valley is about as near as he ever got to this heresy, and even this lacks the particular wrongheadedness necessary to qualify completely for 'Art Nouveau' proper; there is, after all, nothing *mal tourné* about a goldsmith of sufficient imagination using the legitimate materials of his craft in an unconventional way. Even Gaudi's *Sagrada Familia* in Barcelona, with all its fantastic *avant-garde* writhing, the very apotheosis of 'Art Nouveau', is vindicated by the architect's ardent conviction and unfailing inspiration.

This movement in what might be described as the mis-applied arts flourished most successfully in Germany, where it was known as 'Kitsch'; so much so that a certain Professor Pazaurek was moved by the happy thought of founding in Stuttgart the celebrated Kitschmuseum. The history, if it is ever set down, of this crazy collection, and the ultimate fate, in an asylum, of the enterprising professor should make fascinating reading.

Kitsch in Fabergé's work (it has been irreverently suggested that Edelkitsch would be a more suitable name for this bejewelled manifestation) is astonishingly rare, taking into account the impressive quantity of ungainly objects that most of his contemporaries were churning out before he launched his revolutionary programme putting craftsmanship before costliness. By the time this programme had got properly into its stride, no trace at all of this regrettable tendency remained. If we detect now and again a later piece which we feel is 'dated', it is generally not disagreeably so, and does not offend us.

In 1913, the celebrations in connection with the Tercentenary of the rule of the Romanovs were marked by a revival of what is known as the 'Old Russian Style'. This style was a hotch-potch of traditional designs and patterns culled principally from the metalwork, murals, pottery and manuscripts produced at the time of Ivan the Terrible; these designs and patterns themselves were largely a heritage from the pre-Christian Tartars from Asia and the very strong Byzantine influence from the south. It was a bastard idiom reminiscent of the old-fashioned domed and banded baggage chest, the heavily studded portcullis doors of the ancient Russian cathedrals, and the extravagant orientalism of the bulbous domes of St. Basil in the Kremlin. Fabergé redeemed it from its worst excesses by his own seemly sense of order and by the ingenious technical expedient of carrying out many of these pieces in oxidised silver; to finish the metal with a dull satin surface was a particularly felicitous thought—it had the dual effect first of imparting an overall tone value to the object, giving it a much needed sense of unity by reconciling and binding together the often discordant elements in the composition, and secondly it allowed a greater lustre and brilliance to the various Siberian gems with which these pieces were often liberally studded (Pl. 63).

There was, unhappily, no such remedy at hand to save Fabergé from the clumsiness of the neo-Gothic tableware he produced, for instance, for the wealthy Kelch family. These stuffy objects, beautifully made as they are, must remain for all time a stern reminder that even an artist of the most rigid integrity is not always proof against the ill winds and squalls of the aesthetic climate around him. For these, Fabergé worked from designs by the Moscow architect, Scheftel.

The use of *cloisonné* enamel for *kovshi* and large silver pieces for the table is another instance of Fabergé's workshop supplying an already thriving market.

It was while inspecting an embarrassingly complete samovar set executed in this bold manner (cups, bowls, trays, spoons—nothing was left out!) that the Baroness Buxhoeveden, Lady in Waiting to the late Tsarina, Alexandra Feodorovna, was careful to point out that this type of work was sedulously avoided in smart St. Petersburg, being regarded there as primarily intended for export abroad, where the natives—the English, French, and so on—were enchanted by such manifestations of typically Russian art.

The Swiss goldsmiths of the eighteenth century were also not above producing a special commodity for their export business; 'Turkish' boxes, as these are known, are easily recognized by their exotic and flamboyant appearance.

This analogy is not really quite complete, however, as the manufacture of Russian *cloisonné* represented for generations a steady market for silversmiths who sold examples throughout the provinces of their own country quite apart from any question of export.

Fabergé certainly contributed something even to this firmly-rooted art form; besides avoiding the grossest excesses of design, he also greatly extended the range of the actual colours of the enamels, as well as employing much more subtle and attractive colour harmonies.

The Chinese influence in much of Fabergé's work is easily recognized, indeed it is seen in almost every branch of his work. Sometimes an actual salts-bottle or a particularly beautiful carving in jade or agate would be used to form the basis of some agreeable fantasy. The original piece would never be swamped with irrelevant decoration; on the contrary, if it were decided to adopt this course, it was because the designer felt that the full beauty would be enhanced by some addition which he proposed making. The jade powder-box shown on Pl. 66 is a charming example of his success in this field. Following the same principle, Fabergé designed intricately-carved silver-gilt stands for a peacock blue Ch'ien Lung bowl and dish (Pls. 71 and 72) illustrating very clearly that side of his character invariably emphasized by anyone who had personal contact with him; it was a case of the original oriental porcelain first, and his own contribution very much second.

Fabergé pieces were regularly sent to the mandarins in China, and it was probably for this market that these dishes and stands were designed in the first place.

Many of the animal carvings have a distinctly Chinese flavour, although it is easy to overstate the importance of this point, simply because when we think of a pug dog carved from jade, our first obvious comparison is with the Chinese.

Nevertheless, nobody could mistake the aesthetic ancestry of the goose on Pl. 252. In much the same way, the delightful models of flowers and trees are distinctly oriental in their feeling for meticulous detail, and in their resulting inevitability of design, springing from the calm and meditative eye of the creator.

In common with the *ébénistes* and *ciseleurs* of the past, Fabergé often embellished his objects with chinoiserie motifs of outstanding beauty; the smoky topaz box (Pl. 82) is one of the loveliest, as well as one of the most 'sophisticated', examples in this style. This box is almost monochromatic, the stone relieved only by enamels in opaque white, and a particularly effective translucent rust colour which forms a continuous frieze round the cover.

We know that Fabergé had in his home a very comprehensive collection of over five hundred Japanese *netsuké*—those ingeniously and too often tortuously carved ivory buttons that were so reverenced at that time; if they do not now evoke as much of our admiration as they did at the turn of the century, it is certainly not on account of any lack of skilful detail lavished upon them; rather is it because of a superabundance of it which does not accord with our present taste.

Before ending this chapter, reference should be made to the work Fabergé carried out for the Siam Government. This work was, in the main, along the prescribed lines laid down by tradition; the most noteworthy point of interest was the extraordinary quality of the carved nephrite used in many of the objects, such as the impressive bowl, supported by three gold Brahmin mythological figures, made to the order of King Rama VI, which is illustrated on Pl. 76.

The cigarette-case, decorated in the Mogul style, on Pl. 78 was probably made for one of the Maharajas of India and is an astonishing and very beautiful illustration of how Fabergé regarded each new job as an individual battle to be fought and won; I, at any rate, have never come across any other of his pieces made in this way.

It is impossible ever to forget that the Fabergés were by origin a Picardy family, and it is not surprising that the particular style which we have now come to recognize as 'Fabergé' is of mainly French extraction with frequent distinct references to the arts of Germany and China.

Those objects carried out in the 'Old Russian' manner, and the large *cloisonné* pieces, as we have seen, are not, in one sense, 'Fabergé' items at all, though of course they were made in Fabergé's Moscow workshops; they were simply the inevitable stock-in-trade of any silversmith who was in serious business in Russia at that time.

The development of his own style is marked by a shedding of unnecessary decoration and a successful striving after lightness.

But whether one considers an early example of his work, which bears more of the stamp of the period than it does of the creator, or whether one takes a specimen of Fabergé's final and most personal manner, it becomes quite clear that the one unassailable characteristic which is common to both pieces, is the rare quality of liveliness. So often goldsmiths and jewellers, transfixed as it were by the precious nature of their materials, succeed only in producing costly dead things.

One has only to walk into any modern jewellery shop to see too many of these cold moribund objects laid out in stiff rows, silently betraying by their

76. Carved nephrite bowl supported by three silver-gilt traditional Brahmin figures on a nephrite base
Marks not known   Diameter of Bowl at its widest dimension 15″
In the Collection of His Majesty the King of Siam
Reproduced from Mr. Bainbridge's monograph *The Life and Work of Fabergé*, by permission of its
publishers, B. T. Batsford Ltd.

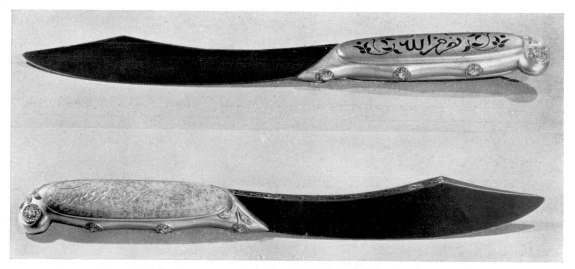

77. Letter-opener with blade in gun-metal, with gold inlaid scrolls and dull gold handle, set on one
side with a large turquoise inlaid with gold lettering, and on the other with a gold plate bearing an
inscription in blue enamel. The handle is set with rose diamond sprays and clusters of cabochon rubies
with rose diamond centres. The inscription is in Slavonic Russian written in Arabic characters and
translated reads: 'Victory through Allah'
Signed: К.Ф.   *In the Collection of Messrs. Berry-Hill*   Length: 9″

78 and 79. Gold cigarette-case richly decorated in Mogul style, enamelled opaque white, and set with a cabochon Siam ruby push-piece. The pattern outside is deeply engraved in the gold, the enamel serving as a background. Inside, a similar pattern has been carved out, probably to reduce the weight of the case. A most unusual technique, and not, as appears at first glance, *repoussé* work
Signed: К. ФАБЕРЖЕ   *From the Collection of the late M. Maurice Sandoz* $3\frac{1}{2}'' \times 2\frac{1}{2}''$

80 and 81. Small box carved from a single turquoise of exceptional colour, decorated with Egyptian motifs in yellow-green gold, and set with four brilliant diamonds and a rose diamond thumb-piece
Signed: К.Ф.   *In the Collection of Mrs. John Hay Whitney* $1\frac{3}{8}'' \times 1\frac{3}{16}'' \times 1''$ height

82 and 83. Carved smoky topaz box with gold mounts enamelled translucent rust and opaque white, the cover engraved with a chinoiserie design
Signed: M.П. $2\frac{1}{2}''$ square $\times 1''$ height
In the Museum of Applied Science and Technology, Sydney, New South Wales

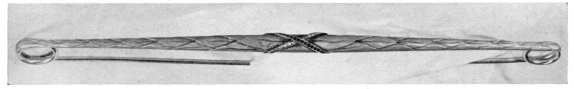

84. Carved dull green gold scarf-pin with rose diamonds set in silver, and sapphires in red gold
Signed: К.Ф.   *In the Collection of Mrs. Eric Low-Beer*   Length: $7\frac{1}{2}''$

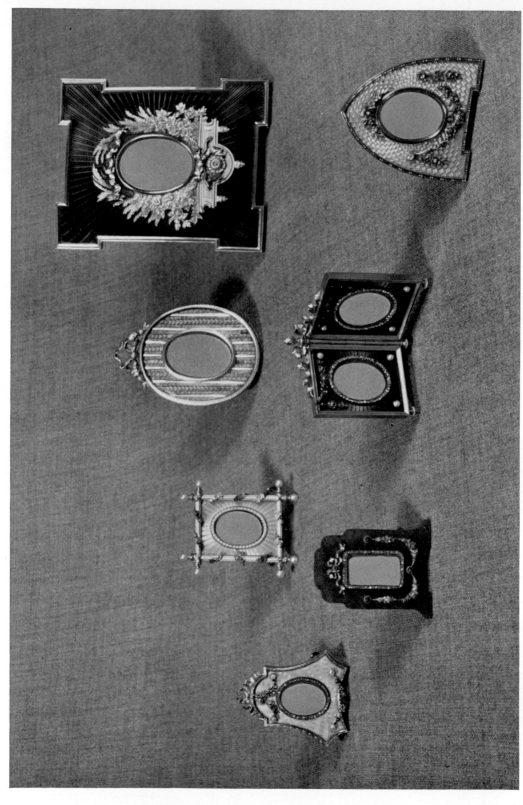

85. A group of miniature-frames in coloured golds and enamels. *Top, left to right:* aquamarine blue, pink, blue, deep violet. *Front, left to right:* nephrite, dark blue, pale green.
In the Royal Collection at Sandringham

86. Four-colour gold and nephrite miniature-frame, the bezel set with pearls and the four white gold pineapple corners with rose diamonds

Signed: К. ФАБЕРЖЕ   *From the Collection of the late M. Maurice Sandoz* $3\frac{3}{4}''$ square

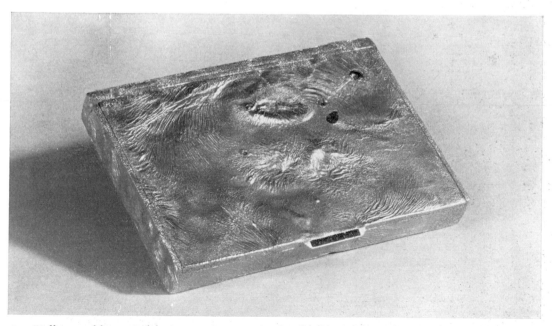

87. Yellow gold *samorodok* cigarette-case set with a brilliant diamond, a cinnamon diamond, a drop ruby and a *pavé* set ruby thumb-piece

Signed: К. ФАБЕРЖЕ   *In a private collection in England* $4\frac{1}{16}'' \times 2\frac{7}{8}'' \times \frac{1}{2}''$

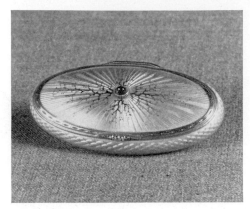

89. Silver-gilt *bonbonnière* enriched with *cloisonné* enamel in olive green, royal blue, orange, white, grey, mauve and coffee
Signed: К. ФАБЕРЖЕ Diameter: 1⅝″
In the author's Collection

88. Silver *bonbonnière* enamelled translucent pale green on an engraved ground with a painted tree design in sepia, and red gold mounts, a rose diamond thumb-piece, surmounted by a cabochon ruby
Signed: Ф.А. Length: 2⅜″
In the Collection of Lady Brabourne

90. Engraved yellow gold double-opening cigarette-case enamelled translucent blue-grey on a *guilloché* field, set with a rose diamond push-piece, and decorated with carved borders made up of dull red gold flowers, dull green gold leaves and polished white gold ties on a granulated yellow gold background
Signed: H.W. Gold mark: 72 3½″ × 2⅜″ × ½″
In a private collection in England

91. A bowenite frame and a gold *bonbonnière*.
Both objects in the Royal Collection at Sandringham
Fuller descriptions in Appendix D

92. Engraved silver tray enamelled translucent cinnamon
Signed: H.W.   Hall-marks shown on Plates 400 and 401 $2\frac{15}{16}''$ square
In the Collection of Messrs. Wartski

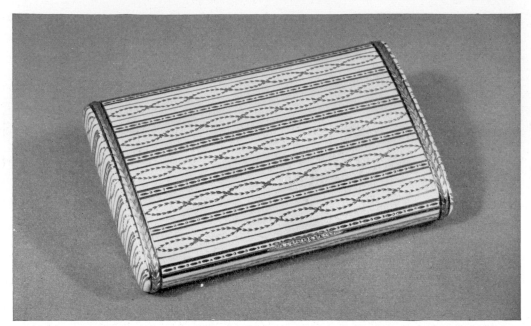

93. Red gold cigarette-case enamelled opaque white, with carved green gold mounts and a looped leaf pattern in green gold, and a rose diamond thumb-piece

Signed: H.W.   Gold Mark: L.U.T. (see Pl. 405) $3\frac{1}{2}'' \times 2\frac{1}{4}'' \times 1\frac{1}{16}''$

In the Collection of Alderman Emanuel Snowman, O.B.E.

94. Silver cigarette-case decorated with *niello* work

Signed: К. ФАБЕРЖЕ   *In the author's Collection* $3\frac{1}{4}'' \times 2\frac{1}{2}'' \times \frac{3}{4}''$

XX. Three boxes and a miniature-frame in enamel
In a private collection in the United States
Full description in Appendix D

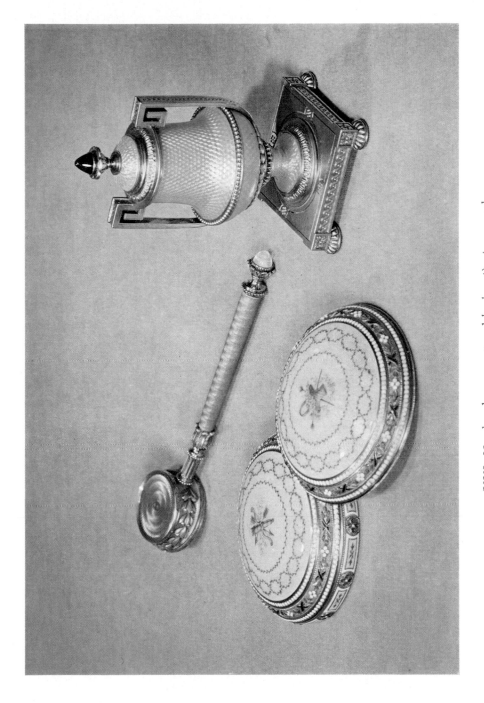

XXI. Hand-seal, gum-pot and *bonbonnière* in enamel
In a private collection in the United States
Full description in Appendix D

95. Double-opening white porcelain sweetmeat box, an imitation by the Imperial Porcelain Factory of Battersea Ware, decorated by Fabergé with gold mounts. Made for the Tsar and marked with the Imperial Crown, the name Nicholas II and dated 1911
In the Collection of Mme Betsy Popoff $3\frac{1}{2}'' \times 2'' \times 1''$

96. Cigarette-box with chamfered corners and a diamond thumb-piece, the lid set with a circular Imperial Porcelain Factory plaque in tones of warm sepia of a lady in profile. The plaque marked on the reverse with the cypher of Nicholas II and the year 1909. The ground enamelled in translucent pale blue over a wave pattern and with green and red gold carved husk borders
Signed: H.W. $4\frac{3}{8}'' \times 3\frac{1}{2}'' \times 1\frac{5}{16}''$
In the Collection of the Hon. Mr. and Mrs. W. H. Watson-Armstrong

97. Nephrite lily of the valley leaf as a dish decorated with a spray of lily flowers in pearls and rose diamonds on a gold stem

No marks   *In a private collection in America*   Length: 5⅞″

98. Silver *niello* cream-jug, decorated in the style of Louis XV, fitted with a carved wood handle painted black. This charming and rare example of Fabergé's use of the *niello* technique was made specially by Wäkewä for the Moscow house, to complete an eighteenth-century tea set

Signed: S.W. and К. ФАБЕРЖЕ   *In the Collection of the Hammer Galleries*   Height: 4″

99. Rhodonite dish with two Catherine coins enamelled translucent pale green within opaque
white enamel borders, mounted as handles with red gold ribbons

Signed: Φ.A.   *In the Collection of Messrs. Wartski*   Length: $6\frac{3}{4}'' \times 3\frac{1}{4}''$ across

100. Engraved silver desk clock in the form of a rose; the small dial is set within a ring of rose
diamonds and the hands are gold

Signed: M.Π.   Silver mark: crossed anchors   Overall length: $5\frac{1}{2}''$
In the Collection of Charles V. Jacobs, Esq.

101 and 102. Obsidian bear with rose diamond eyes   Height: 4″
In the Collection of Prince Theodore Obolensky

103. *Left*: Miniature replica of a samovar in gold. Signed H.W.   Height: 3½″
Right: Coloured gold heart-shaped diamond-set trefoil of miniature portraits enamelled
translucent ruby outside and emerald inside over sunray fields, the enamelled base set with
four fine pearls. Applied with the year 1897 in diamonds to mark the birth of The Grand
Duchess Olga, whose portrait, together with those of her parents, is framed within
Signed: К. ФАБЕРЖЕ   Height: 3¼″
In the collection of Lady Lydia Deterding, Paris

104 and 105. Bowenite rabbit with ruby eyes   Length: $1\frac{15}{16}''$
In the Collection of Captain Dugald Malcolm

106. Two chalcedony carvings of kittens
Left: grey with rose diamond eyes   Length: $2\frac{3}{4}''$ *Right:* pale brown with rose ruby eyes   Height: $1\frac{3}{4}''$
In a private collection in England

107. Bell-push in palisander wood decorated with red and green silver-gilt mounts and set with a moonstone push

Signed: Я.A.   *In the Collection of Messrs. Wartski* $4'' \times 2'' \times \frac{7}{8}''$

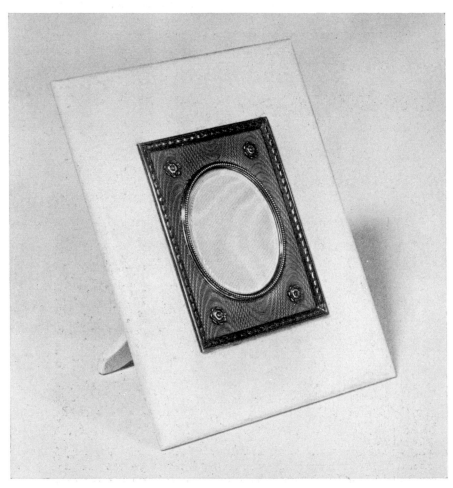

108. Miniature-frame in holly wood with a silver mount enamelled translucent lavender, on an engraved background, suggesting the grain of wood

No marks   *In a private collection in the United States* $3\frac{7}{8}'' \times 4\frac{7}{8}''$

109. Cigarette-case in Viatka birch with tinder attachment and match compartment, with red and green gold mounts, a medallion enamelled steel blue, with the Emperor's crowned initial and a rose diamond border Signed: H.W. $4\frac{1}{4}'' \times 3\frac{1}{4}'' \times \frac{7}{8}''$

From the Collection of the late Lieut.-Col. G. R. Thomson

110. Cigarette-case in palisander wood with carved red and green gold mounts in the manner of Louis XVI, and a cabochon sapphire push-piece Signed: M.Π. *In the Collection of Lady d'Abo* $3\frac{1}{2}'' \times 2\frac{1}{8}'' \times \frac{7}{8}''$

111 and 112. Cigarette-case in palisander wood with tinder attachment and match compartment, decorated with a dull yellow gold panel enamelled opalescent white and set with a ruby, the gold thumb-piece with a cinnamon diamond. This case still contains the original Fabergé price ticket marked 105 roubles (about £10 10s.)

Signed: К.Ф.   Gold mark: Crossed anchors $3\frac{7}{8}'' \times 2\frac{1}{2}'' \times \frac{3}{4}''$

From the Collection of the late Henry Channon, Esq., M.P.

113 and 114. Rock crystal box with a hinged yellow gold lid, engraved and enamelled opalescent white, with a warm sepia enamel painting of Falconet's statue of Peter the Great within a wreath. The lid is bordered by two rings of opalescent enamel beads and a formal pattern of translucent emerald green and strawberry enamel, against a hammered yellow gold background. A continuous leaf pattern is engraved round the box and the bottom bears the crowned monogram of Alexandra Feodorovna

Signed: H.W.   Gold mark: 72   Diameter: $2\frac{15}{16}''$. Height: $1''$

In the Collection of R. Strauss, Esq.

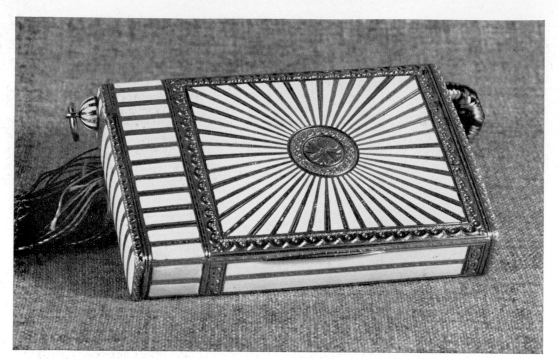

115. Cigarette-case in red and green gold, elaborately chased and enamelled opaque white in a sun-ray pattern with match compartment and tinder attachment

Signed: M.П.   *In the Collection of Max Harari, Esq.* $3\frac{3}{4}'' \times 2\frac{1}{2}'' \times \frac{11}{16}''$

116. Engraved yellow gold double-opening cigarette-case, enamelled translucent rose, and decorated with a pattern of intertwining carved laurel leaves set against opaque white enamel borders, and a brilliant diamond push-piece

Signed: M.П.   *In a private collection* $3\frac{1}{4}'' \times 2'' \times \frac{3}{4}''$

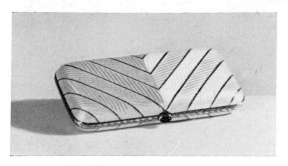

117. Primrose enamelled cigarette-case in
engraved red gold
In the Collection of Peter Otway Smithers, Esq., M.P.

118. Rose and white enamelled silver box for
stamps
In the Collection of Miss F. E. Morrice

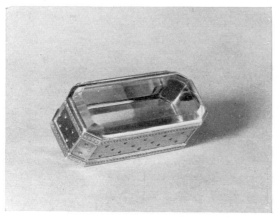

119. Engraved gold box with rock crystal panels
In the Collection of Michael H. Crichton, Esq., O.B.E.

120. Rock crystal cigarette-case
In the Collection of Mrs. Leland Hayward

121. Silver-grey enamelled cigarette-case
In the Collection of Peter Otway Smithers, Esq., M.P.

122. Golden-brown enamelled *bonbonnière*
In a private collection in England

Full descriptions of these objects will be found in Appendix D

123–127. Snuff-box in engraved yellow gold, decorated with two views of Chatsworth painted above and below in translucent warm sepia enamel, and four decorative panels similarly treated and edged with opaque white enamel, within broad bands of hammered gold, enriched with leaf and berry motifs in translucent strawberry and emerald green enamel. This superb box in the Louis XVI manner was commissioned by the Duke of Devonshire

Signed: H.W.   Gold mark: 72 $2\frac{1}{2}'' \times 1\frac{1}{8}'' \times \frac{13}{16}''$

In the Collection of His Grace the Duke of Devonshire

128. Group of objects from the Royal Collection at Sandringham. Full descriptions in Appendix D

129. Dark grey dappled agate snuff-box with red gold mount decorated with chiselled green gold leaf pattern and a briolet cut diamond thumb-piece. The lid is surmounted by a green gold Imperial Eagle, partly tinted red and enamelled opaque black with painted enamel ribbon and shields

Signed: A.H.   Gold mark: crossed anchors $3\frac{1}{8}'' \times 2\frac{1}{8}'' \times \frac{13}{16}''$

In a private collection in England

130. Nephrite box with red and green gold carved mount, the lid enriched with a rose
diamond trellis set in silver, and a foliate wreath containing a miniature painting of
Nicholas II by Zuiev within a border of rose diamonds and surmounted by a diamond
crown

Signed: H.W.   *In a private collection* $3\frac{3}{4}'' \times 2\frac{1}{2}'' \times 1\frac{1}{4}''$

131. Red gold cigarette-case with green gold 'barley pattern' inlaid panels, decorated with
borders of opaque white and royal blue enamel, and a rose diamond thumb-piece

Signed: H.W.   *In the Collection of R. Strauss, Esq.* $3\frac{1}{2}'' \times 2\frac{3}{8}'' \times \frac{5}{8}''$

132. Cigarette-case in ribbed pink gold with cabochon sapphire thumb-piece
Signed: A✶H   *In the Collection of Sir Ralph Anstruther* $3\frac{1}{2}'' \times 2\frac{5}{8}'' \times \frac{5}{8}''$

133. Cigarette-case in ribbed red gold, with rose diamond Imperial Eagle set with a brilliant
diamond centre and a cabochon sapphire thumb-piece
Signed: К. ФАБЕРЖЕ $3\frac{7}{8}'' \times 2\frac{7}{8}'' \times \frac{1}{2}''$
In the Collection of Alderman Emanuel Snowman, O.B.E.

134. Gold cigarette-case set with rose diamonds and enamelled translucent royal blue over a sun-ray ground with carved coloured gold foliate mounts and a diamond bordered miniature portrait of the Grand Duchess Anastasia. Fitted with a brilliant diamond push-piece
Signed: К. ФАБЕРЖЕ   Gold mark: 72 $3\frac{3}{4}'' \times 2\frac{3}{8}'' \times \frac{3}{5}''$
In the Armoury Museum of the Kremlin, Moscow

135. Cigar-box in red and green ribbed gold, an extremely rare piece
Signed: К. ФАБЕРЖЕ   *In a private collection in England* $5\frac{3}{4}'' \times 4'' \times \frac{3}{4}''$

136. Cigarette-tin in silver-gilt of a reddish tint, with a *repoussé* Imperial Eagle and lettering reading: WAR. 1914-15. C. Fabergé. There are two thumb-pieces. The firm produced a number of these austerity cases for use during the war

Signed: К. ФАБЕРЖЕ   *In the Collection of Lady Diana Tiarks* $3\frac{3}{4}'' \times 2\frac{3}{8}'' \times \frac{13}{16}''$

137. Presentation Table Box enamelled green, white and strawberry
In the Wernher Collection, Luton Hoo
Fuller description in Appendix D

139. Clock in engraved red gold, enamelled translucent grey with green gold carved mount, with an opalescent white enamelled dial within a pearl border. The hands are of red gold and an unusual feature of this piece is the name 'Fabergé' painted on the dial

Signed: H.W.   Gold mark: 72   Diameter: 3"

In a private collection in the United States

138. Striking clock in engraved silver enamelled translucent dove-grey and opalescent white, with red, green and yellow gold mounts and a pearl border round the dial, supported on four silver-gilt dolphins

Signed: Я.А.   Height: 8"

In the Collection of C. G. G. Wainman, Esq.

141. Lyre clock, Empire design, in red silver-gilt, with green gilt mounts, and an opalescent white enamelled dial with Indian red enamel numerals, the base in pale green bowenite

Signed: Я.A.   Height: 9"

In the Collection of Mrs. Eion Merry

140. Clock in engraved red gold enamelled translucent peach, with a pale blue border, green and red gold mounts and a pearl bezel   4½" square

Signed: M.П.

In a private collection in England

142. Clock in nephrite with red and green gold carved mounts set with rose diamonds and enamelled translucent pale pink on an engraved ground; the dial set within a pearl border, enamelled opalescent white with red gold hands. The gold XXV indicates that this was an anniversary gift

Signed: H.W.   *In the Collection of Mr. and Mrs. C. J. Byrne* $6\frac{1}{2}'' \times 4'' \times \frac{1}{16}''$

143. *Left: Bonbonnière* carved in smoky quartz to form a slice of crystallized fruit, the gold bezel decorated with translucent strawberry enamel and a band of rose diamonds

Signed: М.П.   Length: $2\frac{9}{16}''$

Right: Bonbonnière carved in pale golden quartz in the form of a crab apple, the gold bezel set with rose diamonds

Signed: М.П.   *In the Collection of R. Strauss, Esq.*   Diameter: $1\frac{5}{8}''$. Height: $1\frac{1}{2}''$

144. Condiment set in dark spinach Siberian jade with silver mounts applied with carved flowers in red gold and comprising oil, vinegar, mustard, salt and pepper with frame fitted on a tray in hammered and carved *art nouveau* style

Signed: ФАБЕРЖЕ   *In the Collection of Messrs. Wartski*   Height: $3\frac{1}{2}''$

145. Nephrite chiming clock with applied yellow gold decorations in Empire taste
Signed: H.W.   *In a private collection in England*   Height: $5\frac{1}{2}''$. Base: $3\frac{1}{8}'' \times 1\frac{7}{8}''$

146. Group of objects from the Royal Collection at Sandringham. Full description in Appendix D

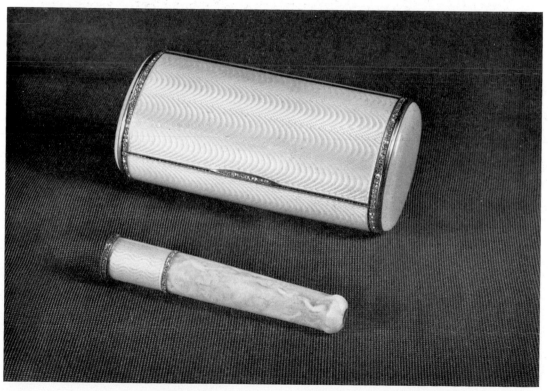

147. Engraved tubular silver cigarette-case and holder enamelled pale blue
In the Collection of Her Grace the Duchess of Leeds
Full description in Appendix D

148. Stamp-damper in the form of a pear, in bowenite with an engraved red gold brush, enamelled translucent sepia and green, and set with a large rose diamond

Signed: ФАБЕРЖЕ   Gold mark: crossed anchors   Height: $3\frac{5}{16}''$

In the Collection of Mrs. Donaldson-Hudson

149. Calendar in engraved silver enamelled translucent pale mauve, with silver-gilt scroll mounts and set with pearls

Signed: M.П.   Height: $4\frac{3}{4}''$

In the Collection of the Marchioness of Milford Haven

unimaginative design the brilliance and sparkle of the gems of which they are composed.

Of all the various qualities Fabergé may or may not possess, this undeniable and invariable liveliness is the one which is the most precious, and which finally entitles him to his honoured position in the history of the goldsmith's art.

CHAPTER IV

Materials and Techniques

The perfect expression of any particular art-form demands the smooth working of the entire technical machinery peculiar to it.

It is not enough that a painter has equipped himself with properly ground colours, suitable brushes and a correctly primed painting surface, if he has not also made sure of an adequate walk-back from his easel.

Oil painting is an activity that requires space, and goldsmithery, especially when allied to enamelling and stone work, is another.

Fabergé appreciated this to the full, and in 1900 moved his entire business to the far roomier premises in Morskaya Street where he was able to house, under one roof, all the most important workshops; Hollming's occupied the first floor, Perchin's (afterwards Wigström's) the second, Holmström's the third, and Thielemann's the top.

Before embarking upon any important new piece, it was his custom to call a round-table conference of all the various specialists who would be required to contribute in some way, at one stage or another, to the final achievement of the job in hand. This is not merely a figure of speech; Eugène Fabergé remembered well the very substantial round table in his father's private office where these plans of action were thrashed out.

Rather as the Editorial Board of a great newspaper meets and confers in order to decide on the 'line' they are to take on a specific news item, so the designer of a Fabergé object was given the opportunity of putting his point of view to the men actually entrusted with the task of carrying out his idea. The goldsmith could decide with the enameller exactly how and when his individual work should be done. Almost certainly the gilder would have to consult both these craftsmen—the goldsmith in order to ascertain the nature and purity of the metal to be used, the enameller to help him decide on the best colour.

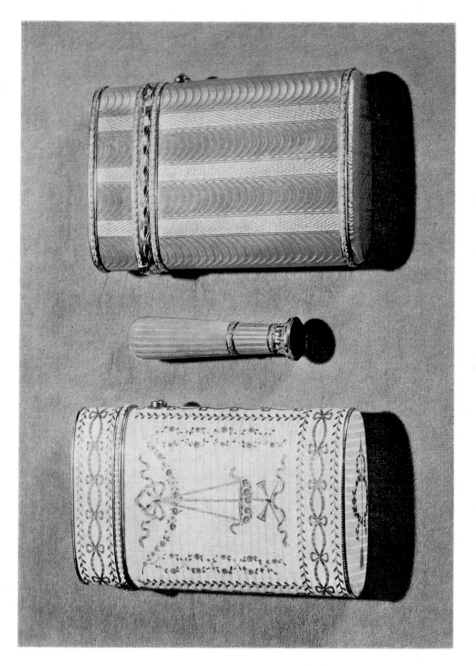

XXII. Two enamelled cigarette-cases and a hand-seal
In a private collection in the United States
Full description in Appendix D

XXIII. Hand-seal, strut clock and a cigarette-case
In the Collection of Mrs. Dennis Hamilton Kyle
Full description in Appendix D

Materials and Techniques

The question of the object, or part of the object 'going through the fire' for the purpose of soldering, is one of the first importance; gem stones, for example, cannot be exposed to a flame without a grave risk not readily undertaken by any experienced craftsman. Thus the goldsmith at this preliminary discussion could plan to solder all the necessary parts having due regard to the requirements of the setter and the enameller; each would be able to perform his own particular function at an appointed time so as to obviate any possible danger of clashing. A modern jeweller, reading this, will appreciate how many dismal catastrophes were avoided by this very sensible precaution.

A special importance attaches to the actual materials used in the manufacture of these objects, and no study of Fabergé's work would be complete without at least a brief description of the most important of these.

THE METALS USED FOR FABERGÉ OBJECTS

Taking the precious metals first, it is clear that to Fabergé, the colour of the gold or silver, no less than the precise shade of the enamel or stone, was a matter of the most deliberate consideration.

There are two methods of obtaining coloured golds, and Fabergé employed both. The metal used by goldsmiths is generally an alloy, as pure 24 carat gold, although used occasionally for small trinkets, is much too soft for ordinary practical purposes. In the gold most often used by Fabergé (56 corresponding to our 14 carat), the nature of the metal added to complete the alloy (10 parts in the case of 14 carat) determines the final colour of the gold.

The colour of the gold alloy is controlled by the precise proportions of pure gold, and mainly pure copper and fine silver; for some special shades other metals, such as pure nickel or palladium, may be introduced. Pure gold combined with fine silver gives a green gold, and with pure copper, a red gold.

The numerous variations of the alloy enable the goldsmith to produce yellow, green, red and white golds in very many degrees of intensity, as well as certain even more *recherché* effects such as blue, orange and grey golds. In the main, however, Fabergé confined his attention to the more usual colours.

The other method of colouring gold, less frequently employed in Morskaya Street, is simply to tint it after the work is finished. It is sometimes difficult to discern which technique has been adopted without disturbing the surface of the metal.

The *quatre-couleur* technique of the eighteenth-century goldsmiths in France was developed to a surprising extent in the St. Petersburg *ateliers,* and this was often combined with the use of enamels or stones to give increased point to the subtle variations between the differently-coloured golds. A characteristic example of this is shown on Pl. 86 where yellow, red, green and white golds are used with nephrite to form a miniature-frame; the four corners in white gold are set with rose diamonds, a finishing touch which adds the last refinement to a piece of unusual beauty. The lime-yellow Easter Egg containing the Coronation Coach (Col. Pl. LXXIII) provides a striking and elaborate instance of the use of coloured golds with enamels. The black double-headed eagles are enamelled on yellow gold, contrasting softly with the chiselled green-gold trellis which links them; this gentle harmony echoes the more obvious contrast between the black and yellow enamels. Observe, too, how well the mat green-gold borders set off the startling brilliance of the enamelled panels they enclose.

Fabergé frequently combined dull or mat golds with polished gold of another colour, producing very lovely effects in this way; a chiselled swag would be carried out in mat green gold and the small bows and ties in polished red gold. One of the most interesting techniques in which he specialized was the manufacture of a rough or molten surface for gold and silver cigarette-cases. This gave the case the appearance of a nugget (*samorodok*), and was obtained by bringing the metal plate almost up to melting point and then deftly removing it from the fire—the sudden cooler temperature shrank the plate and gave it the required surface (Pl. 87). The characteristic satin quality of platinum was exploited on various occasions, perhaps the most important being the Easter Egg set entirely in this metal (Pl. 364). Platinum is a particularly difficult material to work on account of its hard, compressed, non-porous nature.

As well as making a great deal of polished silverware, mostly in the Moscow House, Fabergé was one of the first to make extensive use of oxidized silver, and produce a large quantity of *surtouts-de-table, bratini,* bowls and samovar sets in this medium.

To satisfy a steady demand, it was not unusual to farm such pieces out—they were entitled to the Fabergé mark so long as the article was made from a Fabergé design.

One can detect here, I think, a slight weakening or leakage in the system, and this probably accounts to a certain extent for the rather undistinguished

XXIV. Cigarette-case with match compartment in engraved yellow gold, enamelled translucent royal blue, emerald green and opaque white with opalescent beads, and set with a rose diamond thumb-piece
Signed: H.W.　　　　　　　　　　Gold mark: 72　　　　　　　$3\frac{7}{8}'' \times 2\frac{1}{2}'' \times \frac{5}{8}''$
In the Collection of Mrs. Bert H. Andjel

XXV. Gold-mounted cigarette-case enamelled translucent grey over an engraved ground of floral swags and bow-knots with two borders set with half pearls and another enamelled with translucent green leaves on a *sablé* path, and set with a topaz-quartz push-piece
Signed: H.W.　　　　　　　　　　　　　　　　　　　$8\frac{3}{8}'' \times 1\frac{5}{8}''$
In a private collection in the United States

appearance of some of those pieces produced, as it were, away from the Master's eye. It may be, too, that the long tradition of earlier styles was too firmly rooted to be entirely eradicated, and the results are often an unsatisfactory compromise.

Silver gilt was used, both for its own intrinsic beauty, and also on occasions, as a substitute for gold in the manufacture of inexpensive articles such as parasol tops and so on.

Gun-metal, a blackened form of steel, was not scorned by the Fabergé workshops, indeed the Imperial Easter Egg presented to the Tsarina in 1916 was carried out in this material; it was intended to be a stern metal to match stern times. A few cigarette-cases were also made in gun-metal, but these are seldom found.

Lastly, some mention should be made of the rather commonplace brass *kovshi* and bowls, often set with a coin, that he, in common with most other Russian goldsmiths and silversmiths of the time, made in such great quantities.

THE ENAMELS USED ON FABERGÉ OBJECTS

To attempt a note, however brief, on Fabergé's superb enamels, it is necessary to acquaint the lay reader with some of the principal difficulties inevitably encountered by the craftsman engaged in this work. Enamelling is not a cut-and-dried process learned as one learns how to assemble a wireless set: it is rather an empirical affair of the emotions and instincts, requiring a marvellous combination of the gardener's green fingers, and the touch of a successful pastry-cook to bring off a perfect job. Characteristics of Fabergé enamelling are the even quality and smoothness of its texture, and the purity and fullness of even the most subtle shades.

He specialized in what is known as *en plein* enamelling—this means the smooth covering of comparatively large surfaces, or fields. This type of work allows for no margin of error, and it is for this reason that no serious attempt had been made to revive its practice since the time of the French eighteenth-century goldsmiths who made the beautiful snuff-boxes that are so prized by collectors today.

The Oxford Dictionary tells us that enamel is 'a semi-opaque variety of glass, applied by fusion to metallic surfaces'. The word 'fusion' is the key to the whole operation. For enamel to become malleable, it has to be heated to a certain temperature, and it is precisely this heating that creates the problems that so consistently defeat the modern craftsman. The finest translucent enamel has to be brought up to a heat of about 600 degrees Centigrade— Fabergé's enamellers normally worked at temperatures varying between 700 and 800 degrees; at such tremendous heat, it is obvious that if there has been any slight error or miscalculation in the preparation of the actual enamel or flux, or if the alloy of the metal plate used is not entirely suited to the enamel covering it, disaster, swift and sure, will undoubtedly follow.

In practice, it is astonishing to learn how much heat 14 carat gold, for example, can withstand without coming to grief. It is usually necessary to apply enamel to a part of an object already worked by the goldsmith, and even if the temperature inside the 'muffle' of the kiln were raised to 1,000 degrees Centigrade, the metal would emerge from its ordeal by fire unscathed, as about 1,200 degrees would be needed to affect a gold of this hardness. It is seldom necessary to risk passing gems through the fire, the technique being to cut out the raised settings in advance, then, when the enamel has been applied, the stones may be inserted and the settings closed round to secure them.

Opaque enamel usually requires a lower temperature than translucent, about 300 degrees sufficing. This lower temperature firing is known as '*petit feu*' as opposed to '*grand feu*'.

Translucent enamelling involves the firing of transparent layers of enamel, the fusibility of each carefully matched, on a prepared metal surface. In Fabergé's work this area is generally engine-turned (or sometimes engraved by hand), and is known as a *guilloché* surface. Each layer of enamel, and there may be as many as five or six, has to be baked separately. Sometimes gold leaf patterns known as *paillons* (Pl. 120) or painted decorations or scenes (Pl. 127) appear beneath the surface of such enamels: this very lovely effect is obtained by applying and firing the gold leaf or the enamel on to an already-fired surface of enamel before the top sealing layer of enamel is in turn applied and fired. When the enamel has been baked, it requires careful polishing with a wooden wheel in order to smooth down any irregularities on the surface; this is a highly specialized and extremely laborious operation and one without which the finished article will lack that distinction we have come to connect with Fabergé's work. The enamel is then finished off with the buff.

The characteristic milky quality of some of the translucent enamels, and especially the white, a rich fullness difficult to describe on paper but easy to

XXVI. Red gold strut clock with a carved green gold acanthus border, enamelled translucent pale green against an engraved *moiré* ground with painted enamel sepia swags. The broad margin is enamelled a pale shade of yellow-gold over a pattern of parallel lines and the dial similarly enamelled on a sun-ray field, and both embellished with painted enamel sepia ribbon and foliate motifs. The dial is set within a border of half pearls with gold hands, and the clock is ivory-backed and fitted with a silver-gilt strut Signed: H.W.

$6\frac{7}{8}'' \times 4\frac{1}{16}''$

Privately Owned

recognize in reality, was obtained by a mixture made up in the proportion of about four to six parts of transparent, to one part of opaque enamel, producing a semi-opaque material. This enamel is generally described as opalescent.

Another beautiful feature of some of his enamel pieces is the way the colour appears to alter as the object is turned very slightly; this effect was brought about by simply varying the colours of the layers of enamel. A pale flame-coloured layer of semi-transparent enamel beneath one or more layers of white transparent enamel imparts a particularly enchanting lustre—the round box in the Sandringham Collection on Col. Pl. XXX is an excellent instance of this technique. Also the effect of the light on the separate crystals of which the enamel is composed often gives the impression of a second colour. This variation in colour combined with painting beneath the top surface of enamel is illustrated very well in the lovely Easter Egg made for Barbara Kelch (Col. Pl. LXXXIII). Add to these exquisite variations in colour, the colour and engraved pattern of the gold *guilloché* field—the carcase of the Egg itself, which can be seen through the layers of warm semi-transparent enamel, sometimes indistinctly, at other times very clearly, depending upon the angle of vision and the light, and we begin to get some conception of the thought and careful planning that went into the creation of such an object.

Fabergé's use of the traditional techniques of *champlevé* and *cloisonné* enamelling are illustrated on Pls. 62 and 89.

Very occasionally he made a piece which was enamelled so that, when held up to the light, the small segments or compartments of colour smoulder and blaze in much the same way as do the coloured panes in a stained glass window. This is known as *plique à jour* enamel, and the secret of its intensity of colour is that it is not backed at all, but is used rather as though each of these separate enamelled segments were a gem stone set within a collet consisting of the main framework of the object. A good example of this work may be seen in the Clover Egg on Pl. 338.

Enamellers today, working under the intolerable pressure of modern commercial conditions, are not able to devote the time necessary for such delicate processes, with the result that, not being absolutely sure of their materials, they are beset by very understandable fears.

The modern enameller does not usually dare bring the furnace up to more than about half the temperature required for first-class work. On top of this, he has not got the time—or probably, by now, the ability—to polish the enamel adequately once it has been applied.

It is hardly surprising, therefore, that the cheaper modern enamel toilet set which presents such a consistent and painful offence to the eye bears so little relation to the enamelled objects produced by Fabergé. Indeed they might well be covered by two completely different materials, so wide is the gulf dividing them.

Having outlined some of the principal difficulties lying in the path of the actual enameller, it should be pointed out that he does himself also create fresh difficulties which require great ingenuity and delicacy if they are to be solved. Very often a gold mount, sometimes gem-set and enamelled too, has to be applied by means of pegs or pins to an enamelled surface; the trellis of eagles fixed on the enamelled surface of the Coronation Egg presented just this problem. On this occasion, surprisingly enough, the hard surface of the lime-yellow enamel was carefully drilled to allow the gold pins projecting from the trellis cagework to pass freely through the actual carcase of the Egg, which had itself been drilled in preparation. Once within the Egg the pins were easily bent against the inner shell, firmly securing the trellis mount to the Egg itself. Drilling through an enamel surface in this way, however, is an operation not much relished by goldsmiths—an accident at this stage is generally catastrophic and very costly; a more orthodox method of overcoming this problem would have been to have inserted small removable pegs in the drilled holes before applying the enamel. However, George Stein, who worked in Perchin's workshop, and himself made the model of the Coronation Coach concealed within, remembers very well how the Egg was completely submerged in a tank of water while the enamel was drilled; this was an extra precaution in case the drill became too hot and spoiled the surface.

Before closing this note on the enamels, it seems fitting to relate an experience of Alexander Fabergé who, besides being a very fine sculptor, was himself a skilful painter on enamel. As far as he remembered, it was in 1906 that he travelled to Paris for the express purpose of meeting Houillon, the most celebrated enameller then in France, in order, in his own words, to learn from this recognized master how to improve his craft. Having put forward his request to become an apprentice, Alexander described how he saw the great man gravely tap his magnificent head several times with a long bony finger. 'Are you crazy?' he enquired kindly. 'We in Paris are quite unable to do the

150. White and pink enamelled picture frame
Fuller description in Appendix D
In the Collection of Mrs. Ferrier

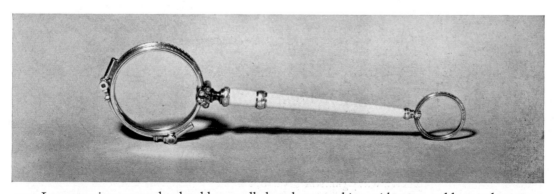

151. Lorgnette in engraved red gold enamelled opalescent white, with green gold carved mounts
and set with brilliant and rose diamonds

Signed: H.W.   *In the Collection of Mrs. Eion Merry*   Length: $5\frac{7}{8}''$

152. Barometer in cylindrical silver case with foliate border to the face, supported on a fluted bowenite column, mounted in silver and with the numerals XXV enclosed in a classical wreath on the front. The column rests on a rectangular base of aventurine quartz, with three silver plaques, the whole supported on silver lions' paw feet
Signed: I.P.   *From the Collection of Messrs. Spink*   Height: 13⅝″

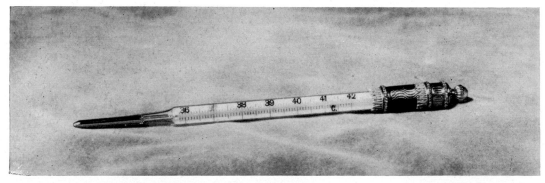

153. Clinical thermometer with red and green gold carved fringe mount with a collar enamelled translucent bright green on a wavy *guilloché* ground, ringed by three rose diamond mounts and a Mecca-stone knop
No marks   *In the Collection of Dr. J. G. Wurfbain*   Length: 6″

154. Barometer in aventurine quartz and red gold, with green gold carved mounts and yellow gold feet and inner bezel set with a cabochon emerald within a rose diamond cluster
Signed: M.Π.   Gold mark: Crossed anchors   Depth: 1½". Diameter: 3¼"
In a private collection in England

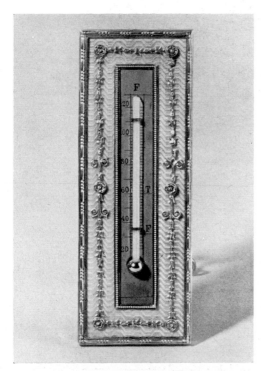

155. Thermometer frame in engraved silver gilt, enamelled translucent pale pink with green and yellow gold mounts
Signed: B.A.   Height: 4¾"
In the Collection of Michael H. Crichton, Esq., O.B.E.

156. Standing thermometer in engraved red and green silver-gilt, enamelled translucent royal blue and supported on a white onyx base with four fluted bun feet
Signed: M.Π. Crossed anchors Height: 11"
In the Wernher Collection, Luton Hoo

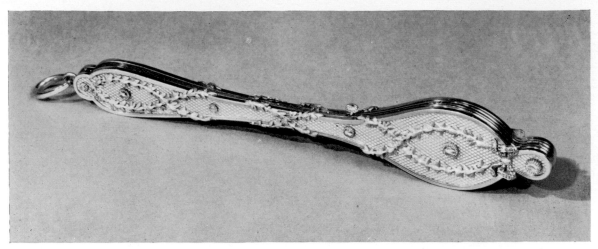

157. Red gold lorgnette enamelled pale translucent mauve overlaid with carved dull green gold trails of
leaves and berries, and set with rose diamond bows and single stones

Signed: M.П.   *In the Collection of Messrs. Wartski*   Length with loop extended: $7\frac{1}{2}''$

158. Pair of opera glasses in engraved red gold, enamelled translucent rose
and opaque white, adorned with carved green gold garlands, and set with
rose diamonds

Signed: M.П.   Height: $3\frac{3}{4}''$

In the Collection of Alexander Schaffer, Esq.

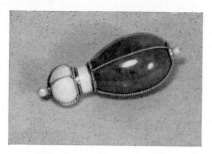

159. Rhodonite scent bottle with yellow gold mounts, enamelled opalescent white, with two pearls
Signed: H.W. Length: 2¼″
In the Wernher Collection, Luton Hoo

160. Shell box in striated agate, with yellow gold fluted lid, and bezel set with a single rose diamond
Signed: E.K. Length: 1⅜″
In a private collection

161. Silver table-bell with an engraved yellow gold handle, enamelled opalescent white, decorated with carved red and green gold mounts, and surmounted by a cabochon ruby
Signed: К. ФАБЕРЖЕ Height: 3¼″
In the Royal Collection at Sandringham

162. Red gold perfume bottle enamelled translucent yellow, and opaque white, with a carved green gold laurel mount, and set with three cabochon rubies
Signed: М.П. Length: 2¾″
In the Collection of Stavros S. Niarchos, Esq.

163. Nephrite ink-pot with red, green and yellow carved gold acanthus leaf mounts
fixed on three legs to a gold-mounted nephrite tray

Signed: H.W.   Gold mark: English control mark   Height: $4\frac{1}{2}''$

In a private collection

164. Three hand seals in rhodonite, Siberian jade and aquamarine
In the Collection of Messrs. Wartski

165. Gold cigarette-case made up of two convex sides enamelled translucent *tête de nègre* on a *guilloché* field and mounted with two brilliant diamond thumb-pieces

Signed: К. ФАБЕРЖЕ   Gold mark: St. George and Dragon $3\frac{1}{2}'' \times 2\frac{1}{4}'' \times \frac{13}{16}''$

In the Collection of E. P. Nomikos, Esq.

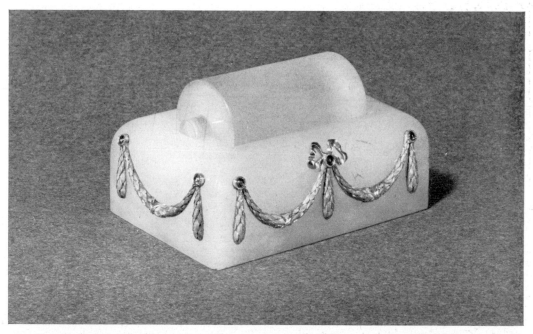

166. Stamp-damper in white onyx, with carved swags in dull green gold with polished red gold ties and bows set with cabochon rubies, and fitted with a rock crystal roller

Signed: Ф.A.   *In the Collection of R. Strauss, Esq.* $2\frac{5}{8}'' \times 2'' \times 1\frac{1}{16}''$ (without roller)

167. Nephrite miniature-frame in the form of a fan, with yellow, red and green
gold mounts, split pearl bezel and a rose diamond

Signed: M.Π.   *In the Royal Collection at Sandringham*   Length: 6¼″

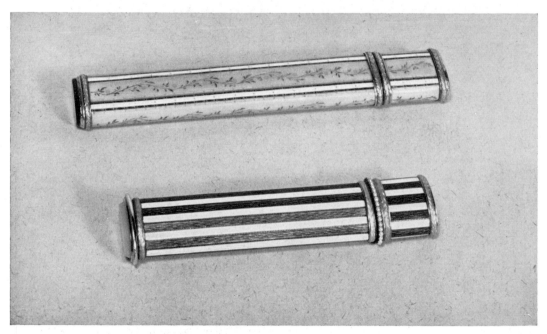

168. Enamelled sealing-wax holders in engraved red gold
In the Wernher Collection, Luton Hoo
Full descriptions of these objects will be found in Appendix D

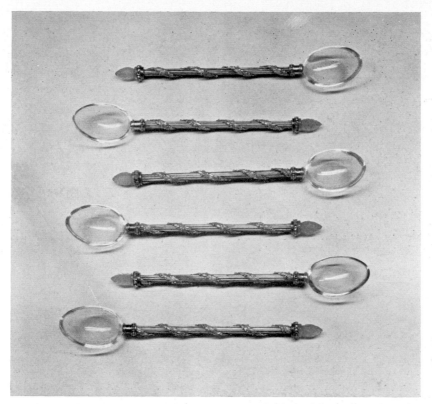

169. Set of six fluted red gold coffee spoons, in the Empire style, with green gold spiral foliate mounts, rock crystal bowls, the tops set with rose diamonds and carved moonstone pineapples

No marks: in original Fabergé case   *In a private collection*   Length of each spoon: 4½″

170. Miniature rock crystal tea-glasses, in yellow gold holders, enamelled with opaque white stripes with green gold carved mounts; handles set with roubles (1756) enamelled strawberry

Signed: M.Π.   Gold mark: crossed anchors   Height: 1¾″

In the Collection of Messrs. Wartski

171. Bowenite and rose enamelled bell-push
In the Collection of Messrs. Wartski

172. White enamelled bell-push
In the Collection of Lady Brabourne

Full description in Appendix D

173. Bell-push in engraved red gold, enamelled translucent strawberry and opalescent white, in radiating stripes, with a moonstone and pearl cluster push, and supported on four fluted bun feet
Signed: M.Π. $1\frac{7}{8}''$ square, $1\frac{1}{8}''$ height
In the Collection of Dr. J. G. Wurfbain

174. Bell-push in engraved silver, enamelled translucent rose with carved acanthus leaves, and a moonstone push, on three bun feet
Signed: A.H.   Height: $1\frac{5}{8}''$
In the Collection of Messrs. Wartski

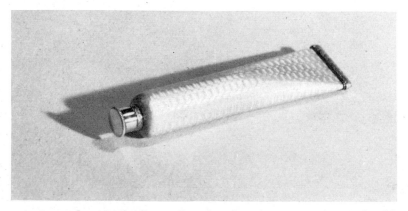

175. Scent *flacon* in the form of a tube of tooth-paste in silver and gold, enamelled translucent pale blue on a *guilloché* ground   Length: $2\frac{3}{4}''$
In the Collection of Her Grace the Duchess of Devonshire

176. Bell-push in the form of a sphinx in lapis lazuli and set with diamonds and rubies, mounted on a carved gold base enamelled opalescent oyster on a *guilloché* field

Signed: К. ФАБЕРЖЕ   *In the Collection of Dr. J. G. Wurfbain*   Base: $4\frac{3}{8}'' \times 2\frac{1}{4}''$

177. *Left:* Square bell-push in bowenite with gold mounts enamelled translucent pink and opalescent white with a cabochon ruby push $2\frac{3}{8}''$ square

Right: Circular bell-push in bowenite with gold mounts and moonstone and diamond cluster push   Diameter: $3\frac{1}{8}''$

Centre: Fan-shaped bell-push in Siberian nephrite with gold mounts and enamelled opalescent white with cabochon ruby push

All signed: М.П.   *In a private collection in England*   Length: $2\frac{9}{16}''$

178. Siberian nephrite cigar-box mounted *en cage* in gold enamelled *champlevé* translucent
strawberry relieved by gold *paillons*
Signed: M.П.   Gold mark: Crossed anchors   Lid: $6\frac{5}{8}'' \times 3\frac{1}{2}''$. Height: $3\frac{7}{8}''$
In the Collection of Robert Strauss, Esq.

179. *Garniture de bureau* consisting of 14 pieces each carved in dark grey Kalgan jasper and mounted in
highly chased *argent oxidé*
Signed: ФАБЕРЖÉ and bearing the maker's mark I.C.A.   *In the Collection of Charles Clore Esq.*

180. Silver-gilt *surtout d'écritoire*, made for the Kelch family in the Empire style. No details
available. Original Fabergé photograph

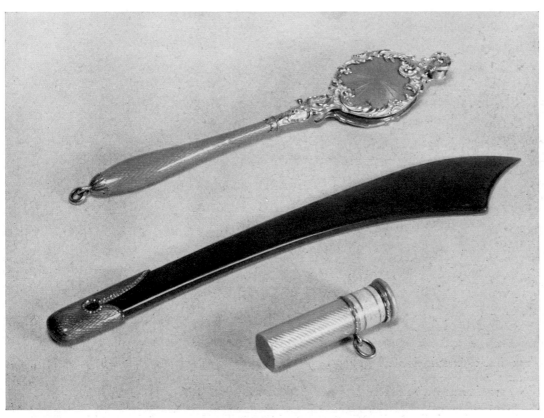

181. Lorgnette, letter-opener and pill-tube
In the Wernher Collection, Luton Hoo
Full descriptions in Appendix D

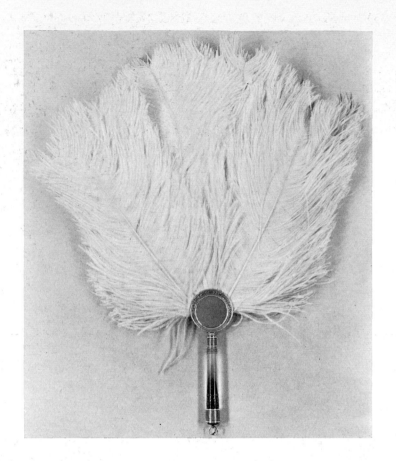

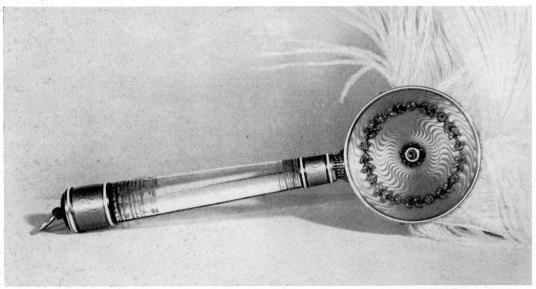

182 and 183. Ostrich-feather fan with engraved rock crystal handle, with red gold mounts, enamelled translucent pink on a *guilloché* ground and opaque white, with rose diamond mounts, and fitted with a mirror enabling the wearer to observe unnoticed those around her

Signed: H.W.   Overall length: 20½″. Length of handle: 7″

In the Collection of Peter Otway Smithers, Esq., M.P.

184. Pair of engraved rock crystal toilet bottles with red and green gold foliate mounts, enamelled translucent pink on a *guilloché* ground and opaque white, the tops set each with a cabochon emerald

Signed К.Ф.   *In the Collection of Madame Seiler*   Height: $5\frac{1}{8}''$

185. Silver and hardstone chess-set
In the Collection of Dr. J. G. Wurfbain
Full description in Appendix D

186. Gold whistle enamelled translucent lilac
on a barley-patterned ground
Gold mark: 72   Length: $1\frac{1}{4}''$
In a private collection in the United States

187. *Garniture de bureau* in pale green bowenite with silver-gilt mounts
Details not known   *Wartski photograph*

things you appear to do so easily in St. Petersburg.' This sincere tribute provides a suitable pendant to any note on Fabergé's wonderful enamels.

THE STONES USED FOR FABERGÉ OBJECTS

The lapidaries working in Russia found everything in their favour; the richest imaginable variety of natural resources was, practically speaking, on their doorstep, from the vivid Siberian emerald to the grey jasper of Kalgan. This astonishing abundance of mineral deposits to be found in the Urals, the Caucasus, Siberia, and elsewhere, must have been a source of great satisfaction to Fabergé, and time and time again he is able to transmit to us his own pleasure in some particularly choice stone by means of an animal carving, or a dish or box.

Almost every stone known to man appears to have been used by his lapidaries. They were not content with material from their own continent either, rich as it was, and stone-dealers from every part of the world were always welcomed at Fabergé's.

As far as precious stones were concerned, he rarely used these unless the purely decorative demands of the particular object called for them. Sapphires, rubies and emeralds were most frequently used *en cabochon,* and nine times out of ten the diamonds he used were rose-cut; he confined his use of brilliant diamonds to specially commissioned and Imperial pieces. Rose-cut diamonds set next to enamel or stone become part of the whole, whereas there is sometimes a danger that brilliant-cut stones, being so much brighter, might appear out of tone unless steps are taken, such as specially designed settings, to prevent this.

Semi-precious gem stones were used a great deal, especially moonstones, cabochon garnets, olivines and stained chalcedonies cut cabochon known as Mecca Stones.

The other stones to which he seems to have been most attracted were rock crystal, jade, bowenite, chalcedony, agate, jasper, rhodonite and quartz, aventurine, lapis lazuli and pale green flecked and opalescent amazonite.

A word or two about the special properties of some of these stones might be useful to collectors.

The early philosophers had a special regard for rock crystal, believing that it was a particularly hard form of ice found exclusively on the highest peaks of the Alps. This thought may have inspired some of Fabergé's happiest creations

E

57

—the Winter Egg for example. He also combined it, in much the same way as the Renaissance craftsmen in Germany and Italy did, with enamel and gems set in gold.

This seems to be the place to correct a misconception held by many collectors. It concerns Fabergé's use of jade. There are, strictly speaking, only two varieties of jade, nephrite and jadeite; both were used by Fabergé, nephrite a very great deal, jadeite only very occasionally. The nephrite he used was the dark green stone found in Siberia. The pale yellow-green stone usually described as 'pale jade' or simply as 'jade' (as opposed to 'Siberian jade') is not a jade at all, but a hard form of serpentine known as bowenite; known, that is to say, since 1822, when G. T. Bowen published his findings in the American *Journal of Science*; until that time, this stone was erroneously thought to be nephrite. Enough time seems to have elapsed since the publication of this valuable document to permit the adoption of the more accurate name by even the most conservative Fabergé collectors. Apart from Rhode Island, U.S.A., where Bowen found it, this form of serpentine is also present in Afghanistan, from which source, doubtless, Fabergé had the stone imported.

Rhodonite or orletz as it is sometimes known, is one of the most beautiful of all the natural stones; it was mined at Ekaterinburg and is characterized by its warm rose colour.

Obsidian, a natural volcanic glass of a grey-black colour which imparts a soft velvety sheen when polished, was peculiarly suited to the carving of animals.

Aventurine quartz, a tawny material mined in the Altai Mountains, also has a particularly attractive surface owing to the gold spangles which become evident when it is polished.

Woerffel's workshops, where so much of the stone work was carried out, must have resembled a miniature Oberstein—the German centre of lapidary activity. Not only were stones cut and polished in these St. Petersburg workshops, they were also stained and even created.

A clever craftsman can alter the natural colour of a stone (or even part of a stone), if it is sufficiently porous, by a staining process. If, for example, a pale agate is immersed in a solution of honey and kept just below boiling point for some days, and if, when the honey is absorbed, the stone is taken out and soaked in sulphuric acid (thus carbonizing the sugar), the result is that the pale agate has become black onyx. By such methods it is possible to obtain very subtle

XXVII. Miniature-frame in the form of a fire-screen
In a private collection in the United States
Full description in Appendix D

XXVIII. Nephrite standing clock
In the Collection of Mrs. India Minshall
Full description in Appendix D

XXIX. Group of objects with a marriage cup and a watering-can
In a private collection in the United States
Full description in Appendix D

tints; the chalcedony duckling shown on Col. Pl. XLII was stained a pale butter-yellow in this way.

Besides the many natural stones available to the firm, a deep crimson material known as purpurine was frequently used with great effect. A worker in the Imperial Glass Factory in St. Petersburg, named Petouchov, discovered the secret of its manufacture. A similar process was known in the eighteenth century to the lapidaries of Murano, to whom also must go the credit for the invention of aventurine glass or 'goldstone'.

The purpurine-like substance found in Italian work however, is considerably lighter both in colour and weight; this is probably due to a smaller proportion of lead in its composition than that used by Petouchov.

The manufacture of purpurine would appear to have been brought about by the crystallization of a lead chromate in a glass matrix. It is a material of great beauty both on account of the intensity and depth of its *sang de boeuf* colour and its spangled glassy texture. The cat on Col. Pl. XXXVIII is carved out of purpurine. The Fabergé workshops seem to have had the exclusive use of this attractive material.

Before starting up with the wheel on a freshly ground piece of stone, the sculptor would generally have before him a wax or plaster model of the subject from which to work. The lapidaries would not necessarily carry out their own ideas; there were about twenty artists and designers in Fabergé's drawing-studio, and it was here that these preliminary wax figures were modelled (Pl. 20).

In some cases—the Sandringham series is an obvious example—the original modelling from nature would be done on the spot and the carving carried out in the St. Petersburg workshops.

Fabergé never hesitated to employ any material, however unorthodox it may have seemed, if it served his purpose, as when the designer of the Dandelion Flower, Col. Pl. LXIV, faced with the problem of how to render the gossamer quality of the puff-ball, had the happy thought of using asbestos fibre.

He had a nice appreciation of the different woods to be found in and around Russia. Karelian birch, palisander, and holly wood in particular were used for many diverse objects including cigarette-cases, miniature frames, and even bell-pushes.

The cases in which Fabergé pieces were delivered were generally made of wood—for the most part, polished white holly wood; they were beautifully made and provided a worthy setting for a precious gift.

CHAPTER V

Objects of Function

Although there is admittedly something faintly absurd in describing a diamond-set, enamel, gold and rock crystal lorgnette as an object of function, the designation serves at least to distinguish such pieces from purely decorative objects such as the models of flowers in pots or the little mechanical toys.

To many Fabergé collectors, it is above all the boxes that have the most irresistible appeal. They can be judged more easily than many of his other works, taking their place as they do, quite naturally, in the long line of fine gold boxes made by master craftsmen from medieval times onward. The persistence of this tradition in Europe affords us a solid basis for comparison, a yard-stick to which we may conveniently refer.

The majority of the boxes are enamelled *en plein* on a *guilloché* field of gold or silver. Apart from snuff-boxes, Fabergé produced boxes of prodigious variety, and for every conceivable purpose: he made boxes for cigarettes, cigars, pills and stamps, boxes to serve as powder compacts, *bonbonnières*, and boxes with no better purpose than to be presented on some ceremonial occasion.

Many boxes were carved from stones, including nephrite, agate, rhodonite, jasper and topaz. Some of the loveliest examples combine the use of rock crystal with either enamel or gem stones, or sometimes both (Pl. 113). On at least one occasion, a piece of turquoise of unusually fine colour was carved to form a small box (Pl. 80). The best of these Fabergé stone boxes, deeply rooted though they are in the Dresden tradition, are immediately recognizable as Russian objects.

The final and most decisive test which can be applied to any modern work of art is to subject it to display next to the acknowledged masterpieces of the past in the same medium. It will be seen at once, and I recommend the reader

XXX. Group of objects from the Royal Collection at Sandringham
Full descriptions in Appendix D

to carry out this trial by comparison for himself, that the Fabergé boxes take their place naturally and easily next to the finest specimens of the goldsmith's art made, for example, in Paris in the eighteenth century. They are, in fact, a culmination of the whole splendid European tradition.

Fabergé cigarette-cases are now so well known and so universally admired both for their beauty and originality of design and for their impeccable craftsmanship that it is hardly necessary to describe these at length. Suffice it to say that they were many years ahead of their time in their formal simplicity, and that they were imitated by his contemporaries, and continue so to be imitated in our own time by fashionable jewellers of taste, with, be it said, a conspicuous lack of success; there is a certain *chic* which eludes them all, and in addition, there do not appear to be many craftsmen left able to make what has become known as a Fabergé hinge (i.e. an invisible one). Also the copies are generally too heavy for comfortable wear—the genuine cases are so well put together that the thicker gauge of metal so beloved by the mediocre crafts-man was never found necessary. They were carried out in an endless variety of engraved and ribbed patterns, and in various colours of gold and silver. An opaque enamel line, blue or white, would sometimes be introduced with striking effect. Fabergé made a large quantity of translucent enamelled cigarette-cases for women's handbags—these were usually in delicate pastel shades.

Fabergé lavished some of his happiest extravagances on the designing of clocks; but however *travaillé* and laden with embellishments they may have been, he never lost sight of the fundamental purpose in hand, and a clock from the House of Fabergé is always a practical and easily-read timepiece. He did not commit the artistic heresies that were constantly being perpetrated around him, when different scales and conflicting styles were time and again concen-trated in a single hideous object. Some of the most attractive clocks he made took the form of Easter Eggs, and these are more fully examined under that heading.

The model he adopted most frequently was the enamelled strut-clock in-tended for table use; within the limits imposed by this pattern, he produced endless variations of design, never once repeating himself. The clocks in this style were of many shapes and sizes—they were generally of translucent enamel and were very often mounted with gold chiselled borders; sometimes, too, the dial was also enamelled. The struts were either gold or more usually silver-gilt, depending to a certain extent upon the metal used for the clock itself. The movements he used were of the finest, and were usually assembled by either Paul Buhré or Henry Moser of Switzerland. The Lyre Clock which is illustrated on Pl. 65 is an eloquent example of how Fabergé seized on an idea and very often ennobled it by an increased clarity of design as well as a more imaginative choice of materials. The beautiful antique clock from the Miatlev collection, which is shown next to this piece and which it does not seem unreasonable to assume he would have seen, is made to appear top heavy in comparison with the even more beautiful modern version, mainly because Fabergé knew that a good design demands one main focal point, in this case the dial, and not, as in the earlier piece with the over-important medallion, two.

Collectors have always been attracted by the finest antique scientific instruments, and it was no doubt an appreciation of their peculiar charm that inspired Fabergé to design a whole series of his own (Pls. 152 to 156). Where the design was dictated by purely utilitarian and scientific considerations, the object was generally very successful indeed, but there were occasions when these requirements were regarded by the maker as purely incidental and the results are sometimes disturbing.

The art of the electric bell-push may be said to belong to Fabergé. His imagination was fired by the endless possibilities opened to him and his craftsmen by the introduction of this new domestic apparatus, and not only were the results original and amusing, but they usually succeeded in being extremely decorative as well. Some table-bells were designed to ring by means of a clapper when pressed; these were domed and fitted with an inner silver lining to give the required pitch and volume.

The table silver produced mainly in Moscow need not detain us too long here, because although it is certainly functional, it is generally not characteristically Fabergé.

Desk ornaments were produced in many different styles and materials, and some of the most felicitous Fabergé pieces take the form of paper-knives, ink-pots, gum-pots, stamp-dampers, sealing-wax holders, taper-sticks, seals, pens and pencils, blotting-pads, pen-trays and even pen-rests.

A bewildering assortment of stones was used for the carving of ash trays and small bowls, and these are among the most charming objects the firm ever made.

It is clear from the number and variety of small strut-frames for miniatures and photographs that have come down to us that the demand for these must have been extraordinarily wide. This is borne out by the testimony of Baroness Buxhoeveden who described how rows of miniature-frames were set out one behind the other in Alexandra Feodorovna's private apartments.

It must be regretfully admitted that the frame was in many cases of a far greater artistic merit than the often painfully inadequate miniature painting it sometimes held; the art of portrait painting in Russia at that time, with a few notable exceptions, was at a very low ebb, and it is fortunate indeed that most owners of such frames chose to preserve the likenesses of their loved ones in the form of charming photographs.

There were many other items, too numerous and diverse to mention in detail, all fulfilling some minor function—scent bottles, fans, crochet-hooks and knitting-needles, *étuis* and *carnets*, complete dressing-table sets, as well as cigarette-holders, cigar-lighters, match-stands and vodka cups. The parasols and walking-sticks carried by Russian ladies and gentlemen of discrimination were generally topped by one of the exquisite conceits from Fabergé's. The very narrowness of the scope offered by this subject seems to have acted as a spur to the designers, and the ingenious variety of attractive parasol- and stick-tops they produced is a real tribute to their imaginative resources and lively sense of invention.

CHAPTER VI

The Jewellery

Owing to his preoccupation with objects of fantasy, Fabergé, as we have seen, turned away more and more from the production of jewellery. The firm, it is true, continued to satisfy the purely commercial demands made upon it; this was, after all, a very profitable side of the business, but much of the jewellery produced to satisfy this market was the usual stock-in-trade of every diamond merchant, and, designed as it was to appeal to the wealthy merchant class, these pieces were often rather dull and conventional. The Moscow shop, more commercially conscious than her exclusive St. Petersburg counterpart, even went so far as to publish an illustrated catalogue (Pl. 21 and Appendix B on p. 139) giving the current prices of both jewels and objects in gold and silver to be sent by post to clients living in the provinces.

Fulfilling the more prosaic requirements of his business, however, did not prevent his designing many really charming and original jewels combining the use of mostly semi-precious gems in rose-cut diamond settings (Pl. 213), as well as a quantity of really dramatic pieces, most of them specially commissioned, which show all the subtlety of composition and delicacy of execution that we associate with Fabergé's work. The tiara on Pl. 219 is an exquisite and extremely rare example of such a piece. Fabergé designed several of the most imaginative of the Crown Jewels in which he set the finest emeralds, sapphires and pearls as well as diamonds of the purest water. Rubies were not liked by members of the Imperial Family owing to the dreaded symbolism of their colour.

More honour attended the celebration of Easter in Russia than even Christmas, and the traditional exchange of Eggs on Easter morning was observed by all classes with equal devotion. The Imperial Eggs were merely a glorified and splendid extension of this established custom.

One of the specialities of the House was the impressive range of small

XXXI. Two brooches and an enamelled ring
In the Collection of Mrs. Kenneth Snowman
Full description in Appendix D

XXXII. Pair of swivel seals
In a private collection in the United States
Full description in Appendix D

188. Nine miscellaneous objects from the Royal Collection at Sandringham
Full descriptions in Appendix D

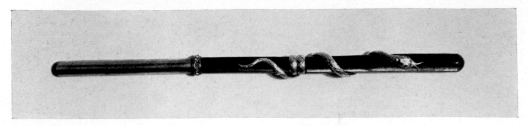

189. Obsidian pen-holder
In the Collection of Messrs. Wartski

190. Green enamelled scent bottle
*In the Collection of Peter Otway
Smithers, Esq., M.P.*

191. Blue enamelled scent bottle designed by
Agathon Fabergé
In the Collection of Messrs. Wartski

192. Chalk holder from *Préférence* set
In the Collection of Messrs. Wartski

Full descriptions of these objects in Appendix D

193. Seven objects from the Collection of Her Majesty Queen Elizabeth the Queen Mother
Full descriptions in Appendix D

194. Parasol handle in bowenite
In the Collection of Villiers David, Esq.

195. Enamelled parasol handle in engraved yellow gold
In the Walters Art Gallery, Baltimore

196. Rock crystal parasol handle
In the Collection of the Marchioness of Milford Haven

Full descriptions of these objects in Appendix D

197. Large silver-gilt *kovsh* with chiselled rococo mounts and engraved panels enamelled translucent strawberry, and surmounted by two crowned eagles bearing in their beaks a spray of berried laurel and a victory wreath. Presented by Nicholas II to Prince Leo Galitzine in 1899, as a prize for the excellent quality of his wine at the Nijni Novgorod Fair in 1896

Signed: I.P.   Weight: 207 oz.   24″ × 12½″ × 15″

In the Collection of Emile Bustani, Esq.

198. Engraved silver cigar-cutter in the form of a fish with pink stained cabochon chalcedony eyes set in red gold. When either of the eyes is depressed, the tip of a cigar placed in the mouth is automatically cut; the cutter is drawn back again by pressing a small button set in the gill

Signed: H.W.   Silver mark: 91   Overall length: 5¼″

In the Collection of A. J. Thomson, Esq.

199. *Above:* Cigarette-case in red gold with match compartment, tinder attachment and cabochon
sapphire thumb-piece. The ribbed sun-ray pattern radiates from a single brilliant diamond
Signed: H.W. $3\frac{5}{8}'' \times 2\frac{7}{16}'' \times \frac{5}{8}''$
Below: Nephrite cigarette-case with match compartment, tinder attachment, rose diamond thumb-
piece and gold mounts enamelled translucent strawberry and opaque white. The lid is surmounted
by a miniature painting of Nicholas II set under a large portrait diamond within a border of rose
diamonds
Signed: H.W.   Gold mark: English Control mark $3\frac{9}{16}'' \times 2\frac{7}{16}'' \times \frac{5}{8}''$
By gracious permission of His Late Majesty, King George VI

200. Lavender enamel and diamond brooch set in gold

201. Pink topaz and diamond brooch set in gold

Both in the Collection of Mrs. E. Tomlin

202. Pearl and diamond bow brooch set in platinum
In the Collection of Mrs. Julius Strauss

203. Mauve enamel and diamond brooch set in gold
In the Collection of Bryan Ledbrook, Esq.

204. Fine Siberian amethyst and diamond brooch
In the collection of Madame Tamara Karsavina

205. Enamel and diamond Iris brooch set in gold
In the Collection of Mrs. G. H. Kenyon

Full descriptions of these brooches in Appendix D

206. Ruby and diamond bracelet set in gold
From the Collection of Miss Woollcombe-Boyce

208. Imperial gold ring set
with diamonds and enamelled
opaque turquoise
Collection of Mrs. Robert Allan

207. Mecca stone and diamond
pendant set in gold
Collection of Bryan Ledbrook, Esq.

209. Pink enamel, pearl and diamond locket set in gold
Collection of Bryan Ledbrook, Esq.

210. Enamel, pearl and sapphire
pendant set in gold
*In the Collection of Mrs. E. Tomlin,
the daughter of Allan Bowe*

211. Gold tie-pin
*From the Collection
of the late Richard
Bradshaw, Esq.*

212. Gold gem-set pectoral cross
Original Fabergé photograph
*In the Collection of Alexander Schaffer,
Esq.*

Full descriptions of these jewels in Appendix D

213. Tourmaline and rose diamond necklet composed of clusters connected by diamond flowers with a pendant fitting to match; set in gold and silver
Signed: A.H.   *In a private collection in England*

214. Drop-diamond pendant necklet and ear-rings *en suite*
No details known   *Original Fabergé photograph*

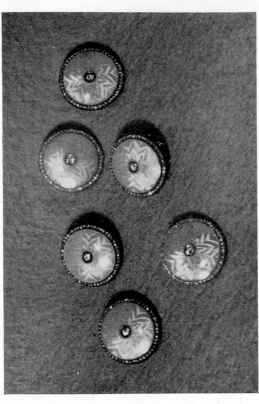

216. Set of six silver buttons enamelled opalescent rose on a radiating
guilloché ground, each with a brilliant diamond centre and a border of
rose diamonds

Signed: M.II.   *In the Collection of Messrs. Wartski*   Diameter: $\frac{13}{16}$"

218. Group of miniature Easter Eggs
In the Collection of Mrs. A. Kenneth Snowman

217. Group of miniature Easter Eggs
In the Collection of Mrs. Emanuel Snowman

217. Replica of a gold bangle from the Scythian Treasure
In the Collection of Mrs. Arthur Sutherland

219. Head ornament in brilliant diamonds, composed of two sprays of Aucuba Variegata, stalks engraved red gold, leaves in rubbed-over silver setting, pierced to suggest veining, backed in gold. Each spray, which is made in two parts, measures $7\frac{1}{2}''$ in length and comprises 14 leaves and 11 berries. The estimated weight of diamonds is over 40 carats, and the quality is superb. Signed: К.Ф.

In the Collection of Mrs. Gerald Grosvenor

220. Yellow gold cuff links enamelled in opalescent tones of apricot to pink on sun-ray backgrounds, with rose diamond borders and brilliant diamond centres
Signed: H.W.   Diameter: $\frac{1}{2}''$
In the author's collection

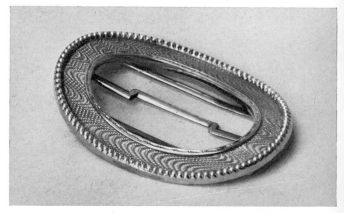

221. Siberian amethyst set with rose diamonds in silver and red gold as a brooch
Signed: A✱H   Length: $1\frac{1}{2}''$
In the Collection of Bryan Ledbrook, Esq.

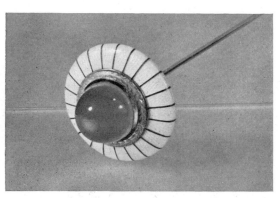

222. Engraved red gold hat-pin enamelled opalescent white, with green gold mount and set with a large blue stained chalcedony
Signed: H.W.   Diameter: $1\frac{1}{2}''$
In the Collection of Messrs. Wartski

223. Engraved silver buckle enamelled translucent pale green, with red gold mounts and set with pearls
Signed: M.Π.   Length: $2\frac{1}{2}''$
In the Collection of Mrs. A. Kenneth Snowman

224. Crochet hook in nephrite with collar enamelled opalescent oyster on a wave patterned field, mounted in red and green gold and set with rose diamonds
Signed: H.W.   *In the Collection of Messrs. Wartski*   Length: $10\frac{3}{8}''$

225. Brilliant and rose diamond-set buckle and six buttons enamelled translucent pale pink over a
guilloché ground en suite

Signed: M.П.   Buckle: $2\frac{7}{8}'' \times 2''$. Diameter of buttons: $1\frac{1}{8}''$

In the Collection of Messrs. Wartski

226. Turquoise tiara set with brilliant and rose diamonds in gold and silver. This piece was made
by Fabergé in 1895

From the Russian Imperial Treasure in the Kremlin

227. Creamy chalcedony swan with cabochon ruby eyes. Length: 2″. Pale coffee-coloured chalcedony pelican with olivine eyes. Height: $2\frac{1}{2}$″. Obsidian sea lion with rose diamond eyes. Length: $2\frac{11}{16}$″. Pale brown chalcedony duck-billed platypus with rose diamond eyes. Length: $2\frac{13}{16}$″. Two nephrite frogs with rose diamond eyes. Lengths: $\frac{13}{16}$″ and $\frac{5}{8}$″. Blue and pink chalcedony sturgeon with rose diamond eyes. Length:$2\frac{3}{4}$″

In the Royal Collection at Sandringham

228, 229. Obsidian king penguin with rose diamond eyes and red gold feet   Height: $3\frac{1}{8}''$
In a private collection in England

230. Group of carvings from the Royal Collection at Sandringham. Full descriptions in Appendix D

231. Baby penguin in agate
In the Collection of the Viscount Rosslyn
Full description in Appendix D

232. Varicoloured agate goat with rose diamond eyes
Length: $2\frac{1}{4}''$
In a private collection in the United States

233. Hippopotamus in grey Kalgan jasper with a dark green patch on the back
and cabochon ruby eyes   Length: $6\frac{3}{4}''$
In the Collection of Messrs. Wartski

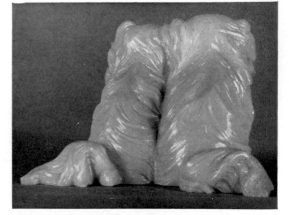

234, 235. Pair of pekinese dogs in grey-brown chalcedony with cabochon ruby eyes   Height: $1\frac{13}{16}''$
In the Collection of the Viscount Astor

XXXIII. Aventurine quartz carving of a sow with cabochon ruby eyes

Length: 5″

In a private collection in the United States

XXXIV. Group of five animal carvings
In the author's collection
Full description in Appendix D

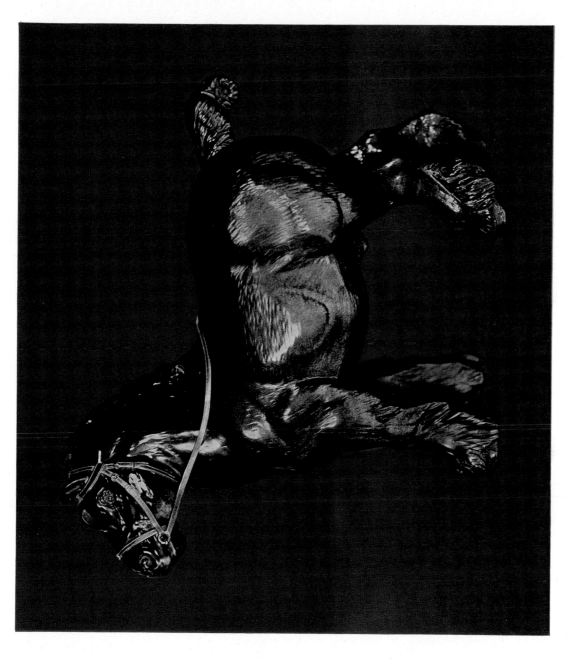

XXXV. A Percheron stallion carved in obsidian with engraved gold bridle and rein set with cabochon ruby eyes
Signed: Fabergé   Height: 5¼″. Length: 6″

In a private collection in the United States

236. Bulldog in varicoloured agate with yellow gold collar enamelled opaque black and set with a rose diamond buckle. Brilliant diamond eyes

In the Collection of Miss Valerie Hobson   Height: $3\frac{1}{2}''$

237. Dalmatian carved from an unusually beautiful piece of pale creamy oatmeal-coloured moss-agate with natural blue-grey moss motifs. The eyes are star-cut rubies

Length: $4\frac{3}{8}''$

In a private collection in the United States

238. Hornbill in grey and white chalcedony with rose diamond eyes and gold claws, perched in a silver-gilt cage
Cage signed: M.П. $2\frac{1}{2}'' \times 2\frac{1}{2}'' \times 3\frac{5}{8}''$
In the Royal Collection at Sandringham

239. Striated agate kiwi with carved gold legs and beak and rose diamond eyes
Signed: H.W. Height: $2\frac{1}{8}''$
In the Collection of Mrs. Rita de Wolfe

240. Brown and blue chalcedony chimpanzee with olivine eyes. Height: $3''$. Blue-grey semi-transparent agate donkey. Height: $3\frac{1}{4}''$. Grey varicoloured chalcedony ostrich with rose diamond eyes and red gold legs. Height: $3\frac{5}{16}''$. Four mice, left to right, dark grey chalcedony with rose diamond eyes. Length: $1\frac{3}{8}''$; white opal with cabochon ruby eyes. Length: $1''$; grey chalcedony with rose diamond eyes, ears and tail set in silver. Length: $1\frac{5}{8}''$; sapphire quartz with rose diamond eyes. Length: $1\frac{5}{8}''$
In the Royal Collection at Sandringham

XXXVI. A superb carving of a Muscovy duck made up of various semi-precious natural stones including speckled brown jasper, pale blue translucent chalcedony and crocidolite with diamond eyes and gold web feet, standing on an aquamarine base.
The gold feet bearing the initials H.W.   Length: $2\frac{1}{5}''$
In the Collection of Major R. Macdonald-Buchanan, C.V.O., M.B.E., M.C.

XXXVII. Group of animal carvings including a litter of piglets
In the Collection of Major R. Macdonald-Buchanan, C.V.O., M.B.E., M.C.
Full description in Appendix D

241. Speckled grey agate mongrel with green and carrot-coloured flecks, with rose diamond eyes   Length: $2\frac{1}{8}''$
In the Collection of Mr. and Mrs. Michael Sobell

242. Topaz bulldog with faceted ruby eyes
Length: $1\frac{5}{16}''$
In the Collection of Captain Dugald Malcolm

243. Grey-brown agate chimpan-zee with rose diamond eyes
Height: $2\frac{1}{2}''$

244. Rhinoceros in spotted red jasper, a material suggesting very well the creature's natural armour
Length: $4\frac{5}{8}''$

Both in the Walters Art Gallery, Baltimore

245. Mink in nephrite   Length: $3\frac{5}{16}''$
In the Collection of the Hon. Mr. and Mrs. W. H. Watson Armstrong

246. Four elephants with rose diamond eyes. *Top left:* in nephrite. Height: 2¼″. *Right:* in obsidian.
Height: 2½″. *Lower left:* in obsidian. Length: 2⅜″. *Right:* in nephrite. Length: 1¹⁵⁄₁₆″
In the Wernher Collection, Luton Hoo

247. Nephrite rogue elephant, with brilliant diamond eyes   Height: 4⅜″. Length: 5″
In the Royal Collection at Sandringham

248. Two elephants and a sparrow in Siberian nephrite
In the Collection of Her Majesty Queen Elizabeth the Queen Mother
Full descriptions in Appendix D

249. Obsidian bear with rose diamond eyes. Height: $2\frac{7}{8}''$. Nephrite frog with gold-set brilliant diamond eyes. Height: $3\frac{3}{4}''$. Nephrite cock with cabochon ruby eyes and yellow gold feet. Height: $4''$. Obsidian walrus with rose diamond eyes. Length: $2\frac{5}{8}''$. Grey jasper elephant with howdah in the form of a tower in red gold enamelled opaque white and Indian red, set with rose diamonds. Signed: M.II. Height: $1\frac{1}{4}''$. This emblem of the Danish Royal House was originally in the possession of Marie Feodorovna.   *In the Wernher Collection, Luton Hoo*

250. Cat in grey Kalgan jasper with
olivine eyes set in yellow gold
Height: $2\frac{1}{4}''$
In the Royal Collection at Sandringham

251. Lapis lazuli duck with gold legs
and ruby eyes
Approximate height: $2''$
Wartski photograph

252. Grey chalcedony goose with yellow gold legs and cabochon ruby eyes
Height: $4\frac{1}{16}''$
Pale coffee and white translucent quartzite guinea-pig with inlaid obsidian
ears and cabochon sapphire eyes   Height: $1\frac{1}{2}''$
In the Royal Collection at Sandringham

XXXVIII. Purpurine carving of a cat set with rock crystal eyes foiled with yellow and
black enamel   Height: 5″
In the Collection of Dr. and Mrs. Leonard Slotover

XXXIX. Agate carving of an ibis
In a private collection in the United States
Description in Appendix D

XL. Crouching jadeite frog
In a private collection in the United States
Full description in Appendix D

XLI. A superbly carved obsidian bison, the surface finished matt with the exception of the muzzle, horns and hooves which are brightly polished

Length: $5\frac{1}{8}''$. Height: $3''$

In a private collection in the United States

253. Mandrill in white chalcedony with ruby eyes
Height: $3\frac{1}{8}''$
In the Collection of the Armoury Museum in the
Kremlin, Moscow

254. A photograph showing visitors examining the Imperial Easter Eggs in the showcase in the
Armoury Museum of the Kremlin

255. *Top*: Edward VII's wire-haired terrier 'Caesar' in white chalcedony with cabochon ruby eyes and gold bell and translucent brown enamelled collar inscribed: 'I belong to the King'. Length: 2¼". *Left*: semi-transparent brown agate bulldog with rose diamond eyes. Length: 2½". *Right*: pale grey chalcedony Clumber spaniel with cabochon ruby eyes. Length: 4⅛". *Front*: varicoloured agate puppy with rose diamond eyes. Length: 1⅞"

In the Royal Collection at Sandringham

XLII. Group of animal carvings from the Royal Collection at Sandringham
Full descriptions in Appendix D

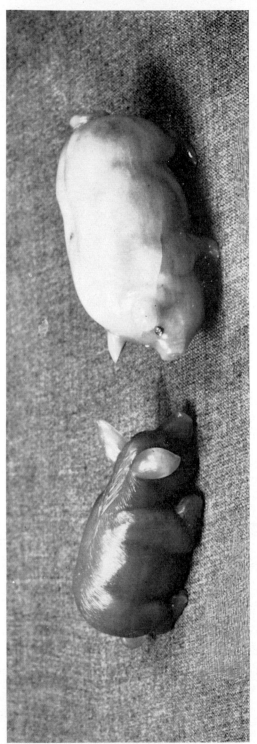

256. *Left*: pink striated agate pig with olivine eyes. Length: $2\frac{3}{4}''$. *Right*: pinky-brown chalcedony sow with rose diamond eyes. Length: $2\frac{7}{8}''$.

258. White and pink chalcedony pig with cabochon ruby eyes
Length: $2\frac{1}{8}''$

257. Varicoloured agate pig with olivine eyes.
Length: $1\frac{3}{4}''$
All in the Royal Collection at Sandringham

259. 'The White Rabbit' from *Alice in Wonderland*, the only known figure from a series carved by Fabergé. In white chalcedony with cabochon ruby eyes   Height: 2¾″
In the Royal Collection at Sandringham

260 The first of all the stone figures designed by Fabergé. Carved in bowenite with cabochon sapphire eyes and a gem-set crown, it caricatures Queen Victoria, and was originally suggested by the Grand Duke Nicolai Nicolaivitch   Approximate height: 1½″
In a private collection

261. Gorilla's head carved in browny-mauve mottled Ural marble as a box with a hinged fluted gold lid set with rose diamonds and a ruby. The brilliant champagne diamond eyes and the large rose diamond teeth are set in gold
Signed: A✶H   Gold mark: 72   4″ × 2½″
In the Collection of 'A la Vieille Russie'

262. King Charles's spaniel's head in white chalcedony with brilliant diamond eyes set within gold rings enamelled opaque black, serving as lid to a round gold box
Signed: M.П.   Diameter: 2¹³⁄₁₆″. Height: 1¹⁵⁄₁₆″
From the Collection of the late M. Maurice Sandoz

263. Chelsea Pensioner made up of various natural stones
In the Royal Collection at Sandringham

264. Russian peasant girl similarly composed of stones
In the Collection of R. Thornton Wilson, Esq.

265. Coachman, another example of this technique

266. An officer of the Imperial Horse Guards in natural stones of colour

Both in the Collection of Alexander Schaffer, Esq.
Full descriptions in Appendix D

267. Sardonyx carvings of a dolphin and a house-fly with diamond eyes
Length of dolphin: $4\frac{3}{4}''$ Length of fly: $2\frac{9}{16}''$
In the Collection of the Armoury Museum in the Kremlin, Moscow

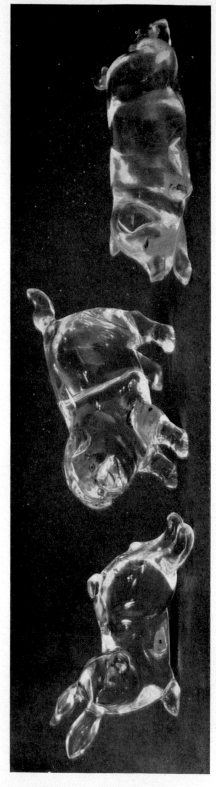

268. Rock crystal carvings of a rabbit, a dog and a pig
Lengths: $3\frac{1}{8}''$, $3\frac{9}{16}''$ and $4\frac{1}{8}''$
In the Collection of the Armoury Museum in the Kremlin, Moscow

XLIII. Carving of a snail in nephrite set with rose diamond eyes   Length: 3¾″. Height: 2″
In the Collection of R. Strauss, Esq.

XLIV. Opal carving of a parrot in a gold cage
In a private collection in the United States
Full description in Appendix D

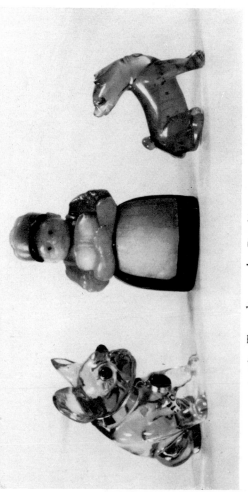

269. Two dogs and a Russian peasant woman
In the Collection of the Armoury Museum in the Kremlin, Moscow
Full descriptions in Appendix D

270, 271. Two views of the showcase containing the Imperial Easter Eggs and a
number of animal carvings and the pansy in the Armoury Museum of the Kremlin

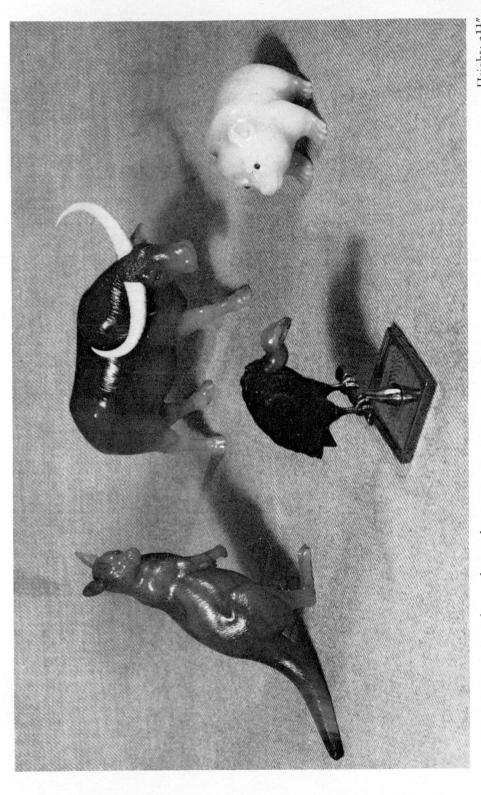

272. Kangaroo in agate with rose diamond eyes   Height: $2\frac{11}{16}$"
Grey chalcedony buffalo with ivory horns and cabochon ruby eyes   Length: 3"
White chalcedony bear with cabochon ruby eyes   Length: 2"
Obsidian vulture with agate head, rose diamond eyes and red gold feet on a red-gilt silver perch   Signed: M.II.   Height: $1\frac{7}{8}$"

In the Royal Collection at Sandringham

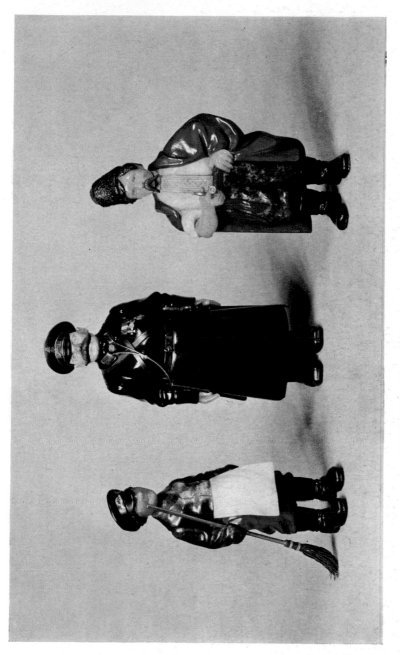

XLV. House boy, policeman and a peasant
In the Collection of Sir William Seeds, K.C.M.G.
Full description in Appendix D

XLVI. Figure of gipsy woman composed of various stones of colour
In a private collection in the United States
Full description in Appendix D

273. A group of animal carvings in the Royal Collection at Sandringham
Full descriptions in Appendix D

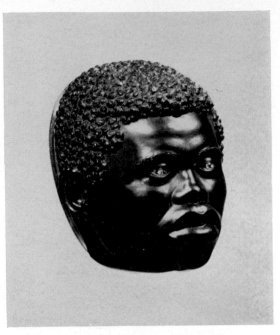

274. Dark sherry agate negro's head
In the author's collection

275. Nephrite Freedom Box
In the Wernher Collection, Luton Hoo

276. Full size palisander wood and
nephrite table
Wartski photograph

277. Jadeite *Magot* with nodding head and
hands
In a private collection

Full descriptions of these four pieces in Appendix D

jewelled, enamelled and even stone eggs which were attached to long gold chains and worn as necklaces. Jewellery for men took the form of tie-pins and cuff-links and dress studs often set with cabochon stone centres.

Enamelled crosses and panagias were also made, but as a rule these were carried out in such a rigidly traditional manner that, like his ikons, they need not necessarily have been made by Fabergé.

Examples of the jewellery are now very rarely found, owing to the fact that much of it had to be sold by refugees for the value of the stones; the Soviets confiscated large quantities during the Revolution, and there must still be many pieces in Russia today of which we know nothing.

The main jewellery workshops were controlled by August Holmström, himself a craftsman of outstanding ability, and A. Thielemann.

The quality that characterizes all the jewellery, however modest the piece may be, is above all the security and precision of the settings. A jewel from Fabergé's was always what the setter at the bench calls a 'clean job'.

CHAPTER VII

The Stone Carvings

The Fabergé lapidaries, naturally enough, very often determined the character and proportion of the final object, but it is not until we get to the stone animals and to some extent the small figures of Russian national types built up from various stones, that we can examine their activities on a stage cleared for them alone.

Fabergé animals—and every species appears to have been attempted, not excluding a few prehistoric creatures—are many and various, but they all seem to share a common amiability and well-being. They are not all equally inspired, but the best of them, and these are the great majority, have an unmistakable vitality and charm.

At this point it is proper to amend our previous estimate of Fabergé the decorative artist—the makers of the animals have a special claim to a different title. They are creative artists in their own miniature field and we must adjust our eye to this new circumstance in order properly to appreciate them.

The House of Fabergé carried out its zoological enterprises in stones found mainly in the Urals and Siberia—nephrite, obsidian, rhodonite, chalcedony, agate, rock crystal and topaz, to list only the most common.

These miniature processions of frogs, pigs and ducks are very much more than mere naturalistic renderings from Nature—they are the direct result of an agile intuition exploiting to the full the material available.

A particularly striking example of this is provided by the opal parrot illustrated on Col. Pl. XLIV, where the fusion of subject and material is so harmonious and appropriate that the markings and brilliant colourings of the bird's plumage are evoked from the natural stone; yet over the whole there is a sense of tranquillity and calm that is strongly reminiscent of antique Chinese carving.

However, the Fabergé craftsman does not rest content until he has probed

XLVII. Carpenter, labourer and a peasant playing a balalaika
In the Collection of Sir William Seeds, K.C.M.G.
Full description in Appendix D

XLVIII. Coachman in lapis lazuli with aventurine quartz face and hands, obsidian hair and beard and dull black slate hat carved with the initial I for Isvoschik, the Russian word for coachman. The buttons and belt in gold, the latter painted in green, blue, yellow, mauve, pink and white enamels

Height: $3\frac{5}{8}''$

In a private collection in the United States

even more profoundly into the essential character of the particular animal with which he is dealing; thus we observe with pleasure how in the case of two rather pathetic little frogs he has, by means of a system of highlights, ingeniously and vividly described the wetness of the creatures (Pl. 227).

Fabergé never forced his medium; in fact Aristotle's plea that 'everything desires to keep its own nature' never found a more ardent practitioner.

The present generation of critics and art-historians has taught us to be very shy of anything that savours of charm—this is the age of the stern seeker after Absolute Beauty, of that alarming figure, the pure aesthete. This philosophy is based on sound enough principles, the condemnation of specious sentimentality and self-pity, but like many other admirable theories, it has been ill used and has suffered cruelly at the hands of its more enthusiastic and gullible devotees, with the result that for many of them a work does not begin to exist artistically unless the theme be either completely abstract or at least a little sordid.

A glance back in time would quickly give us a truer perspective of the unrelenting picture they paint; that we may be immediately attracted to a drawing by Watteau or a melody by Schubert does not necessarily signify any shallow or trifling element either in these works or in ourselves; on the contrary, I suggest that the very opposite is the case, and that this much maligned quality, the ability to charm, is often a characteristic on the credit side when we come to form our estimate of an artist's worth.

So it is with these miniature figures created by the lapidaries of the House of Fabergé, especially, for example, with the obsidian penguin which is illustrated from two aspects (Pls. 228 and 229); this pearl among penguins, complete with flat feet and diamond twinkling eyes set in a pure Hapsburg head, conjures up all the awkward gravity and absurd stateliness that we connect with a visit to the penguin pool at the zoo. Who has not watched entranced the progress of these slippery pillars of dignity as they proceed with measured tread one after the other in solemn file round their enclosure? The craftsman has enshrined for ever this, perhaps the most humorous of God's creatures, in a carving just three inches high. The polish imparted to the obsidian, in order to record the characteristic white shirt-front, is a master stroke of the lapidary's art, and so too is the general impression of 'fishiness' described perfectly by the technically hazardous expedient of polishing to the point when the material, a natural volcanic glass, is made to yield up every subtle nuance of translucent grey and silver.

The Stone Carvings

Nowadays, when creative endeavour is so often expected to be geared to some grandiose social or political credo, when art for art's sake is still looked down upon among the innocent, it is especially gratifying to note how these devoted craftsmen were able to carry on quietly and successfully with no more controversial issue as their platform than a marked affection for the creatures living around them.

It was not Fabergé's job, as court jeweller, goldsmith and lapidary, to find sermons in the stones—his job was to describe the precise manner in which a litter of four agate piglets bunch themselves together to sleep, or to follow, with keen appreciation, the snufflings of an amply nourished chalcedony porker, its beady eyes magically brought to life by tiny diamonds set in the head.

It would be interesting to learn what became of the platinum and gold Noah's Ark set with rubies and diamonds and containing pairs of small stone animal carvings of every description.

A collector who has learned how to distinguish for himself the various gold marks and workmasters' initials which appear on most of the other Fabergé pieces will, it may be contended, be at a loss to recognize the master's hand when it comes to stone animals.

Certainly animal carving, as an art, is as old as the world's history, and since it is not usually practical or even desirable to mark the stone figure itself with initials, how is one to diagnose its origin with any degree of accuracy? Quite often the gold feet of these animals are marked with the initials of Henrik Wigström, whose workshop generally made them; but it should be emphasized that Wigström had nothing to do with the carving of the stone itself.

The key to this problem is largely what for want of a more suitable term may be called 'feeling'—the quality which combines knowledge with love. The Fabergé collector who is indeed completely at a loss when faced by one of these anonymous animals is in rather the same position as the alleged picture expert who never neglects to test the surface of a doubtful masterpiece, minutely examines the back of the canvas, photographs, X-rays and piously stabs it with pins, but never once dreams of merely looking at the picture and using his own judgment in the matter. Yet this is only one stage removed from the collector who will not voluntarily express any opinion at all on a work of art until he has first read the artist's name written below it, thereby enabling him to employ the particular cliché for which he has a preference or which he happens to remember.

In a word, the true connoisseur of Fabergé's work approaches his subject creatively and with his eyes wide open, and does not rely on signposts and fingerprints to guide him. He will come to recognize in time the unerring instinct for the right material, the meticulous treatment of detail, the vigorous sense of movement, and perhaps, above all, the obvious affection for and sympathy with the subject. He will realize also that Fabergé animals can be divided quite easily into two distinct types: there are the completely naturalistic representations—a good example is the goat on Pl. 232, and there are those carvings which are frankly conventionalized caricatures—typical specimens in this manner are illustrated on Pl. 246.

Some reference should be made to the relatively small quantity of Fabergé animals which were built up from a number of different coloured stones. These composite works are very cleverly put together and a striking naturalism is usually attained. This very naturalism generally destroys the model's sense of scale, and instead of an agreeable little piece of original sculpture, we are offered an ingenious midget replica of a live creature—a work of very little artistic value. It may be argued that this is purely a question of taste; however, the real objection to this technique is more serious. The obsidian wings and the rhodonite beak must be applied to the agate body of the bird by means of a cement, and this operation in itself constitutes a real abuse of materials. It should in fairness be conceded, however, that there are notable exceptions even to this general criticism, where the judicious introduction of another stone has succeeded in emphasizing a particular characteristic most successfully without detracting from the sculptural quality of the carving.

The well-known figures of Russian national types were carried out in this way. Painstakingly carved pieces of stone of a suitable colour and texture, each playing their appointed part, were carefully—and invisibly—fitted together, lapis lazuli doing service for a pair of breeches, aventurine representing face and arms, grey jasper from Kalgan for the shirt, and so on. Like the animals they were also executed in two styles, and again like the animals, the purely naturalistic built-up figures succeed only in looking like tiny waxwork effigies or mannikins, whereas the 'cartoon' figures—the Balalaika player on Col. Pl. XLVII is a delightful example—are a source of continuous pleasure and have a great deal in common with theatrical puppets. This series constitutes such a good-humoured joke that, although a purist may justifiably find it unacceptable, one is loth to expose it to an unyielding and merciless criticism; let us say simply that if these irresistible figures had been perpetrated by any lesser man than Fabergé, posterity would have had on its hands an artistic catastrophe of the first order. They were put together in Wigström's workshop. It may be noted here in conclusion, that the Pitti Palace houses a number of similarly constructed stone figures which may well have inspired the Russian series.

Besides carving animals and figures, however, the services of the lapidaries were required for many other purposes. Innumerable boxes were made, mainly of stone with gold mounts; cups, *kovshi* and bowls as well as *tazze* and other large ornaments were always in great popular demand, and one may be sure that the workshops in Karavannya Street devoted to these larger-scale activities were usually working at full capacity.

XLIX. Enamelled scent bottle and buttercup and an ant-eater in striated agate

Buttercup: In the Collection of Robert Strauss, Esq.

Scent Bottle: From the Collection of the late Marquess of Portago

Ant-eater in the Collection of Mrs. Arthur Sutherland

Full descriptions in Appendix D

CHAPTER VIII

Toys and Flowers

Those pieces for which no practical use whatever can be found, and whose *raison d'être* is purely decorative, are possibly the most charming items in Fabergé's entire repertoire.

The stone carvings, jewellery and Easter Eggs are discussed under their own headings, and so we are left with the replicas, including the miniature pieces of furniture, the tiny mechanical toys, some of the most ingenious serving as the surprises inside the Imperial Eggs, and the models of flowers in stone pots.

Taking it as almost axiomatic that Fabergé is at his best in small things, it is not difficult to appreciate that the faithful translation in miniature of objects familiar to us in their natural dimensions endows them with a special charm.

The escritoire from the collection of Her late Majesty Queen Mary (Col. Pl. LIV) is an exquisite illustration of the careful way in which the designer has selected the most suitable materials to give an accurate if, on such a tiny scale, a necessarily conventionalized rendering of the original.

The very grain of the wood, for instance, is suggested in the engraving of the gold beneath the translucent red-brown enamel. Again, what a felicitous thought it was to use a ball of rock crystal to represent the globe in the splendid replica at Sandringham (Pl. 280).

Reproduced on Plates 289 and 290 are pictures of the diamond-set replicas of the Imperial Regalia, consisting of two crowns, orb and sceptre set in platinum, displayed in the Hermitage.

An unerring instinct for materials is fundamental to the success of such small objects, which, approaching as they do the domain of jewellery, call for the use of stones and metals beautiful in themselves.

Whether, in about 400 B.C., Archytas of Tarentum really did make a wooden pigeon that flew is questionable; what is quite certain however, is that craftsmen all over the world have for centuries been fascinated with the idea of building the perfect automaton. History abounds in instances of man's occasional successes, frequent failures and deliberate evasions such as Baron von Kempelen's notorious Chess Player.

The Swiss have come nearest to technical perfection in the production of conjurers, wizards, *escamoteurs,* musicians, acrobats and the like, but in doing so they have paid the heavy price of artistic perdition.

One of the first impressions to strike a visitor to the fantastic exhibition of *automates* in the Neuchâtel Museum is the excessive size of these disquieting robots; instead of being agreeable mechanical toys, which we could all enjoy, they turn out to be life-size and, collected together, present a silent assembly of articulated waxworks, dead, dusty and faintly menacing. There is even a particularly precocious and sinister baby by the Swiss designer Jaquet-Droz which, when wound up, writes, with an eye to the tourist trade, 'Soyez les bienvenus à Neuchâtel'.

Fabergé, on the other hand, understood very well man's love for the miniature, and his automatic elephants, sedan-chairs and so on are always charming playthings.

Alexander Fabergé, confirming this, explained how, in the case of the mechanical peacock contained in the rock crystal Egg (Pl. 356), the first model made was almost as large as a real peacock, the next rather smaller, and so on through about three or four diminishing sizes, in order to be quite sure of the complicated mechanism on such a small scale. Fabergé never set out merely to astound with his mechanical toys, his aim was rather to charm and divert.

In Russia, where the winters are long and pitiless, the first signs of spring take on a special significance, and the flower becomes a symbol of happiness and renewed hope. Special trains used to bring spring flowers from the South of France on blocks of ice to brighten the Court Balls. In recognizing this special significance, Fabergé created some of his most lovely compositions. These pots of flowers are the ultimate refinement of his art—in them he has shed all unnecessary and disturbing elements, and, naturalistic to an astonishing degree, they yet may be justifiably regarded as the most typically 'Fabergé' of all his pieces.

At one point early in the third act of Rimsky Korsakov's opera *The Invisible City of Kitesh,* as the orchestra spins a dark and fragile web of magic, single, separate and distinct bell notes ring out with crystal clarity; they

278. Large nephrite *kovsh* and a maize-enamelled cigarette case
From the Collection of the late M. Maurice Sandoz
Full description in Appendix D

279. Large nephrite dish mounted with two engraved yellow gold handles in the
Louis XV style enamelled translucent strawberry and lavishly set with rose diamonds
Signed: M.Π.   Gold mark: Crossed anchors $17\frac{1}{2}'' \times 10\frac{1}{2}'' \times 1''$
In the Wernher Collection, Luton Hoo

280. Scale model of a terrestrial globe
In the Royal Collection at Sandringham

281. Miniature grand piano
Original Fabergé photograph

Full descriptions in Appendix D

282. Miniature tankard with cover in engraved red gold and inset with hammered
yellow gold panels, on four ball feet

Signed: M.Π.   Overall length: $3\frac{1}{2}''$

In the Collection of Alexander Schaffer, Esq.

L. Sedan chair in engraved red gold, with panels enamelled translucent rose on sun-ray backgrounds with sepia-painted symbols of the arts; opaque white and translucent emerald green enamelled and *sablé* borders, carved yellow gold mounts, engraved rock crystal windows and lined with mother of pearl

Signed: M.II.   Gold Mark: 72   Height: $3\frac{5}{8}''$

In a private collection in the United States

LI. Miniature gold salt chair with cabochon rubies and rose diamonds, the brocade simulated in painted enamel. The seat forms
the lid of a receptacle, the hinge of which is cleverly concealed.
Signed: К. ФАБЕРЖЕ   Height: 4"
Both in the Collection of Mrs. India Minshall

LII. Miniature salt chair in jade mounted in varicoloured
chased golds. The seat, as well as both sides of the
back, is in translucent enamel naturalistically simulating
brocade, the front outlined with half pearls.
    The seat opens to disclose the interior of the hollowed-
out jade receptacle
Signed: H.W.   Gold Mark: 72   Height: 3 $\frac{1}{8}$"

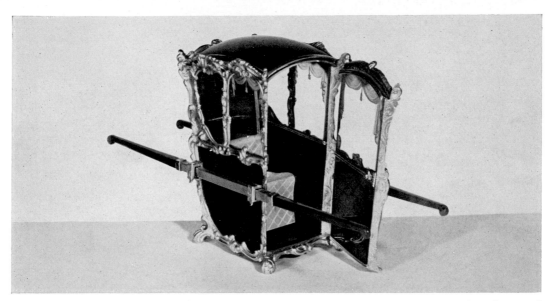

283. Sedan Chair in nephrite with red and green gold *repoussé* mounts, engraved rock crystal
windows and mother of pearl seat

Signed: M.П.   *In the Collection of Miss Woollcombe-Boyce*   Height: $3\frac{1}{8}''$

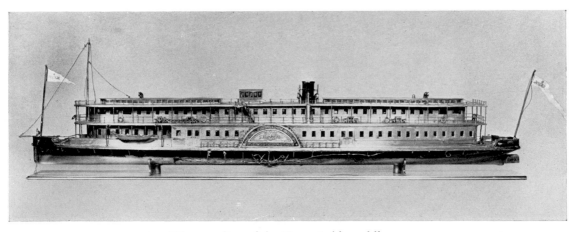

284. Silver replica of the Tsarevitch's paddle-steamer
In the Collection of the Hammer Galleries
Full details in Appendix D

285. Spray of cornflowers, a rock crystal seal and a miniature Louis XV desk
In the Collection of Her Majesty Queen Elizabeth the Queen Mother
Full descriptions in Appendix D

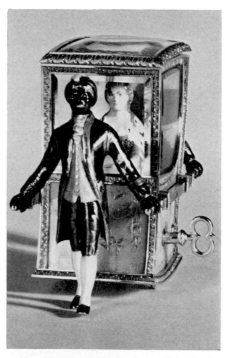

286. An action photograph of the
mechanical Sedan Chair shown on
Colour Plate LIII

LIII. Mechanical sedan chair in engraved red gold enamelled translucent yellow with green gold mounts and rock crystal windows and roof. A miniature gold figure of Catherine the Great in her Imperial robes enamelled in natural translucent colours and wearing a rose diamond crown and order, is seated within. The chair is borne along by two scarlet-coated 'Court Arabs' in gold and enamels, who walk naturalistically when the clockwork mechanism is wound with a small gold key. Another view on Pl. 286

Signed: H.W.   Overall length: 3¼". Height: 2⅝"
This piece bears the signature FABERGE in Latin characters indicating that it was made for the English or French market
In the Collection of Charles Clore, Esq.

287, 288. Miniature grand piano in engraved silver enamelled opalescent white with painted arabesques in sanguine, pale green and turquoise enamel, and red and green gold carved mounts

Signed: К. ФАБЕРЖЕ　　　　　　　　　　　　　　　　　　　Length: $4\frac{1}{8}''$

From the Collection of the late M. Maurice Sandoz

289, 290. Two views of the replicas of the Imperial Regalia in diamonds set in platinum

Large Crown Height: $2\frac{7}{8}$". Diameter: $2\frac{5}{8}$". Smaller Crown Height: $1\frac{1}{2}$". Diameter: $1\frac{7}{16}$". Height of sceptre: $6\frac{1}{4}$". Diameter of orb: $1\frac{3}{4}$"

Signed: ФАБЕРЖЕ

In the Hermitage Collection, Leningrad

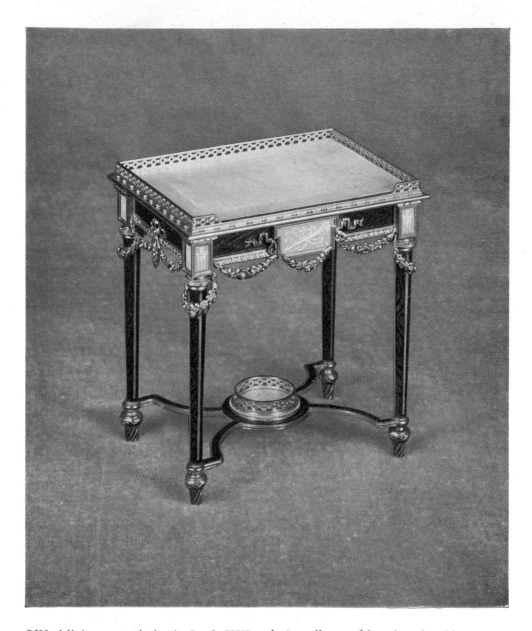

LIV. Miniature escritoire in Louis XVI style in yellow gold with red gold mounts, enamelled translucent red-brown on a ground specially engraved to simulate the grain of the veneer. Decorated with opaque turquoise enamel panels with eight painted Imperial cyphers of Marie Feodorovna and classical motifs in *grisaille*. The hinged mother of pearl top is engraved with four double-headed eagles, and the small circular panel below, with a rose

Signed: M.Π.   Height: $3\frac{1}{2}''$. Top: $3\frac{1}{4}'' \times 2\frac{3}{8}''$

From the Collection of Her late Majesty Queen Mary

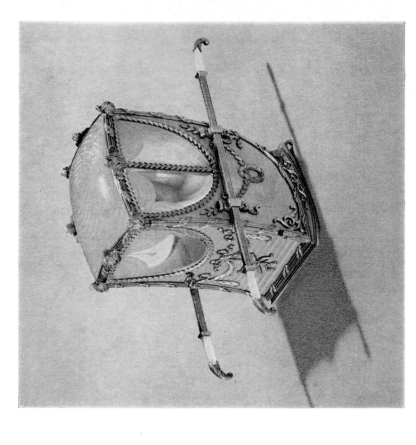

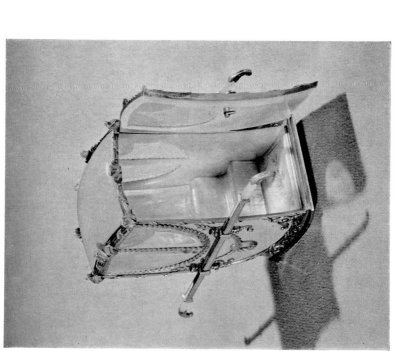

LV. and LVI. Sedan chair in engraved red gold, enamelled translucent pale pink on a *moiré guillochage* with carved green gold and mother of pearl mounts, engraved rock crystal windows, and lined with engraved mother of pearl

Signed: H.W.   Height: 3″

In a private collection in the United States

291. One of a small group of eighteenth-
century flower models, this one in silver, set
with diamonds and pearls, which are displayed in the Gold Room of the Hermitage.
Fabergé must undoubtedly have been influenced by these examples in his own work
Height: 13¾″

292. Holly, with berries in purpurine, stalk in dull green gold, and leaves in dark nephrite in a
rock crystal glass

No marks   Height: 5⅞″
Pine tree engraved dull red gold set with rose diamonds, in a bowenite vase supported on an
aventurine quartz platform. This model was taken from nature at Sandringham
No marks   *Both in the Royal Collection at Sandringham*   Height: 5⅛″

293. Catkins in spun green gold, stalk in dull red gold and leaves in carved nephrite. No marks. Height: 5⅞″. Rowan tree with purpurine berries, dull red gold stem and pale nephrite leaves. No marks. Height: 9″. Wild Cherries in purpurine, blossom in opaque white enamel with rose diamond centres, stalks in dull red gold and leaves in nephrite. No marks. Height: 5⅜″. All in rock crystal pots

In the Royal Collection at Sandringham

LVII. *Bonbonnière* with articulated dancing peasant figures
In a private collection
Full description in Appendix D

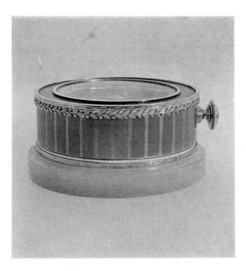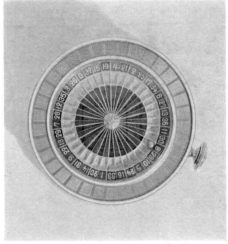

LVIII and LIX. Miniature working model roulette wheel enamelled translucent
grey-blue against a *guilloché* ground with two-colour gold mounts, the main bezel
chased with husks, and resting on an onyx base

Diameter: $2\frac{3}{4}''$

In a private collection in the United States

LX and LXI. Box in engraved red gold, enamelled opalescent white with carved green gold borders framing movable painted ivory puppets set in the lid and base against dull black oxidised silver backgrounds. This box was made to commemorate a gala performance of Tchaikowsky's opera *The Queen of Spades*; the two dancing figures depict characters from the pastoral interlude in the second act

Signed: H.W.   *In a private collection in England* $2\frac{1}{2}'' \times 2\frac{3}{16}'' \times 1''$

294. *Left:* Rosebuds in opaque pink and translucent green enamel, stalk in red gold, leaves carved in nephrite, in a rock crystal pot
No marks   Height: $5\frac{1}{2}''$
Right: Bleeding-heart in rhodonite and white chalcedony, dull green gold stalks, carved nephrite leaves, in a rock crystal pot
No marks   Height: $7\frac{3}{4}''$
In the Royal Collection at Sandringham

295. Gypsophila with flowers in translucent green enamel with rose diamond centres, engraved dull green gold stalk, moss in yellow and red gold in a nephrite jar. Formerly in the Collection of Queen Olga of Greece

No marks   Height: 7″

In the Wernher Collection, Luton Hoo

296, 297. Hoya Bella (Honey Flower) with flowers in pale parchment-coloured opaque enamel with pale orange veining and translucent green enamel calyx and rose diamond centres, engraved dull green gold stalk, carved nephrite leaves in a rock crystal pot

Signed: ФАБЕРЖЕ   Height: 7½″

In the Collection of R. Strauss, Esq.

LXII. Group of flowers in rock crystal pots
In the Collection of Mr. and Mrs. Alexander Schaffer
Full descriptions in Appendix D

298. Naturalistically enamelled pansy in gold in a rock crystal pot engraved
with a Roman X on one side and the names of the five Imperial children on
the other. Given on 7th December, 1904 by the Tsar to his wife to commemorate their tenth Wedding Anniversary, each of the five petals swivels
round to reveal an oval miniature portrait of one of the children within a
diamond border

Signed: H.W.   Height: $5\frac{15}{16}''$

In the Armoury Museum of the Kremlin, Moscow

299. Carnation in yellow gold enamelled translucent red bronze, the engraved green gold
stalk, leaves and bud enamelled translucent green, in a rock crystal pot

No marks *In the Royal Collection at Sandringham* Height: $7\frac{1}{4}''$

LXIII. Basket of lilies of the valley in yellow gold. Nine sprays of lilies with engraved green gold stalks, carved nephrite leaves and pearl and rose diamond flowers grow in a bed of spun green gold 'moss' composed of clipped wire polished and unpolished in patches

The following is a translation of the Russian inscription engraved underneath the basket:

To Her Imperial Majesty, Tsarina Alexandra Feodorovna
from the Iron-works management and dealers in the Siberian iron section of the Nijegorodski Fair in the year 1896

Signed: H.W.   Gold mark: crossed anchors   Height: $7\frac{1}{2}''$
Wartski photograph

LXIV. Green gold dandelion 'seed-clock' composed of strands of asbestos fibre, spun platinum and rose diamonds, with two nephrite leaves in a carved rock crystal pot

Height: $5\frac{5}{8}''$

In a private collection in the United States

300. Japonica with flowers in pinky white opaque enamel with rose diamond centres, engraved dull green gold stalk, carved nephrite leaves in a rock crystal pot
No marks   *In the Royal Collection at Sandringham*   Height: $6\frac{3}{4}''$

301. Pansy, wild rose and daisies in a flower-pot

302. Cranberry, pansy and a small raspberry plant
Both groups in the Royal Collection at Sandringham
Full descriptions in Appendix D

LXV. Gold basket of Lilies of the Valley with a looped gold handle, the basket composed of plaited gold wire and the flowers growing from rough gold moss, in oriental pearls and the leaves in carved nephrite

Signed: **M.П.**   Height: $3\frac{1}{4}''$

In a private collection in the United States

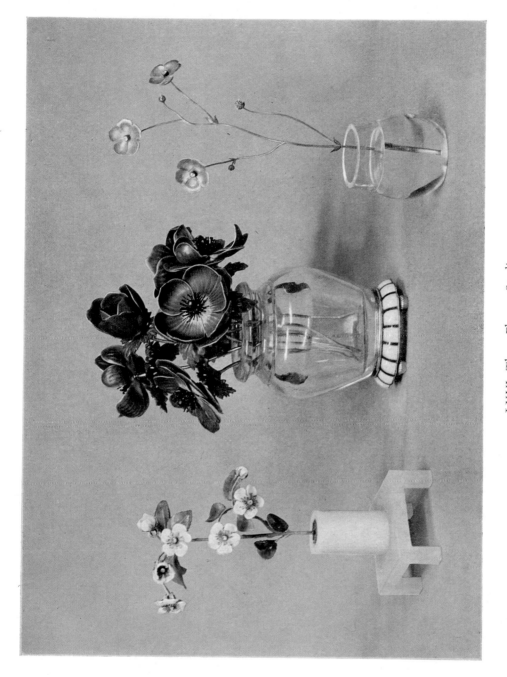

LXVI. Three Flower Studies
In the Collection of R. Strauss, Esq.
Full description in Appendix D

303. Chrysanthemum, lilies of the valley, mock–orange and a rose
In the Royal Collection at Sandringham
Full descriptions in Appendix D

304. Spray of buttercups in gold enamelled translucent yellow and green, and cornflowers enamelled translucent blue with diamond centres, with green gold stalks and leaves in a rock crystal jar. A diamond, ruby, and black enamelled bee set in red gold, is poised on one of the buttercups   Height: 9″

In the Collection of Her Majesty Queen Elizabeth the Queen Mother

LXVII. An engraved rock crystal jar set with a gold mount, enamelled translucent strawberry and pale opalescent pink, supported on four bun feet, containing seven separate sprays of wild strawberries in purpurine with pale yellow gold stalks, carved nephrite leaves and five flowers in chalcedony, nephrite and gold

Signed: ФАБЕРЖЕ   *In the Collection of R. Strauss, Esq.*   Height: 6¾″

suggest very vividly, as they are intended to suggest, the sudden miraculous appearance of flowers in an enchanted forest. The pleasure we feel when we are shown one of Fabergé's little flower studies has in it something of the delighted surprise that the maiden Fevronia must experience in the opera when she wakes up to find herself in her Paradise Garden.

The essentially ephemeral quality of the single sprays is generally accentuated by their being placed, as though casually, in what appear to be simple glass pots or jars filled with cold water. Upon closer inspection, however, the impression of the water is discovered to be a simple stratagem contrived by the lapidary, for both the liquid and the container are one solid block of skilfully carved rock crystal.

From delicately engraved gold stalks, nephrite leaves sprout, carved and veined with an oriental devotion to detail; the tiny gold rivets which hold them in place are not seen. The petals of the flower itself are sometimes represented by translucent or opaque enamel on gold, at others, by carved stones. In earlier examples the leaves are often rendered in gold and enamel.

Sometimes, in the more conventionalized models, small rose diamonds or other gem stones are used to illuminate the centre of a flower, and, when these catch the light, owing to the constant almost imperceptible trembling of the most delicate examples, a marvellous sense of life and movement is attained.

The flowers are sometimes signed, but this whole question is discussed more fully in Chapter X.

There is a cunningly designed pansy in the Kremlin each of whose five petals when opened reveals a tiny portrait of one of the Tsar's children (Pl. 298). Fabergé also designed a delightful sprig of pear blossom, the emblem of the Queen's Own Worcestershire Hussars, which was presented to the regiment in 1900 by the Countess of Dudley, and represents today one of their most prized possessions.

A genuine Fabergé flower can stand up to the most searching examination in all its parts; in fact one good test of authenticity is the way the flower grows naturally from the stalk (Pl. 297). The Germans produced quantities of flowers —as they did animals—which are often put up for sale, possibly in good faith, as Fabergé pieces. Careful inspection, however, coupled with a certain amount of judgment based on experience of the genuine article, can generally be relied upon to prevent mistakes.

CHAPTER IX

The Imperial Easter Eggs

When the ancient Pagan rites and ceremonies came to be Christianized, the egg, regarded always as the manifestation of fertility and the life-force, was quite naturally sublimated into the symbol of the Resurrection, and in the same way, the various spring cults and festivals in honour of the rebirth of the Sun, and therefore of life itself, became Easter. It is clear then that the custom of exchanging eggs at Easter time is one that has grown from the most deeply planted roots.

We can trace the actual painting of eggs with religious subjects from the thirteenth century, but it was not until the early sixteenth century, when François I of France, an enthusiastic patron of the arts, was given an egg-shell containing a wood carving of the Passion of Christ, that the custom of presenting really elaborate 'surprise' Easter Eggs was established.

Perhaps the most significant examples of the Easter Egg as a work of art, and those most relevant in our study of Fabergé, are those made in France during the seventeenth and eighteenth centuries.

The gilded and painted eggs that were brought to Louis XIV on Easter morning were presented by him to his courtiers and servants with a great deal of pomp and ceremony, but under Louis XV both the giving and the decorating of Easter eggs was undertaken in a rather more lighthearted spirit. More often than not, the recipient of an egg was regaled by the distinctly broad couplets daintily encircling it.

Some of the finest artists in France, Watteau, Boucher and Lancret, for example, directed their talents towards the painting of egg shells, resulting, as a rule, in some elegantly conceived composition of a gallant and rather improper nature. One of these rare painted eggs was sold in Paris at the Salle Drouot in 1914 for 25,000 gold francs.

Louis XV presented Madame du Barry with a particularly large egg which

LXVIII. Serpent Clock Egg
Presented to Marie Feodorovna by Alexander III
Made between 1885 and 1890
In the Collection of Messrs. Wartski
Full description in the catalogue of Imperial Easter Eggs

had been richly gilded by his court jeweller, and concealed a beautifully modelled cupid. I can find no exact details of the white-enamelled egg made for one of the princes of Spain by a Paris goldsmith; the Gospel was inscribed on the outside of this egg and it is reported to have contained a small automatic cockerel which sang two distinct melodies.

One Easter, Louis XVI presented Madame Victoire de France, the daughter of Louis XV, with what appeared to be simply two duck eggs, but turned out, on closer inspection, to contain each an agreeable little scene with a group of figures modelled in wax showing episodes of an authentic drama; this concerned the courage and nobility of the seventy-year-old Louis Gillet in rescuing a simple country girl from the clutches of two desperadoes, and then refusing to accept any reward whatever, having brought her safely home to her parents (Pls. 307, 308).

Fabergé showed himself very Russian in his own strongly developed love of novelty and the curious in art, although this never found expression in anything as engagingly scandalous as the earlier French examples. As Eugène Fabergé once put it to me: 'Papa était plutôt solide.'

Before embarking upon a detailed examination of the Imperial Easter Eggs, surely one of the most extraordinary series of gifts ever conceived and brought to reality, we must attune our minds to the particular circumstances prevailing at the time—especially as these are so far removed from those of our own day.

'Every artist', writes Lord David Cecil, 'constructs his work within certain conventions, which we must accept before we are in a position to estimate his success. Some of the most famous ineptitudes of criticism are due to a failure to realize this obligation.'

It requires an imaginative effort of an heroic order for us, with our rigidly controlled economy, to visualize the scene at the Palace on Easter morning when the Tsarina, having exchanged the greeting 'Christ is risen' and the traditional three kisses with her husband, opened the case containing Fabergé's latest *tour-de-force* designed for the supreme purpose of giving her pleasure.

To find any possible parallel for these royal gifts, we have to think back to the days of Melchior Dinglinger and the treasures he created for the Elector of Saxony; to James Cox and the fabulous collection of mechanical clocks he made for Ch'ien Lung's Imperial Palaces at Peking, Yuan Ming Yuan, and Jehol, where, as Mr. Simon Harcourt-Smith tells us, 'the passage of the hours was marked by a fluttering of enamelled wings, a gushing of glass fountains and a spinning of paste stars.'

Just how the first Imperial Easter Egg came to be made has been the subject of conjecture for some time, although it has been generally assumed that Fabergé sought and obtained an interview with Alexander III, and proposed that a very special egg be made for the Empress, to look exactly like an actual hen's egg, but containing in reality some delightful surprise; the Tsar was evidently not then given any further details but was so delighted when he saw the result that he commissioned Fabergé forthwith to make a surprise Easter Egg for him to present every year. The Egg (Pl. 313) contained a gold yolk, which in turn held a coloured gold hen inside which a diamond Imperial Crown lay concealed; within this Crown was hung a miniature ruby egg.

In the face of some new evidence, however, it appears as though we may have to revise this version of the events which led up to this first Egg. I reproduce photographs of an egg containing a similar series of surprises culminating finally in a diamond ring which since the eighteenth century has been in the possession of the Danish Royal Family (Pls. 309 and 310); I am grateful to Mr. Gudmund Boesen of Rosenborg Castle in Copenhagen, for the fascinating and illuminating historical note of this piece which he has given me, and which appears as Appendix C on p. 142.

The Empress Marie Feodorovna, who was born Princess Dagmar of Denmark, would certainly have known this attractive object in her native home, and might well have spoken of it to her husband. He was at this time especially anxious to find any diversion or pleasure that might supplant for a while the indelible picture that haunted his wife's imagination of the recent gruesome scene, the deathbed of the murdered Tsar Alexander II, at which she was present; it is more than likely that he asked Fabergé to make just such an object, containing this time not a ring but an Easter Egg. In this way he would not only be giving his wife a very special Easter present, but one which would remind her of happier times spent at home in Denmark.

Taking 1884 as the year the first Egg was presented, eleven of these splendid objects would have been made for Alexander III who died on 1st November, 1894. Nicholas II announced on his accession to the throne that he intended following his father in everything; he lived up to this piece of wishful thinking quite literally at any rate in the matter of the Easter Eggs, and the arrangement was even extended to include an Egg for the Dowager Empress as well as the

LXIX. Spring Flowers Egg
Presented to Marie Feodorovna by Alexander III
Made between 1885 and 1890
In a private collection in the United States
Full description in the catalogue of Imperial Easter Eggs

one to be made every year for Alexandra Feodorovna. Thus two Eggs were made annually from 1895 right up to 1917, making a total of 57 in all. Carl Fabergé himself brought the Easter Eggs to the Emperor; those for the Dowager Empress were delivered by one of his principal assistants until his sons were old enough to take on this job.

Bell-pushes, seals, boxes and even miniature-frames were also made in the form of eggs, so that they should be suitable as Easter presents.

Besides the Imperial Eggs, Fabergé made a number of very beautiful ones for presentation to the Prince and Princess Youssoupoff, to Madame Barbara Kelch, a wealthy eccentric, and to Fru Emanuel Nobel, whose husband was the nephew of Alfred Nobel.

With one or two notable exceptions, such as the Eggs for 1912 and Marie Feodorovna's Egg for 1914, it is, as we should expect, the earlier examples that are the most frankly derivative; although, as we have seen, even these bear the unmistakable imprint of their creator's personality.

Every time we are made to catch our breath and, as if under a spell, are held enchanted before some new miracle of delicacy and inventiveness, we are acknowledging the debt we owe to the liveliness of the imagination of Carl Fabergé. This noble procession of Imperial gifts, instead of remaining intact to decorate a room in a Royal Palace, a coherent and unique collection, has, as we know, been tragically broken up and scattered to the four corners of the earth.

It was with the idea in mind of recreating this sense of a story unfolding, year after year, that I have attempted to compile an illustrated catalogue of the Easter Eggs as far as possible in the order they were presented. There are still many gaps, several dates about which it is difficult to be certain, and a number of inadequate photographs of Eggs, which, being the only known surviving records we have of the originals, I have not hesitated to include. Research has been obscured by the Revolution in Russia, but I feel that there are still fragmentary clues to be picked up, and it may be that the publication of all the facts that are known may have the effect of stirring someone's memory somewhere and bringing to light fresh evidence.

Catalogue of
Imperial Easter Eggs

THE FIRST IMPERIAL EASTER EGG
(Pls. 313–316)

Presented to Marie Feodorovna by Alexander III
Probable date, 1884

★

This was the very first of all the Fabergé Easter Eggs, and the pleasure that it gave to both the Tsar, who presented it, and the Tsarina, who received it, established a custom which was to continue without interruption until the violent end of the Romanov dynasty.

The shell of the Egg is gold, enamelled opaque white, and polished to give the effect of a hen's egg. The two halves are held together by a bayonet fitting; when these are opened, a yellow gold yolk with a dull sandblasted surface is revealed. Inside this yolk, which opens in the same way as the shell, sits a yellow and white tinted gold hen as though in a nest. Each feather is most beautifully engraved, and two cabochon ruby eyes are set in the head; the beak and comb are carried out in red gold. By lifting the head, the hen opens on a hinge at the tail. Originally, the diamond replica of the Imperial Crown was contained within the hen, and when this was opened, a tiny ruby pendant was found hanging inside.

A detailed account of the historical circumstances which probably united to bring about the designing of this first Egg is set out on p. 76.

There are no marks at all on this Egg.

Shell: $2\frac{1}{2}''$ length × $1\frac{13}{16}''$ across. Thickness $\frac{1}{8}''$ of hollow shell.
Yolk: $1\frac{9}{16}''$ diameter.
Hen: $1\frac{3}{8}''$ length × $1\frac{1}{3}''$ height.

In the Collection of Lady Grantchester.

RESURRECTION EGG
(Pl. 317)

Presented to Marie Feodorovna by Alexander III
Made between 1885 and 1890

*

In the form of a monstrance, this Resurrection Egg is one of Fabergé's masterpieces; exquisitely made in the manner of the Italian Renaissance, it is essentially a jewel.

The three gold figures in the group are enamelled with natural opaque colours— white drapery and lilac-coloured wings. The grass and the ground upon which the group is arranged are enamelled pale green and brown with yellow flecks, and this base is surrounded by a narrow belt of rose diamonds. The door of the Tomb is enamelled to simulate marble with a coral-coloured handle. The whole Resurrection scene is contained within a superbly carved rock crystal Egg, the two hemispheres held together by a line of rose diamonds. The plinth supporting the Egg is enamelled translucent strawberry and green and opaque white with opaque black-painted enamel motifs, and opaque cerulean blue. The gold used is yellow, and the piece is set with eight brilliant diamonds in opaque black enamel collets; an Indian pearl is set on each of the four main panels of the base which is richly set with rose diamonds, and a large pearl serves as the shaft of this Egg. The photograph of this piece shows how carefully the gold *cloisons* separating, for instance, the translucent strawberry and opaque white enamel round the edge of the base have been chased.

Signed by Michael Perchin.
Gold Marks: 56 and crossed anchors.
Height $3\frac{7}{8}'' \times 1\frac{3}{4}''$ across base.

In the Collection of Lady Grantchester.

SERPENT CLOCK EGG
Colour Pl. LXVIII

Presented to Marie Feodorovna by Alexander III
Made between 1885 and 1890

*

Designed as a clock in the Sèvres tradition, this piece is one of the loveliest examples of Fabergé's use of the *quatre-couleur* technique in gold. The Egg itself is enamelled translucent royal blue contrasting with the opalescent white enamel of the base, which is made up of three panels to each of which are applied motifs in four colours of gold of the Arts and Sciences. Round the shaft supporting the Egg a diamond-set gold serpent is coiled, the head and tongue pointing the hour.

Signed by Michael Perchin.
Gold Marks: 56 and crossed anchors.
Height: $7\frac{1}{4}''$.

In the Collection of Messrs. Wartski.

EGG WITH TWELVE MONOGRAMS
(Pl. 318)

Presented to Marie Feodorovna by Alexander III
Made between 1885 and 1890

★

Easter Egg in gold and painted royal blue enamel divided by bands of rose diamonds and richly decorated with a scroll pattern. The crowned monograms of Alexander III and Marie Feodorovna in rose diamonds, appear each six times round the Egg, which is velvet lined.

The surprise has been lost.

Signed by Michael Perchin.
$3\frac{1}{4}'' \times 2\frac{1}{4}''$.

In the Collection of Mrs. Herbert May.

BLUE ENAMEL RIBBED EGG
(Pl. 319)

Presented to Marie Feodorovna by Alexander III
Made between 1885 and 1890

★

In three colours of gold and enamelled translucent royal blue, the egg is surmounted by an Imperial Crown set with sapphires and diamonds. Not an entirely successful design, despite some fine carving, this piece appears top-heavy owing partly to the excessive length of the finial, and partly to the inadequate base, which must originally have been much more substantial. The onyx steps supporting the Egg are, in the author's opinion, a justified addition to, or completion of, this light spiral gold stem.

The surprise has been lost.

305. Rock crystal clock made in Dresden by Heinrich Hoffmann *circa* 1560 with a scene showing Orpheus, under a tree, charming the animals by his music

306. Early eighteenth-century silver-gilt covered goblet set with cameos

It is interesting to compare these examples from the Green Vaults in Dresden with the Fabergé Eggs illustrated on Plates 317 and 373

307, 308. One of a pair of Easter Eggs presented
by Louis XVI to Madame Victoire, the daughter
of Louis XV
In the Musée Lambinet, Versailles

309, 310. An old French Ivory Easter Egg
In the Royal Collection at Rosenborg, Copenhagen
By kind permission of H.M. the King of Denmark
See Appendix C and full description in Appendix D

311, 312. Two views of the celebrated Peacock Clock in ormolu, by James Cox (died 1788), which inspired the Fabergé Easter Egg given to the Dowager Empress in 1908
In the Hermitage Museum, Leningrad

THE IMPERIAL EASTER EGGS

Illustrated in the order of their presentation by Alexander III and Nicholas II
A *catalogue raisonné* with full descriptions of the Eggs accompanies the plates

313-316. The First Imperial Easter Egg
Presented to Marie Feodorovna by Alexander III
Probable date 1884
In the Collection of Lady Grantchester

317. Resurrection Egg
Presented to Marie Feodorovna by Alexander III
Made between 1885 and 1890
In the Collection of Lady Grantchester

LXX. Diamond Trellis Egg
Presented to Marie Feodorovna by Alexander III
Probable date, 1892
In a private collection in England
Full description in the Catalogue of Imperial Easter Eggs

318. Egg with Twelve Monograms
Presented to Marie Feodorovna by Alexander III
Made between 1885 and 1890
In the Collection of Mrs. Herbert May

319. Blue Enamel Ribbed Egg
Presented to Marie Feodorovna by
Alexander III
In the Collection of Stavros S. Niarchos, Esq.

320. Danish Silver Jubilee Egg
Presented to Marie Feodorovna by Alexander III
Date 1888
Present whereabouts unknown

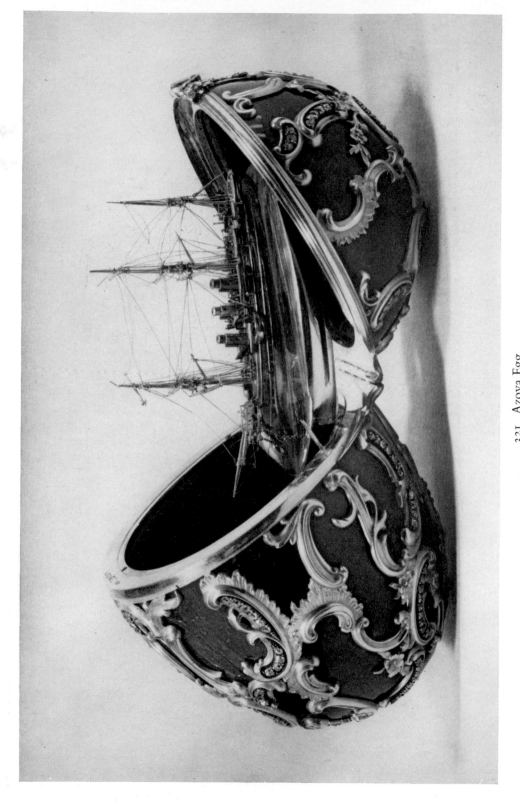

321. Azova Egg
Presented to Marie Feodorovna by Alexander III
1891
In the Armoury Museum of the Kremlin, Moscow

LXXI. Caucasus Egg
Presented to Marie Feodorovna by Alexander III
Dated 1893
Privately Owned
Full description in the catalogue of Imperial Easter Eggs

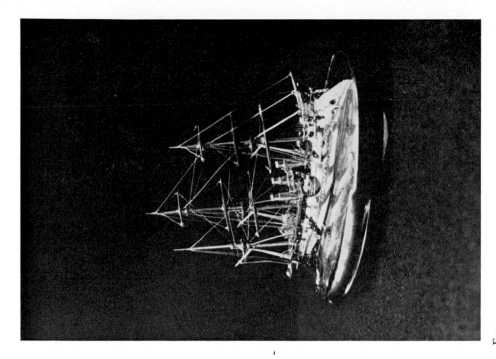

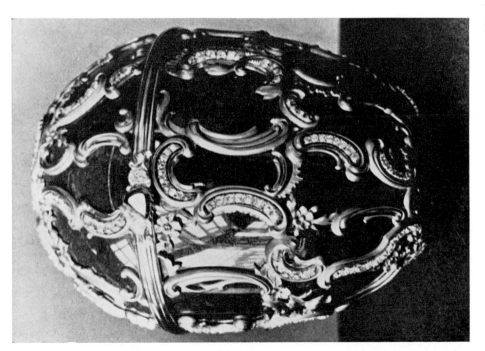

322, 323. Azova Egg
Presented to Marie Feodorovna by Alexander III
1891
In the Armoury Museum of the Kremlin, Moscow

324. Egg-shaped Casket in chalcedony decorated with enamel mounts by Le Roy of Amsterdam
Early eighteenth century
In the Green Vaults Collection formerly in Dresden

325. Rosebud Egg
Presented to Alexandra Feodorovna by Nicholas II
Dated 1895
Present whereabouts unknown

LXXII. Egg in the Renaissance Style
Presented to Marie Feodorovna by Alexander III
Dated 1894
In the Collection of Alexander Schaffer, Esq.
Full description in the Catalogue of Imperial Easter Eggs

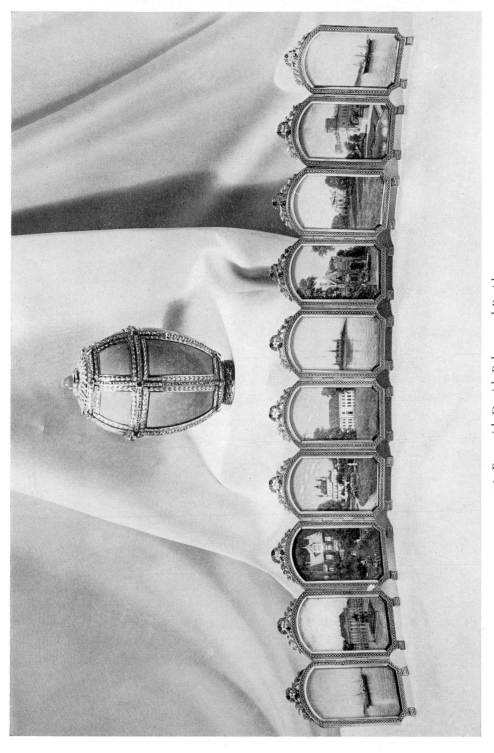

326. Egg with Danish Palaces and Residences
Presented to the Dowager Empress Marie Feodorovna by Nicholas II
Probably 1895
In a private collection in the United States

327. Egg with Revolving Miniatures
Presented to Alexandra Feodorovna by Nicholas II
Probable date 1896
In the Lillian Thomas Pratt Collection of the Virginia Museum of Fine Arts

328. The Winter and Anitchkov Palaces

329. Tsarskoe Selo and Rosenau, Coburg

330, 331. Pelican Egg
Presented to the Dowager Empress Marie Feodorovna by Nicholas II
Dated 1897
In the Lillian Thomas Pratt Collection of the Virginia Museum of Fine Arts

332. Madonna Lily Egg
Presented to Alexandra Feodorovna by Nicholas II
Dated 1899
In the Armoury Museum of the Kremlin, Moscow

333. Pansy Egg
Presented to the Dowager Empress Marie Feodorovna by Nicholas II
Dated 1899
In a private collection in the United States

Signed by Michael Perchin.
Gold marks: 56 and crossed anchors.
Height: $4\frac{1}{4}''$.

In the Collection of Stavros S. Niarchos, Esq.

DANISH SILVER JUBILEE EGG
(Pl. 320)

Presented to Marie Feodorovna by Alexander III
Date 1888

★

Given on the occasion of the Silver Jubilee of King Christian IX of Denmark, the father of the Tsarina, this gold Egg is surmounted by a Danish Royal Elephant and supported by three Danish heraldic lions. Enamelled opalescent white and pale blue and profusely set with precious stones, this Egg, which stands on an elaborate plinth, is decorated with swags and laurel leaves, a diamond-set fillet, carved gold masks and the Empress's monogram in diamonds. The Egg contains a double-sided miniature screen on a stand showing portraits by Zehngraf of King Christian on one side and his Queen Louise on the other. Each miniature is surmounted by a diamond crown and initial.

Approximate height: 10″.
No details of marks available.
It is not known if this Egg is still in existence.
Original Fabergé photograph.

SPRING FLOWERS EGG
Colour Plate LXIX

Presented to Marie Feodorovna by Alexander III
Made between 1885 and 1890

★

Supported on a circular carved and fluted bowenite base, mounted with red and green gold scrolls and chased acanthus leaves and set with rose diamonds, the gold Egg is enamelled translucent strawberry on a guilloché field. It is richly embellished with carved green gold rocaille decoration in the Louis XV manner and the red gold rim which bisects the Egg is set with rose diamonds, as are the two surmounting fasteners. When these are divided the Easter Egg opens to reveal the surprise, an exquisite basket of Spring flowers resting on a small gold circular plinth.

The flowers are carved in milky chalcedony with olivine centres set in green gold, and the gold leaves are enamelled translucent green over an engraved ground. The basket, which is carved in platinum, is elaborately pierced and set with a profusion of rose diamonds, as is the handle. This flower-basket motif was used again much later by Fabergé in his Winter Egg of 1913. As in the case of all the early Imperial Easter Eggs, this example is smaller than those which were made in 1896 and after.

Signed by Michael Perchin.
Gold Mark: Crossed anchors.
Height of Egg: 3″.
Height of Basket: $1\frac{5}{16}$″.

In a private collection in the United States.

AZOVA EGG
(Pls. 321, 322 and 323)

Presented to Marie Feodorovna by Alexander III
Dated 1891

★

Made to commemorate the Tsarevitch's recent voyage round the world in the cruiser *Pamiat Azova*, which sailed in 1890 and returned in the following August. The Egg itself is carved from a solid piece of heliotrope jasper, and is decorated in the Louis XV style with yellow gold scrolls set with brilliant diamonds and chased gold flowers; the broad fluted gold bezel is set with a drop ruby clasp. A tiny replica in gold of the *Pamiat Azova* set on a piece of aquamarine is contained inside the Egg. The model of the cruiser is the work of August Holmström himself, and the minute attention to detail and the delicacy of the craftsmanship are of the highest order; it is carried out in red and yellow golds and platinum.

Signed by Michael Perchin.
Gold Mark: 72.
Length of Egg: $3\frac{7}{8}$″.
Height of Egg: 3″.
Length of ship: $3\frac{1}{16}$″.

In the Armoury Museum of the Kremlin in Moscow.

DIAMOND TRELLIS EGG
Colour Plate LXX

Presented to Marie Feodorovna by Alexander III
Probable date 1892

★

Carved in bowenite and encased in a fine and gently undulating net or trellis of rose diamonds, the pale yellow-green colour of the serpentine with its opalescent finish adds to the overall delicacy of this elegant object by Fabergé's chief jeweller. The Easter Egg is hinged and set at the top with a large rose diamond.

Signed by August Holmström.
Gold mark on bezel: crossed anchors.
Height: $4\frac{1}{4}''$.

In a private collection in England.

CAUCASUS EGG
Colour Plate LXXI

Presented to Marie Feodorovna by Alexander III
Dated 1893

★

Mounted with *quatre-couleur* gold floral swags held by rose diamond bows, this splendid engraved gold Egg in Louis Quinze style is enamelled a translucent crimson, four pearl-bordered oval doors each bearing a diamond set numeral of the year 1893 within a diamond wreath, reveal painted views of Abastouman, a mountain retreat high in the Caucasus, signed by Krijitski. It was here that the Grand Duke George Alexandrovitch, the younger brother of Nicholas II, was obliged to spend the greater part of his life owing to his ill health. When the Egg is held to the light, through portrait diamonds at the top and base, a miniature of the Grand Duke in naval uniform is seen.

Signed by Michael Perchin.
Gold Marks: 72 and crossed anchors.
Height: $3\frac{5}{8}''$.

In the Collection of Dr. Armand Hammer.

EGG IN THE RENAISSANCE STYLE
Colour Plate LXXII

Presented to Marie Feodorovna by Alexander III
Dated 1894

★

Based quite frankly on Le Roy's masterpiece in the *Grüne Gewölbe* at Dresden, this Easter Egg in the Renaissance style is carved from a large block of milky grey agate to form a jewel casket. A scalloped border in rose diamonds at the top of the cover encloses a strawberry-coloured translucent enamel medallion with the year in diamonds. The Egg, which is mounted horizontally on an enamelled gold base, is richly decorated with a trellis pattern and numerous other gold motifs enamelled strawberry, emerald green, cerulean blue and opaque white and is set with an abundance of rose diamonds and cabochon rubies. The clasp is set with rose diamonds. Carved gold lions' heads holding rings in their mouths are mounted at either end of this, the last Easter Egg given to Marie Feodorovna by her husband. The surprise has been lost.

In comparing Fabergé's work with Le Roy's, note how carefully the modern goldsmith has carried out an almost identical composition in a far lighter vein, by means of a subtle appreciation of the basic egg shape and a careful adjustment of the scales as instanced by the gentle curve added to the trellis pattern, and the more substantial base in relation to the casket as a whole.

Signed by Michael Perchin.
Gold marks: 56 and crossed anchors.
$3\frac{3}{4}'' \times 5\frac{1}{2}'' \times 3\frac{3}{4}''$.

In the Collection of Alexander Schaffer, Esq.

ROSEBUD EGG
(Pl. 325)

Presented to Alexandra Feodorovna by Nicholas II
Dated 1895

★

Engraved gold Egg enamelled translucent strawberry red and segmented by narrow bands of opaque white enamel; it is enriched with carved gold mounts in the form of swags and rose diamond set Cupid's arrows. A gold rosebud enamelled in natural opaque and translucent colours is concealed inside the Egg; this in turn opens to disclose a diamond and ruby-set Imperial Crown within which hangs a small ruby egg pendant.

84

The Egg, the first to be given to Alexandra Feodorovna, is surmounted by a small miniature portrait of Nicholas II, and the year is set in the base beneath a rose diamond.

No marks known.
Height of Egg: 3″.

Present whereabouts and condition unknown.

EGG WITH DANISH PALACES AND RESIDENCES
(Pl. 326)

Presented to the Dowager Empress Marie Feodorovna by Nicholas II
Probably 1895

★

A star sapphire within a cluster of rose diamonds and carved gold laurel leaves surmounts this *trois-couleur* gold Egg which is enamelled a translucent pink on a *guilloché* pattern of repeated crosses. The Egg is divided into twelve panels by broad bands consisting each of a line of rose diamonds within continuous laurel leaf borders carved in gold; an emerald is set at each intersection of the lines of rose diamonds.

A folding screen of miniature paintings framed in varicoloured gold is recessed within the Egg. Painted on mother-of-pearl by Krijitski and dated 1891, eight of the ten panels depict palaces and residences in Denmark where the Dowager Empress, as Princess Dagmar, spent her childhood; the paintings at either end of the screen show the Imperial yachts *Standart* and *Poliarnaya Svesda*. The natural mother-of-pearl is vividly revealed when the miniatures are held up to the light.

The date 1895 is written in ink on the outside of the velvet case containing this Egg.

Signed by Michael Perchin.
Gold Marks: 56 and crossed anchors.
Height: 4″.

In a private collection in the United States.

EGG WITH REVOLVING MINIATURES
(Pls. 327–329)

Presented to Alexandra Feodorovna by Nicholas II
Probable date, 1896

★

The two halves of this rock crystal Egg are held together by a narrow rose diamond and translucent emerald green enamelled gold mount, culminating at the top with an elaborately set Siberian emerald weighing 27 carats, cabochon and pointed. The Egg is supported on a circular rock crystal plinth decorated with *champlevé* enamel of various colours and richly set with rose diamonds; the monograms of the Tsarina, as the Princess Alix of Hesse-Darmstadt before her marriage, and as Alexandra Feodorovna, Empress of Russia, surmounted each by their respective crown, appear as separate continuous formal patterns encircling this plinth. Twelve miniature paintings signed by Zehngraf, elegantly framed in gold, revolve round a fluted gold shaft which passes through the centre of the Egg when the cabochon emerald set in the top is depressed and turned. The miniatures show Royal Residences in Germany, England and Russia associated with the life of the Tsarina and include views of various palaces in and around Darmstadt and Coburg in Germany, Windsor Castle, Osborne House and Balmoral in Great Britain and the Alexander, Anitchkov and Winter Palaces in Russia.

Signed by Michael Perchin.
Gold Marks: 56 and crossed anchors.
Height: $9\frac{3}{4}''$.

In the Lillian Thomas Pratt Collection of the Virginia Museum of Fine Arts.

CORONATION EGG
Colour Plate LXXIII

Presented to Alexandra Feodorovna by Nicholas II
Dated 1897

★

This superb red gold Egg, enamelled translucent lime yellow on an engraved field, is enclosed by a green gold laurel leaf trellis work cage mounted at each intersection by a yellow gold Imperial double-headed eagle enamelled opaque black, and set with a rose diamond. A large portrait diamond is set in the top of the egg within a cluster of ten brilliant diamonds; through the table of this stone, the monogram of the Empress is seen, the crowned 'A' described in rose diamonds, and the Russian, 'F' in cabochon rubies set in an opaque white enamel plaque. Another, smaller, portrait diamond is set within a cluster of rose diamonds at the end of the Egg, beneath which the date is inscribed on a similar plaque.

The surprise concealed inside this elaborate shell is an exact replica of the Imperial coach used in 1896, at the Coronation of Nicholas and Alexandra in Moscow. In yellow gold and strawberry coloured translucent enamel, the coach, one of the most splendid achievements of the goldsmith's art, is surmounted by the Imperial Crown in rose diamonds and six double-headed eagles on the roof; it is fitted with engraved rock crystal windows and platinum tyres, and is decorated with a diamond-set trellis in gold and an Imperial eagle in diamonds on either door. It is perfectly articulated in all its

LXXIII. Coronation Egg
Presented to Alexandra Feodorovna by Nicholas II
Dated 1897
In the Collection of Messrs. Wartski
Full description in the catalogue of Imperial Easter Eggs

parts, even to the two steps which may be let down when the doors are opened, and the whole chassis is correctly slung. The interior is enamelled with pale blue curtains behind the upholstered seats and footstool, and a daintily painted ceiling with a turquoise-blue sconce and hook set in the centre. The meticulous chasing and carving of this astonishing piece was carried out with the naked eye without even the aid of a loupe. George Stein, who made the coach while he was employed in Perchin's workshop, explains that at that time, when he was a young man of twenty-three, his sight was so good that he could easily detect a flaw in a diamond by simply holding it up to the light. He evidently spent about fifteen months on this model, paying many exploratory visits to the famous Coach Museum in St. Petersburg before starting the work. His pay was considered lavish at the rate of 5 roubles (or 10 shillings) a day—days which were sometimes sixteen hours long; Stein only earned three roubles a day at Kortmann's, his previous place of employment, but the conditions were better there than at Fabergé's before the removal to new premises in 1900. The yellow and black shell of the egg is a reference to the sumptuous Cloth of Gold robe worn by the Tsarina at her Coronation.

The name Wigström, Perchin's assistant, is roughly scratched on the inner surface of the shell.

Signed by Michael Perchin.
Gold Marks: 56 and crossed anchors.
Height of Egg: 5″.   Length of Coach: $3\frac{11}{16}$″.

In the Collection of Messrs. Wartski.

PELICAN EGG
(Pls. 330 and 331)

Presented to the Dowager Empress Marie Feodorovna by Nicholas II
Dated 1897

★

To celebrate the centenary of the founding of the Institutions of the Empress Marie, wife of Paul I, this engraved gold Egg is surmounted by a pelican in opalescent white enamel and diamonds feeding her young in the nest, a symbol of maternal care; it is engraved with classical motifs, the commemorative dates 1797–1897, and the inscription 'Visit our vineyards, O Lord, and we shall live in Thee'.

The Egg itself unfolds into an extending screen of ivory miniatures each within a pearl border, depicting the institutions founded principally for the education of the daughters of the nobility, of which the Dowager Empress was Patroness. When closed the panels fit so well together that this 'surprise' is effectively concealed; the Egg is supported on a varicoloured four-legged stand decorated with the crowned heads of eagles, crossed arrows, and other classical ornaments.

Signed by Michael Perchin.

Gold Marks: 56 and crossed anchors.

Height: $4\frac{1}{8}''$.

In the Lillian Thomas Pratt Collection of the Virginia Museum of Fine Arts.

LILIES OF THE VALLEY EGG
Colour Plate LXXIV

Presented to the Dowager Empress Marie Feodorovna by Nicholas II
Dated 5th April, 1898

★

Gold Egg enamelled translucent rose on a *guilloché* field and supported on four dull green cabriolet legs composed of overlapping leaves veined with rose diamonds. The Egg is surmounted by a rose diamond and cabochon ruby Imperial Crown set with two bows and quartered by four lines of rose diamonds and decorated with lilies of the valley carried out in pearls and rose diamonds, the stalks lightly engraved green gold and the leaves enamelled translucent green on gold. The 'surprise' consists of three oval miniatures of Nicholas II in military uniform, and the Grand Duchesses Olga and Tatiana, his first two children, signed by Zehngraf within rose diamond borders which are drawn out of the top of the Egg by means of a geared mechanism, and spread into a fan when a gold-mounted pearl button at the side is turned; a turn in the opposite direction automatically folds and returns the miniatures back to the interior of the Egg. The date is engraved on the reverse of the miniatures.

Signed by Michael Perchin.

Gold Marks: 56 and crossed anchors.

Height when closed $5\frac{15}{16}''$, when extended $7\frac{7}{8}''$.

In the Collection of Messrs. Wartski.

MADONNA LILY EGG
(Pl. 332)

Presented to Alexandra Feodorovna by Nicholas II
Dated 1899

★

This, one of the most pleasing of all the Eggs and startling in its *panache*, takes the form of a clock with a revolving dial. The four-colour gold Egg is enamelled translucent daffodil yellow, and is richly set with diamonds.

LXXIV. Lilies of the Valley Egg
Presented to the Dowager Empress Marie Feodorovna by Nicholas II
Dated 1898
In the Collection of Messrs. Wartski
Full description in the catalogue of Imperial Easter Eggs

334, 335. Pine Cone Egg
Presented to the Dowager Empress Marie Feodorovna by Nicholas II
Dated 1900
In a private collection in the United States

336. Trans-Siberian Railway Egg
Presented to Alexandra Feodorovna by Nicholas II
In the Armoury Museum of the Kremlin, Moscow

337. Apple Blossom Egg
Probably presented to the Dowager Empress Marie Feodorovna by Nicholas II
Circa 1901
In a private collection in the United States

338. Clover Egg
Probably presented to Alexandra Feodorovna by Nicholas II
1902, date given by Kremlin Armoury Museum
In the Armoury Museum of the Kremlin, Moscow

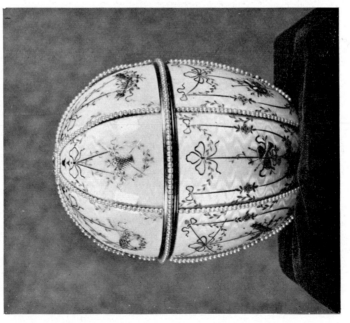

339, 340. Gatchina Palace Egg
Probably presented to the Dowager Empress Marie Feodorovna by Nicholas II
Circa 1902
In the Walters Art Gallery, Baltimore

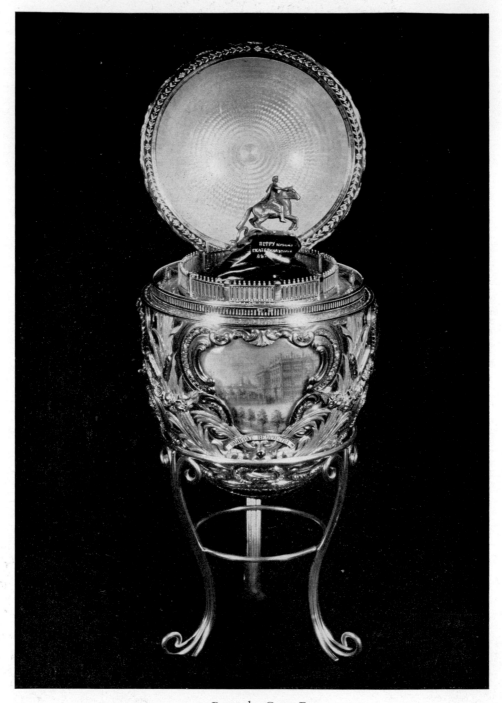

341. Peter the Great Egg
Presented to Alexandra Feodorovna by Nicholas II
Dated 1903
In the Lillian Thomas Pratt Collection of the Virginia Museum of Fine Arts

342. Gold and enamel *nécessaire* in the form of an egg set with
brilliant and rose diamonds, and containing a watch. Made in 1757
by a Parisian goldsmith for the Empress Elizabeth whose cypher is
embodied in the decoration, this beautiful object clearly inspired
Fabergé and the result is seen in the Peter the Great Egg (Pl. 341)
Height: 3¼"

In the Hermitage Collection, Leningrad

343, 344 and 345. Photographs showing interior mechanism of the Chanticleer Egg
(Colour plate LXXVI)

346. Uspensky Cathedral Egg
Presented to Alexandra Feodorovna by Nicholas II
Dated 1904
In the Armoury Museum of the Kremlin, Moscow

It stands on an onyx platform decorated with coloured gold scroll mounts, rosettes and the year in diamonds, and is designed as a vase with red gold scrolls serving as extra supports at either side. The belt of the dial which divides the Egg is enamelled opaque white with diamond set numerals and the hours are pointed by the head of an arrow in a drawn bow. The gold rim of the vase is carved as a cluster of roses; a bunch of Madonna lilies carved from quartzite and each set with rose diamonds sprouts from the vase. A small enamelled egg was hung from the green enamel foliage of this bunch of flowers as a further personal surprise gift for the Tsarina.

Signed by Michael Perchin.
Gold Marks: 56 and *Kokoshnik*.
Height: $10\frac{1}{2}''$.

In the Armoury Museum of the Kremlin in Moscow.

PANSY EGG
(Pl. 333)

Presented to the Dowager Empress Marie Feodorovna by Nicholas II
Dated 1899

★

Supported on a spiral twist of silver-gilt leaves and twigs set with rose diamonds, this carved nephrite Egg, designed in the 'Art Nouveau' style, is decorated with opaque violet enamelled pansies, symbols of remembrance and affection.

Within is a gold easel surmounted by a diamond-set Star of Bethlehem inside a wreath over the year; the easel is fluted and embellished with carved gold floral and torch motifs and is set with gems and pearls. On it rests a heart-shaped plaque enamelled opalescent white on a sun-ray *guilloché* background and bordered by rose diamonds set in silver and surmounted by the Romanov crown also in diamonds. Eleven tiny translucent strawberry enamelled gold covers, each bearing its own monogram, are connected by a large diamond 'M' to form a decoration for the front of this plaque. When a button is pressed, the enamelled covers open simultaneously to reveal eleven miniatures of the immediate Imperial Family. Reading vertically, those in the first row are: Grand Duke George, younger brother of the Tsar, Grand Duke Alexander, husband of the Grand Duchess Xenia, the Tsar's sister. In the second row are Tsar Nicholas II and Grand Duchess Irina, subsequently Princess Youssoupoff, daughter of Grand Duke Alexander and Grand Duchess Xenia; in the third row, Grand Duchess Olga, the first child of the Tsar and Tsarina, Grand Duchess Tatiana, their second child, and Grand Duke Michael, youngest brother of the Tsar. The fourth row shows the Tsarina and Grand Duke Andrew, brother of Grand Duchess Irina, and the fifth, Grand Duchesses Olga and Xenia, sisters of the Tsar.

Signed by Michael Perchin.
Silver Marks: 88 and the *Kokoshnik*.
Height: 5¾″.

In a private collection in the United States.

CUCKOO EGG
Colour Plate LXXV

Presented to Alexandra Feodorovna by Nicholas II
Dated 1900

★

Easter Egg Clock in dull yellow, green and red golds, enamelled translucent violet on a zig-zag *guilloché* field, and opalescent white, and set with pearls and rose diamonds. The dial, which is encircled by pearls set in red polished gold, is enamelled with translucent emerald green trefoils, and the rose diamond numerals are set on pale greenish white opalescent enamel within opaque white enamel rings. A yellow gold leaf pattern surrounds the central pivot on which the red gold hands revolve.

The Egg is supported on an elaborate base set with three large rose diamonds by a central shaft and three struts enamelled opalescent white.

When a button at the back of the clock is pressed, the circular pierced gold grille which surmounts it opens, and a cuckoo, plumed with natural feathers, set with cabochon ruby eyes, and standing on gold legs, rises crowing on a gold platform, the beak and wings moving authentically, until, the crowing finished, it descends once again into the Egg, and the grille closes down. Surmounting this grille, the date 1900 is inscribed beneath a portrait diamond.

Signed by Michael Perchin.
Gold Marks: 56 and *Kokoshnik*.
Height: 8⅛″.

In the Collection of Messrs. Wartski.

PINE CONE EGG
(Pls. 334 and 335)

Presented to the Dowager Empress Marie Feodorovna by Nicholas II
Dated 1900

★

Designed as a pine cone, a symbol of the Resurrection, this beautiful Egg is composed of overlapping scales, each one enamelled translucent royal blue on an engraved gold ground and edged with graduated rose diamonds. A four-leaf clover design at one

LXXV. Cuckoo Egg
Presented to Alexandra Feodorovna by Nicholas II
Dated 1900
In the Collection of Messrs. Wartski
Full description in the catalogue of Imperial Easter Eggs

end is made up of pear-shaped portrait diamonds, each covering a numeral of the year; the other end finishes with a star pattern in diamonds with a large centre stone.

A tiny dull grey metal automatic elephant within suggests the armorial bearings of the Danish Royal House whose Princess Dagmar went to Russia as the bride of the Tsarevitch Alexander Alexandrovitch. A mahout with an elephant-hook is seated on a gold diamond-set rug, enamelled translucent strawberry and emerald, which is spread across the creature's back. When it is wound, the elephant slowly advances shifting its weight from one side to the other, turning its head and switching its tail.

Signed by Michael Perchin.
Gold Marks: 56 and *Kokoshnik*.
Height of Egg: $3\frac{3}{4}''$.

In a private collection in the United States.

TRANS-SIBERIAN RAILWAY EGG
(Pl. 336)

Presented to Alexandra Feodorovna by Nicholas II
Probable date 1901

★

A map of the route of the Trans-Siberian railway as it was in 1900, from St. Petersburg to Vladivostock, engraved on silver, each station marked by a precious stone, forms a broad belt around this translucent green enamelled gold Egg decorated with blue and orange enamel mounts. The Egg is surmounted by a three-headed eagle in gold bearing the Imperial crown and is supported by three Romanov Griffins each brandishing sword and shield, and mounted on a white onyx base.

The Egg is opened on a hinge where the enamelled top meets the silver map, and within is concealed, in three sections, a faithful miniature replica of the Trans-Siberian Express, the engine and tender in platinum and gold, and five coaches in gold, minutely chiselled to give every detail; the three parts may be connected to form a train which runs along when the clockwork locomotive is wound up above the driving wheels. The last coach is designed as a travelling church, others are marked 'Smoking' and 'For Ladies only'. The Trans-Siberian Railway, begun in 1891, was completed, in the main, by 1900, and this ingenious Egg, probably given in the following year, commemorates the ceremonial opening.

An engraved gold plaque bears the following inscription beneath the Imperial crown:

'The Grand Siberian Railway in the Year 1900.'

Signed by Michael Perchin.
Height of Egg: $10\frac{3}{4}''$.   Length of train: $15\frac{11}{16}''$.   Height of train: $\frac{9}{16}''$.

In the Armoury Museum of the Kremlin in Moscow.

APPLE BLOSSOM EGG
(Pl. 337)

Probably presented to the Dowager Empress Marie Feodorovna by Nicholas II
Circa 1901

★

A solid piece of carved nephrite forms the astonishingly thin polished shell of this Egg; it stands on four carved gold feet naturalistically fashioned as twisted branches which spread upward and enclose it. These branches, which are carried out in green and red gold, bear fruit blossoms and buds in pink mat enamel set with pink foiled diamonds. Designed as a jewel case, the 'surprise' has been lost.

Eugène Fabergé put the date of this Egg in the Victorian style at about 1901.

Signed by Michael Perchin.
Gold Marks: 56 and *Kokoshnik.*
Height: 4⅜″.

In a private collection in the United States.

CLOVER EGG
(Pl. 338)

Probably presented to Alexandra Feodorovna by Nicholas II
1902, *date given by Kremlin Armoury Museum*

★

The shell of this exquisite Egg is composed of closely packed clover leaves carried out in *plique à jour* green enamel, dull green gold and diamonds massed so closely together that the settings are quite invisible. A cabochon ruby and diamond cluster is set at the point of this egg which is further decorated by a pattern of *calibré* ruby ribbons. The supporting tripod is carried out in the same style as the egg itself.

The surprise originally contained within has been lost.

Signed by Michael Perchin.
Gold Mark: 72.
Height: 3⅜″.

In the Armoury Museum of the Kremlin in Moscow.

Catalogue of Imperial Easter Eggs

GATCHINA PALACE EGG
(Pls. 339 and 340)

Probably presented to the Dowager Empress Marie Feodorovna by Nicholas II
Circa 1902

*

Enamelled opalescent white on a gold *guilloché* carcase, this superb Egg is divided into twelve panels by lines of pearls. Portrait diamonds are set at either extremity, but unfortunately both the monogram and the year which, presumably, they once covered, have disappeared. Classical motifs painted in enamel in each of the segments refer to the various fields of endeavour actively and consistently encouraged by Marie Feodorovna. When the egg is opened, a wonderfully detailed model of the Gatchina Palace, near St. Petersburg, is revealed; it is carried out in four colours of gold, and bears the most searching scrutiny, showing trees, bridges, cannon, turrets and so on. This piece must be accounted one of Fabergé's most delightful compositions. Under the model of the palace, Marie Feodorovna's favourite residence, a velvet-lined space originally concealed some precious jewel now separated and lost.

Signed by Michael Perchin.
Gold Marks: 56 and *Kokoshnik*.
Height: 5″.

In the Walters Art Gallery, Baltimore.

PETER THE GREAT EGG
(Pl. 341)

Presented to Alexandra Feodorovna by Nicholas II
Dated 1903

*

This Easter Egg commemorates the Bicentenary of the founding of the city of St. Petersburg in 1703; in Louis XV style, it is elaborately enriched with a rococo cagework of diamond and ruby set scrolls, and shells, foliage and bullrushes in green gold set with square-cut rubies. The dates 1703 and 1903 in rose diamonds appear on either side of the lid of the Egg.

Linked by *quatre-couleur* gold swags of roses, four miniature paintings by Zuiev show Peter the Great, the wooden hut which he is traditionally said to have built himself, Nicholas II and the Winter Palace.

Opaque white enamel ribbons inscribed with relevant historical details encircle the upper and lower portions of this Egg.

As the Egg is opened, a mechanism within raises a miniature replica in gold, on a sapphire pedestal, of Falconet's monument on the Neva of Peter the Great on horseback; it is surrounded by a carved gold railing which is itself encircled by chains and posts pinned to an engraved gold pavement within a raised gold bezel in the form of a wall. The replica was modelled by Malychev.

The inside of the lid of the Egg is enamelled translucent yellow on a *guilloché* pattern of concentric circles, thus making the surprise even more effective.

This was the last Easter Egg made by Perchin for the Tsarina.

Signed by Michael Perchin.
Gold Marks: 72.
Approximate height: 6″.

Reproduced from Mr. Bainbridge's *Monograph on the Life and Work of Fabergé* by kind permission of its publishers, B. T. Batsford Ltd.

In the Lillian Thomas Pratt Collection of the Virginia Museum of Fine Arts.

CHANTICLEER EGG
Colour Plate LXXVI and Monochrome Plates 343–345

*Probably presented to the Dowager Empress Marie Feodorovna by Nicholas II
Probable date, 1903*

★

In the French classical manner, this graceful Egg is enamelled a translucent Cambridge blue on a shimmering *guilloché* surface of gold. Heavy carved green gold laurel swags hang from a circular pierced red gold grille at the top and a line of pearls within borders of carved green gold leaves and berries forms a belt around the centre of the egg; this belt is interrupted by the opalescent white enamelled dial of the clock set in red gold within a ring of pearls. The hands are of gold and the numerals are painted in blue enamel. The Egg is mounted on a four-sided pedestal decorated with applied red and green gold devices of the Arts and Sciences. The four main concave panels are enamelled translucent Cambridge blue and the remaining ones bordering them, and the fluted shaft supporting the Egg, are in opalescent white.

This clock is mechanically a step in advance of the earlier example in violet enamel (Col. Pl. LXXV).

The diamond-set cockerel in gold and varicoloured enamels which rises from the interior of the egg, flapping its wings and crowing, does not do so at the pressure of a button, but automatically at each hour. When it has announced the time, it disappears beneath the grille which closes down over the top of the egg.

LXXVI. Chanticleer Egg
Probably presented to the Dowager Empress Marie Feodorovna by
Nicholas II
Probable date 1903
In a private collection in the United States
Full description in the catalogue of Imperial Easter Eggs

Signed by Michael Perchin.
Gold Marks: 56 and *Kokoshnik.*
Height: 11″.

In a private collection in the United States.

USPENSKY CATHEDRAL EGG
(Pl. 346)

Presented to Alexandra Feodorovna by Nicholas II
Dated 1904

*

This, the most ambitious of the Imperial Eggs, represents the Uspensky Cathedral where the Tsars of Russia were crowned. Reminiscent of Dinglinger's work in Dresden, the walls, towers and staircases are clustered round the central opalescent white enamel Egg, the top of which takes the form of a graceful yellow gold cupola. The turrets of the Kremlin are described in red gold and the roofs are enamelled translucent light green. There are chiming clocks on two of the towers, the dials each measuring approximately half an inch in diameter. Through the windows of the Egg can be seen a minutely accurate representation of the interior of the cathedral with its rich carpets, decorations and High Altar. The melody of the traditional hymn 'Ijey Cheruvime' is played when a button at the back of the Egg is pressed. The clockwork mechanism is wound by a gold key $2\frac{1}{2}$″ long. Tiny enamelled ikons decorate the walls of the cathedral.

The Egg, which rests on a white onyx base, is consciously designed as a triangle and is built up of other smaller triangles

Engraved at the foot of the model: ФАБЕРЖЕ 1904.
Height: $14\frac{1}{2}$″.

In the Armoury Museum of the Kremlin in Moscow.

ALEXANDER III COMMEMORATIVE EGG
(Pl. 347)

Presented to the Dowager Empress Marie Feodorovna by Nicholas II
Date 1904

*

Designed to commemorate the death, ten years before, of her husband Alexander III, this platinum Egg was the first to be completely carried out in mat enamel, in this instance white. Stripes, in possibly black mat enamel, appear to be painted over this white ground, unless these are simply reserved gold lines.

The Egg is richly set with rose diamond garlands, borders and classical motifs. Portrait diamonds are set at either end, doubtless covering the monogram of the Dowager Empress and the year.

Within the Egg, a miniature gold bust of Alexander III on a lapis lazuli pedestal is concealed.

Marks not known.
Height of Egg: $3\frac{3}{4}''$.
Original Fabergé photograph.

Present whereabouts unknown.

COLONNADE EGG
Colour Plate LXXVII

Presented to Alexandra Feodorovna by Nicholas II
Probable date, 1905

*

Conceived as an arcadian Temple of Love, this charming Rotary Clock Egg commemorates the birth of the long-awaited heir to the throne in 1904. A silver-gilt cupid representing the Tsarevitch surmounts the gold Egg, which is enamelled opalescent pale pink on an engraved ground and is encircled by the broad band of a translucent white enamelled dial set with rose diamond numerals; a diamond set pointer projects from a colonnade in pale green bowenite, which supports the Egg. The base of this colonnade, which is made up of six gold-mounted Ionic columns, is set with coloured gold carved mounts and a broad band of pale pink enamel. Four silver-gilt cherubs, representing the Tsar's four daughters, are seated at intervals around this elaborate base and are linked by floral swags chiselled in *quatre-couleur* gold.

Two carved platinum doves are perched on a white enamel plinth raised within the circle of columns.

Signed by Henrik Wigström.
Gold Marks: 56 and *Kokoshnik*.
Height: $11\frac{1}{4}''$.

From the Collection of Her late Majesty Queen Mary.

LXXVII. Colonnade Egg
Presented to Alexandra Feodorovna by Nicholas II
Probable date 1905
From the Collection of Her late Majesty Queen Mary
Full description in the catalogue of Imperial Easter Eggs

347. Alexander III Commemo-
rative Egg
Presented to the Dowager Em-
press Marie Feodorovna by
Nicholas II
Date 1904
Original Fabergé photograph

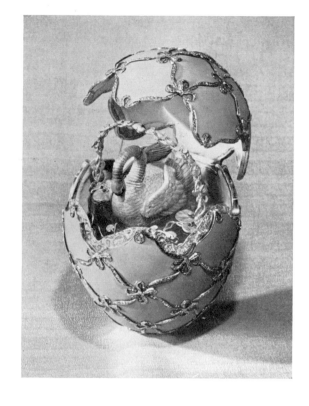

348, 349, 350. Swan Egg
Presented to Alexandra Feodorovna by Nicholas II
Dated 1906
From the Collection of the late Maurice Sandoz

351. Rose Trellis Egg
Presented to either his Wife or Mother by Nicholas II
Dated 1907
In the Walters Art Gallery, Baltimore

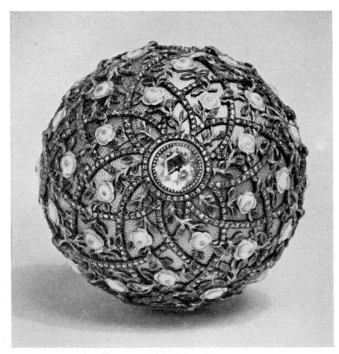

352. Enlarged photograph showing top of the Egg

353, 354, 355. Alexander Palace Egg
Presented to Alexandra Feodorovna by Nicholas II
Dated 1908
In the Armoury Museum of the Kremlin, Moscow

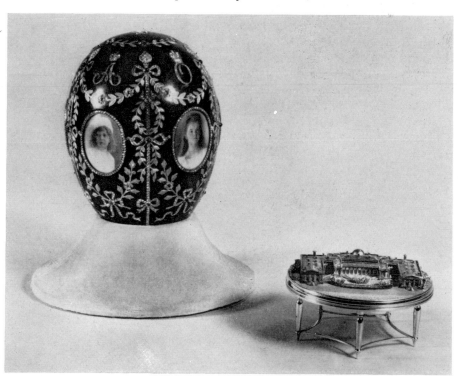

356. Peacock Egg
Presented to the Dowager Empress Marie Feodorovna by
Nicholas II
Dated 1908
From the Collection of the late M. Maurice Sandoz

357. View of Peacock showing tail fully spread

359, 360. Standart Egg
Presented to Alexandra Feodorovna by
Nicholas II
Dated 1909

In the Armoury Museum of the Kremlin, Moscow

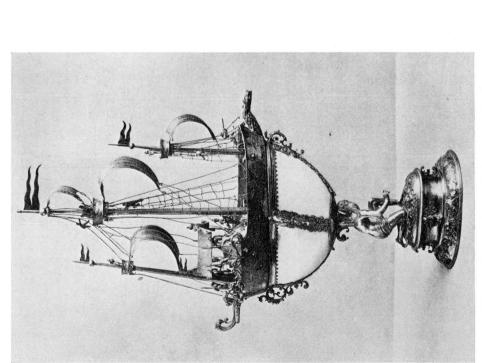

358. Nautilus shell with silver-gilt mounts in the form of
an armed frigate, supported by a kneeling figure of Nep-
tune on an oval base, by the sixteenth-century Nuremberg
goldsmith Jürg Ruel

Formerly in the Green Vaults Collection in Dresden

361. Egg with Love-Trophies
Presented to Alexandra Feodorovna by Nicholas II
Probable date 1910 or 1911

362. Miniature-frame
contained in Egg with
Love-Trophies

363. Orange Tree Egg
Presented to the Dowager Empress Marie Feodorovna by
Nicholas II
Dated 1911
In a private collection in the United States

364. Alexander III Equestrian Egg
Presented to The Dowager Empress Marie Feodorovna by Nicholas II
Date 1910
In the Armoury Museum of the Kremlin, Moscow

365 A, B, C and 366 A, B, C. Fifteenth Anniversary Egg
Presented to Alexandra Feodorovna by Nicholas II, dated 1911
In a private collection

Catalogue of Imperial Easter Eggs

SWAN EGG
(Pls. 348–350)

Presented to Alexandra Feodorovna by Nicholas II
Dated 1906

*

This gold Egg is mat enamelled mauve within a twisted ribbon trellis of rose diamonds with a four-looped bow at each intersection. The top, carefully designed to conceal the division when closed, is surmounted by a large portrait diamond covering the year; another is set in the base. Lifted from the Egg by a handle formed of water lilies in four colours of gold, a miniature lake is revealed composed of a large aquamarine, also richly decorated with water lilies, upon which rests a superbly chased platinum swan.

When wound up under one wing, chased gold webbed feet guide the bird along its course; it wags its tail characteristically. The head and arched neck are proudly raised then lowered and the wings are opened and spread to display each feather separately.

Gold Marks: 56.
Height of Egg: 4″.

From th Collection of the late Maurice Sandoz.

ROSE TRELLIS EGG
(Pls. 351 and 352)

Presented to either his Wife or Mother by Nicholas II
Dated 1907

*

Gold Easter Egg in pale green translucent enamel latticed with rose diamonds and decorated with opaque light and dark pink enamel rose blooms and translucent emerald green leaves. A portrait diamond is set at either end of this very charming Egg, the one at the base covering the date; unfortunately the monogram has disappeared from beneath the other.

An oval jewelled locket was originally concealed in the Egg, but now, unfortunately, only its impression on the satin lining remains.

Signed by Henrik Wigström.
Gold Marks: 56 and *Kokoshnik*.
Height: $3\frac{1}{15}$″.

In the Walters Art Gallery, Baltimore.

Catalogue of Imperial Easter Eggs

ALEXANDER PALACE EGG
(Pls. 353–355)

Presented to Alexandra Feodorovna by Nicholas II
Dated 1908

*

Surmounted by a beautifully cut triangular diamond, this attractive Siberian nephrite Egg is decorated with yellow and green gold mounts and set with cabochon rubies and diamonds. Five miniature portraits of the Tsar's children form a belt encircling the Egg; each one is set within a frame of rose diamonds and is surmounted by the appropriate initial in diamonds. Concealed within is a coloured gold model of the Alexander Palace, the favourite home of the Imperial Family in Tsarskoe Selo, the roofs enamelled pale translucent green and the grounds decorated with bushes in spun green gold wire, the whole set out upon a miniature gold table with five legs.

Signed by Henrik Wigström.
Gold Marks: 72 and *Kokoshnik*.
Height of Egg: $4\frac{5}{16}''$.

In the Armoury Museum of the Kremlin in Moscow.

PEACOCK EGG
(Pls. 356 and 357)

Presented to the Dowager Empress Marie Feodorovna by Nicholas II
Dated 1908

*

A delightful conception in the style of Louis XV, this rock crystal Easter Egg, engraved with the monogram of the Dowager Empress and the year, each within a formal border, is supported on a silver-gilt scroll base. Within the egg a mechanical gold and enamelled peacock, one of Fabergé's most ingenious creations, is seen perched in the branches of a tree in gold with flowers in enamel and precious stones. The Egg falls into two halves each set with a carved silver-gilt mount when opened at the top by means of a clasp. The peacock, when lifted from the branches, wound up, and put on a table, struts proudly about, placing one foot carefully before the other, moving its head and, at intervals, spreading and closing its varicoloured enamel tail.

Signed by Henrik Wigström.
Gold Mark: 56.
Height of Egg: 6″.
Length of Peacock: $4\frac{3}{4}''$.

From the Collection of the late M. Maurice Sandoz.

STANDART EGG
(Pls. 359 and 360)

Presented to Alexandra Feodorovna by Nicholas II
Date 1909

★

This rock crystal Egg is mounted in gold richly enamelled and set with gems; it is supported on a rock crystal pedestal similarly decorated, two intertwined lapis lazuli dolphins forming the shaft. The eagles perched on either side of the horizontally-set egg are also carved in lapis, and these surmount two pearl drops.

When this Egg in Renaissance style is opened, a faithful replica in gold of the nine-teenth-century yacht *Standart* is revealed set on a large piece of aquamarine to give the impression of sea.

Derived from Jürg Ruel's sixteenth-century masterpiece in the Dresden collection, this Egg is one of the most brilliant of the series. It is sadly marred, however, by the ridiculous little ship within, which besides being quite out of scale with its surroundings, strikes a completely anachronistic note, and very nearly wrecks an excellent design. Eugène Fabergé put the date of this Egg at about 1908, and it may well have been made to commemorate the part played by the Tsarina when, on 11th September, 1907, the yacht struck a rock and appeared to be sinking fast and, as Baroness Buxhoeveden tells us in her *Life and Tragedy of Alexandra Feodorovna:* 'The Empress arranged that the children and the ladies' maids should be first lowered into the boats. Then she rushed into the cabins, tore the sheets off the beds and tossed all valuables into them, making huge bundles of the most necessary and precious things. It was all done in about a quarter of an hour. The Empress was the last woman to leave the yacht.'

Signed by Henrik Wigström.
Height: 6⅛″.
Original Fabergé photograph.

In the Armoury Museum of the Kremlin in Moscow.

EGG WITH LOVE TROPHIES
(Pls. 361 and 362)

Presented to Alexandra Feodorovna by Nicholas II
Probable date, 1910

★

Gold Egg in the style of Louis XVI enamelled pale blue, decorated with elaborate formal bands in carved gold and opaque white enamel, and surmounted by an elegant finial in golds of colour, enamel, rubies, pearls and rose diamonds in the form of a basket of roses, the whole supported upon four quivers revealing the diamond-set tops of arrows. The quivers are linked by heavy carved swags of roses in coloured golds and enamel and are set on a bowenite base with gold and enamel mounts and four half-ball feet.

A gold heart-shaped miniature-frame in enamel and diamonds is concealed within the Egg. The strut of this frame, which contained originally a miniature portrait of Nicholas II, is formed from the signature Niki.

Marks not known.
Approximate height of Egg: 9″.
Approximate height of frame: 3½″.
The present whereabouts of this Egg are not known.

Photographs by courtesy of 'A la Vieille Russie'.

ALEXANDER III EQUESTRIAN EGG
(Pl. 364)

Presented to the Dowager Empress Marie Feodorovna by Nicholas II
Dated 1910

*

Made presumably to perpetuate the memory of the Tsar Alexander III, this, the first Egg to be set entirely in platinum, is one of the most beautifully designed of all. The Egg itself is carved from a solid piece of rock crystal and is surmounted by a diamond-set platinum lacework fillet, a large rose diamond at its centre and bordered by a tasselled fringe.

The Egg is supported upon the wings of four carved platinum *amoretti* set on a carved rock crystal shaped base.

Two vertical motifs, each slung with carved decorative swags, join the hemispheres of the Egg.

Through the engraved crystal can be seen a miniature equestrian statue of Alexander III in dull green gold on a lapis lazuli plinth; it is a tiny replica of Prince Troubetskoy's well-known work.

Signed: К. ФАБЕРЖЕ.
Height: 6⅛″.

In the Armoury Museum of the Kremlin in Moscow.

Catalogue of Imperial Easter Eggs

FIFTEENTH ANNIVERSARY EGG
(Pls. 365 and 366)

Presented to Alexandra Feodorovna by Nicholas II
Dated 1911

*

The following is based on a translation of the description given with a photograph of this Egg printed in *Stolitza Y Usadba* (Town and Country) 'The Journal of Elegant Living', a magazine published in what was then Petrograd. This particular issue, dated 1st April, 1916, gave special prominence to a series of photographs of nine of the Tsarina's Easter Eggs:

Red gold Egg commemorating the fifteenth anniversary of Nicholas II's Coronation; it is enamelled opalescent oyster with heavy carved husk borders enamelled translucent emerald green with diamond ties at the intersections. The surface is covered with a series of miniature paintings on ivory by Zuiev depicting notable events of the reign; these are set under carved rock crystal panels and represent:

1. The ceremonial procession to the Uspensky Cathedral.
2. The actual moment of the Holy Coronation.
3. The Alexander III bridge in Paris at the opening of which His Imperial Majesty was present.
4. The House in the Hague, where the first Peace Conference took place. Huis ten Bosch.
5. The ceremonial reception for the member of the first State Duma in the Winter Palace.
6. The Emperor Alexander III Museum.
7. The unveiling of the Peter the Great monument in Riga.
8. The unveiling in Poltava of the monument commemorating the 200th year of the founding of Poltava.
9. The removal of the remains of the sainted Serafim Sarovski.

The paintings are framed by narrow opaque white enamelled borders and oval portrait miniatures of the Imperial Family are set in opalescent oyster enamelled mounts over *guilloché* fields and rimmed by rose diamonds.

Fabergé's signature appears twice in pale blue enamel in three parts (ФА, БЕР, ЖЕ) of a ribbon on the plaques showing the dates 1894 (the date of the wedding) and 1911, below pink bouquets. The carved acanthus mounts encircling the rose diamond cluster at the culot of the Egg, and the portrait and rose diamond cluster at the top, under which is the Imperial Cypher A.Ф. beneath the crown, are in dull green gold.

There are no gold marks.
Height: 5″.
In a private collection.

Catalogue of Imperial Easter Eggs

ORANGE-TREE EGG
Colour Plate LXXVIII and Monochrome Plate 363

Presented to the Dowager Empress Marie Feodorovna by Nicholas II
Date 1911

★

In the form of an orange tree growing in a tub, this Easter Egg is a remarkable example of the jeweller's art. Based on a solid block of nephrite and surrounded by four gold-mounted nephrite posts connected by swinging chains of translucent emerald enamelled gold leaves half covering pearls, a white quartz tub, set with cabochon rubies and pearls, trellised in gold and decorated with carved gold swags, is filled with hammered gold soil. As if growing from this soil, a naturalistically modelled gold tree trunk supports the egg-shaped foliage composed of single carved nephrite leaves each engraved to show the veining. White opaque enamel flowers with brilliant diamond centres and various gem stones including topaz, amethysts, pale rubies and champagne diamonds representing fruit, are set at random amongst the leaves. Within this nephrite foliage, four main limbs branch from the trunk, and a complex network of smaller branches grows from these, each finally passing through tiny drilled collets concealed behind each leaf. When a small button is pressed, the top leaves spring up and a feathered gold bird rises from the interior of the tree, sings and then automatically disappears. The key to the mechanism is hidden among the leaves and may be located only by the gem set in the top, which appears to be simply another fruit.

No marks.
Height: $10\frac{1}{2}''$.

In a private collection in the United States.

TSAREVITCH EGG
(Pls. 367–369)

Presented to Alexandra Feodorovna by Nicholas II
Dated 1912

★

Designed in the style of Louis XV, this egg is carved from a solid block of lapis lazuli of superb quality, and is enclosed in an elaborately carved and chased gold cage-work composed of conventionalized motifs including scrolls, shells, baskets of flowers, winged cherubs and the Imperial double-headed eagle beneath a canopy hanging from a fretted arch. The crowned Imperial monogram and the year are shown under a rectangular portrait diamond surmounting the egg; a large brilliant diamond is set in the base.

LXXVIII. Orange Tree Egg
Presented to the Dowager Empress Marie Feodorovna by Nicholas II
Dated 1911
In a private collection in the United States
Full description in the catalogue of Imperial Easter Eggs

Inside the egg, a crowned double-headed Imperial eagle, richly set back and front with rose diamonds, frames an oval miniature painting of the Tsarevitch Alexey; this important jewel is supported on a diamond-set base with four diamond leaves, curled to serve as feet. The reverse side frames a miniature showing the back of the eight-year-old Prince.

Here in this whole composition is a striking instance of the beauty of the frame, surpassing by far the picture it holds, for it must be confessed that the miniature portrait, which is understandably not signed, provides in its weakness of execution, a melancholy anti-climax to a good design.

Signed by Henrik Wigström.
Gold marks: 56.
Height of Egg: $4\frac{3}{4}''$.

In the Lillian Thomas Pratt Collection of the Virginia Museum of Fine Arts.

NAPOLEONIC EGG
(Pls. 370–372)

Presented to the Dowager Empress Marie Feodorovna by Nicholas II
Dated 1912

*

In the Empire style, this green and yellow gold Egg commemorates the hundredth anniversary of the War of the Motherland waged against Napoleon. Military emblems and double-headed eagles carved in gold decorate the translucent emerald green with which the *guilloché* surface of the Egg is enamelled, and these are framed by broad bands of chiselled gold leaves and rosettes applied to translucent strawberry enamel.

In addition to the profusion of rose diamonds with which this magnificent Egg is set, portrait diamonds at either end cover the crowned monogram of the Dowager Empress and the year.

Within the Egg is a folding screen of six signed miniatures by Vassily Zuiev, each showing members of the regiments of which Her Imperial Majesty was honorary Colonel; the back of each panel bears an inscription identifying these, and is set with her monogram and crown in rose diamonds on a green enamel plaque set in the centre of a translucent white enamel sunburst pattern.

Signed by Henrik Wigström.
Height of Egg: $4\frac{5}{8}''$.

In a private collection in the United States.

Catalogue of Imperial Easter Eggs

ROMANOV TERCENTENARY EGG
(Pl. 373)

Presented to Alexandra Feodorovna by Nicholas II
Dated 1913

*

This Egg, one of Fabergé's most astonishing pieces, commemorates three hundred years of Romanov rule. Enamelled opalescent white on gold, it is decorated with a pattern of chased gold double-headed eagles and ancient and contemporary Romanov crowns, framing at intervals eighteen miniature likenesses of the most notable Romanov rulers, within rose diamond borders; these are painted on ivory by Zuiev.

The Egg, which is removable, rests on a pedestal in the form of a three-sided Imperial eagle in pale gold, the three talons holding respectively the Sceptre, Orb and the Romanov Sword. Supporting this, the circular gem-set purpurine base, mounted in gold, represents the Russian Imperial Shield.

Within the Egg is a blue steel globe divided into two halves, one hemisphere showing the map of the Russian Empire in 1613, the other in 1913; the blue steel represents the sea, and the land masses are described in coloured golds.

Portrait diamonds are set at either end of this Egg, the one in the top covering the Tsarina's monogram, that in the base the year.

Signed by Henrik Wigström.
Gold Marks: 72 and *Kokoshnik*.
Height: $7\frac{5}{16}''$.

In the Armoury Museum of the Kremlin in Moscow.

WINTER EGG
(Pl. 374)

Presented to the Dowager Empress Marie Feodorovna by Nicholas II
Dated 1913

*

This enchanting composition consists of an Egg carved from a block of rock crystal with frost flowers engraved on the inside and carried out in diamonds outside. Each half of the Egg, which opens on a hinge, is rimmed with brilliant diamonds; it is surmounted by a moonstone covering the date, and is set throughout in platinum. Within the Egg, a rose diamond and platinum basket of snowdrops hangs by the handle from a hook; the flowers are executed in white quartz with gold-set olivine centres, the leaves in pale nephrite, stalks in gold and the earth in spun gold. The Egg, which is removable, rests on a rock crystal block of ice set with brilliant and rose diamonds; it is held firmly

367. Tsarevitch Egg
Presented to Alexandra Feodorovna by Nicholas II
Dated 1912
In the Lillian Thomas Pratt Collection of the Virginia Museum of Fine Arts

368. Fabergé photograph showing original
stand

369. Photograph showing back
of Imperial Eagle

370. Napoleonic Egg
Presented to the Dowager Empress Marie Feodorovna
by Nicholas II
Dated 1912
In a private collection in the United States

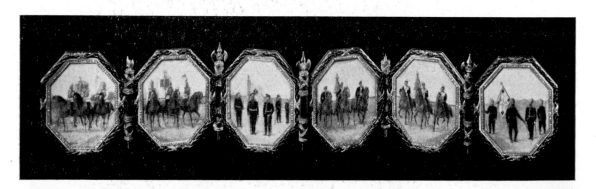

371, 372. Photographs showing front and back of folding screen of miniatures contained within the Egg

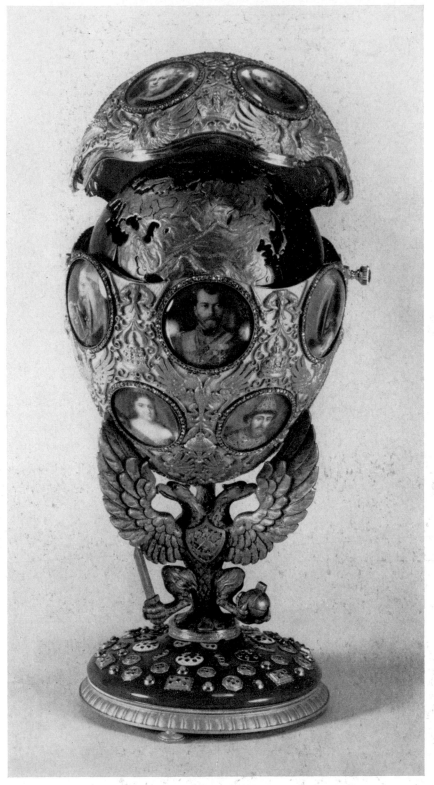

373. Romanov Tercentenary Egg
Presented to Alexandra Feodorovna by Nicholas II
Dated 1913
In the Armoury Museum of the Kremlin, Moscow

374. Winter Egg
Presented to the Dowager Empress Marie Feodorovna by Nicholas II
Dated 1913
In the Collection of Bryan Ledbrook, Esq.

LXXIX and LXXX. Mosaic Egg
Presented to Alexandra Feodorovna by Nicholas II
Dated 1914
*From the Collection of Her late Majesty Queen Mary and reproduced here by gracious permission of
Her Majesty The Queen*
Full description in the catalogue of Imperial Easter Eggs

375, 376 and 377. Nicholas II Equestrian Egg
Presented to Nicholas II by Alexandra Feodorovna
Dated 1913
From the Collection of the late Harry H. Blum, Esq.

378. Red Cross Egg with Resurrection Triptych
Presented to Alexandra Feodorovna by Nicholas II
Dated 1915
In the Collection of Mrs. India Minshall

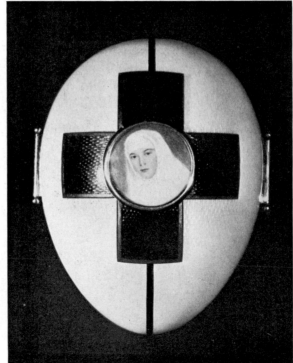

379, 380 and 381. *Centre:* View of Egg closed
Left and right: Views showing miniature paintings of Saints Tatiana and Olga

LXXXI. Grisaille Egg
Presented to the Dowager Empress Marie Feodorovna
by Nicholas II
Dated 1914
In the Collection of Mrs. Herbert May
Full description in the catalogue of Imperial Easter Eggs

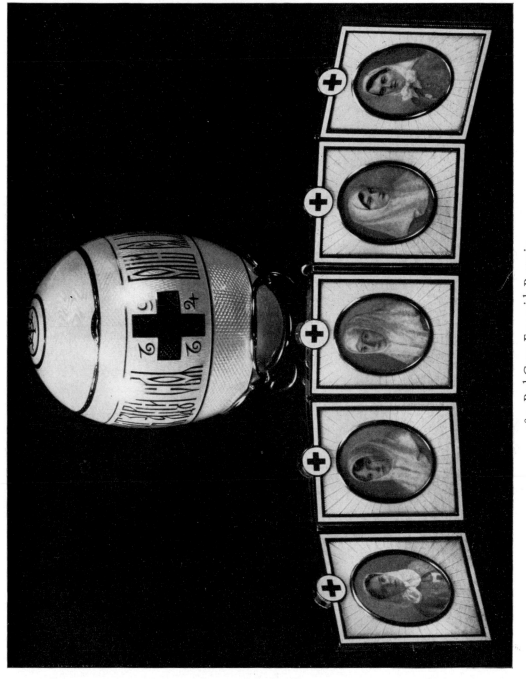

382. Red Cross Egg with Portraits
Presented to the Dowager Empress Marie Feodorovna by Nicholas II
Dated 1915
In the Lillian Thomas Pratt Collection of the Virginia Museum of Fine Arts

383. Steel Military Egg
Presented to Alexandra Feodorovna by Nicholas II
Dated 1916
In the Armoury Museum of the Kremlin, Moscow

384. Steel Military Egg, another view

385A

385B

385E

385C

385D

385F

385 A—F. Cross of St. George Egg showing decorative details. Dated 1916
From the Collection of Her late Imperial Highness the Grand Duchess Xenia

386. An original water-colour design dated 1917 for an Easter Egg in the form of
a clock, which was never made

387. Ice Egg
Presented by Dr. Emanuel Nobel to a friend
In a private collection in the United States

388. Egg with Twelve Panels. Photograph showing the
initials of Barbara Kelch
From the Collection of Her late Majesty Queen Mary

389. Photograph showing open position of carved gold tripod contained
in the Rocaille Egg

390. Bonbonnière Easter Egg
Probably presented to Barbara Kelch by her husband
Dated 1903
In a private collection in the United States

391 and 392. Miniatures of the two sons of Prince Felix
Youssoupoff from the Egg in Plate 393

393. Youssoupoff Easter Egg
Presented to the Princess Zénaïde Youssoupoff on the twenty-fifth anniversary of
their marriage by her husband, Prince Felix Youssoupoff
From the Collection of the late M. Maurice Sandoz

394. St. Petersburg gold mark showing firm's name, workmaster's initials, sometimes upside down, gold mark and crossed anchors and sceptre state mark, in use before 1896. From box on Plate 119

395. Similar mark but with higher grade of gold (72). From box on colour Plate IX

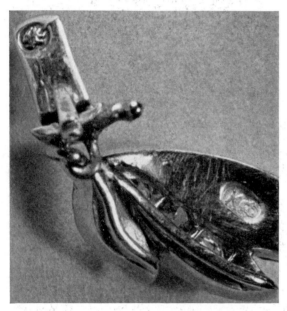 

396. St. George and Dragon mark used in Moscow before 1896 and initialed signature of the House, often used for stamping jewellery where space was limited. From bracelet on Plate 206

397. Moscow mark found on silver carafe showing the initials of an unknown workmaster

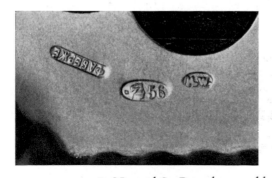 

398. Normal St. Petersburg gold mark after 1896 showing the *Kokoshnik*.

399. Normal Moscow silver mark after 1896. From cigarette-case on Plate 94

400, 401. English control marks together with normal Russian silver marks. Both from tray on Plate 92

402. Mark found on a jug designed by Fabergé, Moscow, showing the initials of Hall Inspector Alexander Sevjer

403. Mark showing the name of the designer Agathon Fabergé together with the initials of the work-master who actually made the piece. From a gold mounted bell push
The initials Я.Л. which appear beside the *Kokoshnik* are those of the Hall Inspector—in this case Jakob Ljapunov

404. Mark showing the highest grade of silver used (91)
405. Soviet mark showing initials L.U.T. The initial on the right is probably that of the examiner From cigarette-case on Plate 93

406. Silk lid-lining with Imperial Eagle over the words Fabergé,
St. Petersburg, Moscow, London

407. Group of Fabergé cases in wood, and the velvet-coloured case for the Lily of the Valley Egg
(Colour Plate LXXIV)

in position by a projecting pin which fits into the bottom of the Egg. Sacheverell Sitwell has described this piece as a 'Winter Egg' and the surprise it contains is particularly felicitous with its promise of spring. This is one of the best examples of Fabergé's use of gems to express his composition as opposed to their introduction merely as an enrichment.

The Egg itself bears no marks, but the bottom of the basket of flowers is engraved 'Fabergé 1913'.

Height of Egg: 4″.
Height of Basket: 3¼″.

In the Collection of Bryan Ledbrook, Esq.

NICHOLAS II EQUESTRIAN EGG
(Pls. 375–377)

Presented to Nicholas II by Alexandra Feodorovna
Dated 1913

*

This Egg was a special gift presented during the Romanov Tercentenary celebrations by the Tsarina to her husband. Enamelled pale green on an engraved silver field, it is supported on a white onyx and silver gilt pedestal set with rose diamonds. A latticed canopy of brilliant and rose diamonds and cabochon rubies culminating in a cabochon emerald surmounts the Egg, which is divided into two halves; applied to one half is a miniature portrait of the Tsarina in court dress within a border of brilliant diamonds surmounted by the Imperial crown and flanked on either side by the dates 1613 and 1913 in rose diamonds; the other half is decorated with a magnificent double-headed eagle set in brilliant diamonds with a brilliant canary diamond of approximately five carats as its centre. When the emerald set in the top is pressed, a catch is released, and the two hinged halves of the Egg fall apart to reveal a carved miniature equestrian statue in oxidised silver of Nicholas II carrying the flag. The carving stands on a silver roadway set with rose diamonds to suggest cobbles. The interior of the Egg is gilt.

This Egg is unique, not only because it was given by the Tsarina to her husband, but also because it was made in the workshop of Victor Aarne.

Signed by Victor Aarne.
Marks: 88 and *Kokoshnik.*
Height: 3⅞″.

From the Collection of the late Harry H. Blum, Esq.

Catalogue of Imperial Easter Eggs

MOSAIC EGG
Colour Plates LXXIX and LXXX

Presented to Alexandra Feodorovna by Nicholas II
Dated 1914

*

An Easter Egg the skeleton of which consists of a system of yellow gold belts to which is applied a platinum network partially pavé set with diamonds and coloured gems including sapphires, rubies, emeralds, topaz quartz and green (demantoid) garnets in flower patterns. The Egg is divided into five oval panels by these gold belts which are set with half pearls within lines of opaque white enamel and five brilliant diamonds are set at each intersection; it is further decorated by grilles of rose diamond scrolls and the rounder end is set with a moonstone beneath which may be seen the gold initials of the Tsarina in Russian characters inlaid in an opaque pale pink enamelled plaque serving as a foil.

The surprise concealed within, and held in place by two gold clips, consists of a gold, pearl and translucent green and opaque white enamelled pedestal set with diamonds and green garnets and surmounted by a diamond Imperial Crown, supporting a plaque, on one side of which is shown, painted in pale sepia *grisaille* enamel, the profiles of the five Imperial children against a background of engraved vertical parallel lines enamelled opalescent rose Pompadour. The reverse is enamelled with a pale sepia basket of flowers against a pale green background around which the year 1914 and the names of the children are written in sepia on the opaque ivory enamelled border.

The gold surface underneath the pedestal is engraved with a sun in splendour design and the name, presumably in error, G. Fabergé, 1914. Designed as a jewel, this beautiful Egg was made in Holmström's workshop and is engraved C. Fabergé.

Length of Egg: $3\frac{5}{8}''$.
Width: $2\frac{3}{4}''$.
Height of Pedestal: $3''$.

From the collection of Her late Majesty Queen Mary and reproduced here by gracious permission of Her Majesty The Queen.

GRISAILLE EGG
Colour Plate LXXXI

Presented to the Dowager Empress Marie Feodorovna by Nicholas II
Dated 1914

*

In the French Classic manner this gold Egg is decorated with eight *grisaille* panels, enamelled translucent pink, and set within pearl borders edged by narrow opaque white enamel bands. Painted by Vassily Zuiev, they show representations of the Muses. The various arts of peace are also recalled in the exquisitely chiselled four-colour gold mounts composed of the symbols of music, the fine arts, literature, the theatre, and science. The Egg is set with rose diamond ribbon and laurel leaf mounts, and portrait diamonds at either end cover the crown and monogram of the Dowager Empress at the top, and the year at the base.

The Egg was intended to be used as a jewel case. The original surprise has been lost.

Signed by Henrik Wigström.
Marks: 56 and *Kokoshnik.*
Height: 4¾″.

In the Collection of Mrs. Herbert May.

RED CROSS EGG WITH RESURRECTION TRIPTYCH
(Pls. 378–381)

Presented to Alexandra Feodorovna by Nicholas II
Dated 1915

★

In white opalescent enamel on an engraved silver-gilt ground, this Egg bears a large red translucent enamel cross on either side, in whose centres are set circular painted miniature portraits of the Grand Duchesses Tatiana and Olga in Red Cross uniform. The front cross with the portrait of Tatiana serves as a clasp securing the double opening doors, which open to reveal a triptych painting by Prachov of the Resurrection of Christ in the centre with the Saints Olga and Tatiana painted on the side panels. The two remaining panels of the doors are inscribed, one with the crowned monogram of the Tsarina and the other with the year. The indifferent painting of the two unsigned exterior miniatures does not prepare one for the rather impressive triptych concealed within the Egg, thus in this case the 'surprise' is a double one. In order to save the Emperor money, the cost of this war-time egg was kept down to about £200.

Signed by Henrik Wigström.
Gold Marks: 72 and *Kokoshnik* (mounts only in gold).
Height: 3⅜″.

In the Collection of Mrs. India Minshall.

RED CROSS EGG WITH PORTRAITS
(Pl. 382)

Presented to the Dowager Empress Marie Feodorovna by Nicholas II
Dated 1915

✴

Like its counterpart presented to the Tsarina, this Egg is enamelled opalescent white on a *guilloché* surface of silver-gilt and is decorated with a broad band composed of two translucent red enamel crosses with the dates 1914 and 1915, the first commemorating the beginning of the Great War, the other marking the year of its presentation, and a conventionalized inscription, also in red enamel which, translated, reads:

> *Greater love hath no man than this,*
> *that a man lay down his life for his friends.*

The Egg contains a screen of five oval miniature portraits, painted on mother-of-pearl, each set in an opalescent white enamelled panel mounted in gold. The portraits are painted by Zuiev and show the Grand Duchess Olga Alexandrovna, sister of Nicholas II, Grand Duchess Olga Nikolaevna, his eldest daughter, the Tsarina Alexandra Feodorovna, Grand Duchess Tatiana Nikolaevna, second daughter of the Tsar, and Grand Duchess Marie Pavlovna, cousin of Nicholas II, each wearing the uniform of the Red Cross whose symbol surmounts the individual panels.

This Egg pays tribute to the service rendered to the Red Cross by Marie Feodorovna, first as Tsarievna (Crown Princess), during the Russo-Turkish War of 1877, and then as President of the Organisation from the beginning of her reign until the fall of the Dynasty.

Signed by Henrik Wigström.
Gold Marks: *Kokoshnik.*
Height of Egg: $3\frac{1}{8}''$.

In the Lillian Thomas Pratt Collection of the Virginia Museum of Fine Arts.

STEEL MILITARY EGG
(Pls. 383 and 384)

Presented to Alexandra Feodorovna by Nicholas II
Dated 1916

✴

In steel, this war-time Egg bears the crowned initials of the Tsarina and the year in gold, and is poised on the points of four miniature artillery shells ringed with yellow gold bands set vertically on a nephrite base. Within the Egg, which is surmounted by the

Imperial Crown in yellow gold and is circumscribed by two red gold bands, a white gold or steel easel supports a gold frame enamelled with an opaque white line and cross, containing a miniature painting by Zuiev showing the Tsar and his son conferring with the staff generals at the front. Eugène Fabergé said this Egg was originally executed in blackened steel, but the surface now has the appearance of brightly polished steel or silver.

Signed by Henrik Wigström.
Gold Marks: 72 and *Kokoshnik*.
Height of Egg only: 4″.

In the Armoury Museum of the Kremlin in Moscow.

CROSS OF ST. GEORGE EGG
(Pl. 385)

Presented to the Dowager Empress Marie Feodorovna by Nicholas II
Dated 1916

★

This Egg was made to commemorate the recent presentation of the Order of St. George to the Tsarevitch and the Cross of that Order to his father.

In opalescent white enamel, the surface of this silver Egg is trellised with a simple laurel leaf pattern forming panels within which military crosses of St. George are painted. The egg is encircled by the black and orange-striped ribbon of the Order of St. George, which was awarded in recognition of outstanding courage; from two of the bows of this ribbon, which is carried out in enamel, hang silver medallions which may be raised upwards by pressing small buttons set beneath them, to reveal painted miniatures set in the main shell of the Egg. One medallion showing the Tsar's head covers the portrait of the Tsarevitch and the other showing the Cross of St. George, the portrait of the Tsar. The crowned initials of the Dowager Empress appear raised within a round carved border at the top of the Egg, while the year is similarly applied to the base.

Marks not known.
Approximate height: $3\frac{1}{4}$″.
Original photograph from catalogue of Russian Exhibition, London, 1935.

From the Collection of Her late Imperial Highness the Grand Duchess Xenia.

THE IMPERIAL EASTER EGGS FOR 1917

*

Permission was not given for these Easter gifts to be delivered to the Imperial Family. One of these Eggs was carved from Karelian birch wood. No other details are known.

A typewritten list in the author's possession based on the St. Petersburg Stocklist No. 1455 of 11th/12th June, 1913, briefly describes seventeen of the Imperial Eggs. They are shown on Colour Plates LXXV, LXXVII and LXXVIII, and on Monochrome Plates 320, 321, 332, 336, 341, 346, 347, 356, 360, 364, 367, 370, 373 and 374.

LXXXII. Small strawberry-coloured Easter Egg
Presented to Barbara Kelch by her husband, Alexander Ferdinandovitch Kelch
Dated 1898
In a private collection in the United States
Full description in the catalogue of specially commissioned Easter Eggs

Some Specially Commissioned
Easter Eggs

SMALL STRAWBERRY-COLOURED EASTER EGG
Colour Plate LXXXII

Presented to Barbara Kelch by her husband, Alexander Ferdinandovitch Kelch
Dated 1898

*

Easter Egg in engraved gold, enamelled translucent strawberry and set with rose diamonds with two portrait diamonds covering the initials B.K. and the year. The egg contains a yolk and white in opaque enamel, inside which is concealed a gold hen in varicoloured enamels set with rose diamond eyes; this in turn opens to disclose a tiny folding easel surmounted by a heart-shaped diamond and a cabochon ruby, and bearing a bevelled rock crystal within a rose diamond frame. The miniature it once contained is now missing.

Signed by Michael Perchin.
Gold Mark: crossed anchors.
Height: $2\frac{1}{4}''$.

In a private collection in the United States.

EGG WITH TWELVE PANELS
Colour Plate LXXXIII

Presented to Barbara Kelch by her husband
Dated 1899

*

Easter Egg enamelled pale translucent pink and opaque white on a yellow gold *guilloché* surface decorated with twelve panels, each with a painted enamel motif in pale violet and divided by broad bands of opaque enamel Indian red roses and translucent green enamel leaves on a dull hammered gold background, and set with rose diamonds. The initials of Barbara Kelch appear under a portrait diamond set in the top; the date of its presentation, 1899, under another in the base.

Signed by Michael Perchin.
No gold marks.
Height: $3\frac{1}{2}''$.

From the Collection of Her late Majesty Queen Mary.

ROCAILLE EGG
Colour Plate LXXXIV

Presented to Barbara Kelch by her husband
Dated 1902

★

Supported on its side by three scrolled feet, this gold *rocaille* egg is adorned with palm trees, floral swags, and scroll mounts set with rose diamonds. The engraved surface is enamelled translucent emerald green. Within, a carved gold tripod is surmounted by an engraved heart enamelled translucent rose and showing on one side the initials B.K. and on the other the year. When a diamond button is pressed, the heart opens out into a fan of three frames bordered by rose diamonds and opaque white enamel. The miniatures originally contained in these frames are now missing.

Signed by Michael Perchin.
Height of Egg: $4\frac{3}{4}''$.

In a private collection in the United States.

BONBONNIÈRE EASTER EGG
(Pl. 390)

Probably presented to Barbara Kelch by her husband
Dated 1903

★

Strongly reminiscent of the Gatchina Palace Egg (Pls. 339, 340), this, one of the last of Perchin's eggs, differs mainly from the earlier piece by reason of its *guilloché* pattern and the addition of emeralds to the lines dividing the surface of the enamel.

Two pieces of pink stained chalcedony cut cabochon are set within rings of rose diamonds at either end. Classical motifs are painted in enamel in each of the segments.

An oval striated agate *bonbonnière* is concealed within the egg. The lid is set with a rectangular portrait diamond covering the year, and the chased gold hinge and clasp are set with cabochon rubies; inside rests a tiny egg pendant, patterned with enamel

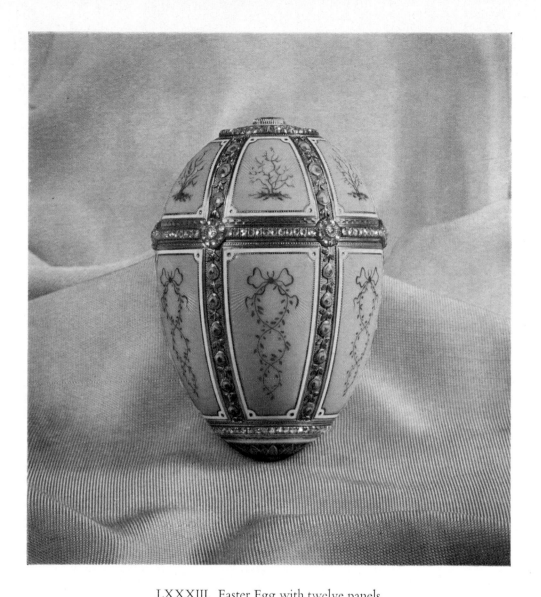

LXXXIII. Easter Egg with twelve panels
Presented to Barbara Kelch by her husband
Dated 1899
From the Collection of Her late Majesty Queen Mary
Full description in the catalogue of specially commissioned Easter Eggs

painted flowers to match the large egg. Both Eugène and Alexander Fabergé took the view that this is not an Imperial Egg, but one of the Kelch series.

Egg signed by Michael Perchin.
Gold Marks: 56 and *Kokoshnik* and French control mark.
Pendant signed by August Hollming and stamped 56.
Height of Egg: 5″.

In a private collection in the United States.

ICE EGG
(Pl. 387)

Presented by Dr. Emanuel Nobel to a friend
Date not known

★

Easter Egg with frost patterns engraved on silver and enamelled opalescent white, rimmed with pearls. Within, a diamond-shaped pendant watch rests on a rock crystal cushion set with ice motifs in rose diamonds in platinum.

No marks, apart from French control mark.
Height: $2\frac{3}{4}$″.

In a private collection in the United States.

YOUSSOUPOFF EASTER EGG
(Pls. 391–393)

Presented to the Princess Zénaïde Youssoupoff on the twenty-fifth anniversary of their marriage by her husband Prince Felix Youssoupoff

★

In the form of a clock in engraved yellow and red gold, enamelled translucent pink and opaque white and set with diamonds, emeralds, rubies and pearls, on a white onyx base. Three miniatures depict Prince Felix and his sons.

Signed: ФАБЕРЖЕ.
Gold Mark: 56 and *Kokoshnik*.
Height: $9\frac{5}{8}$″.

From the Collection of the late Maurice Sandoz.

Egg reproduced from Mr. Bainbridge's Monograph on the Life and Work of Fabergé by permission of its publishers, B. T. Batsford, Ltd.

CHAPTER X

Gold Marks and Workmasters' Initials

Goldsmiths' and workers' marks did not fascinate Fabergé; anyone having handled and examined even a small number of his pieces soon detects the casual esteem in which he held them. How many times when trying to discover the craftsman responsible for a certain object, has one found how frustrating this artistically endearing characteristic can be in practice. It is by no means uncommon to find only half a mark impressed —the punch having been only partially applied, the other half remaining unused in the air. A notable example of this is provided by the Easter Egg made for Barbara Kelch (Pl. LXXXIII)—a particularly lovely piece which would not appear to merit such cavalier and arbitrary treatment.

When, however, a mark does appear, and when, further, it is a good mark, both decipherable and complete, there are several conclusions to be drawn from it.

RUSSIAN STATE MARKS ON GOLD AND SILVER OBJECTS

St. Petersburg and Moscow each had their own separate cyphers which are easily distinguishable. To take St. Petersburg first, since it was here that Fabergé's main workshops were set up; during the period that concerns us, when the Fabergé *atelier* was in production, the gold mark of the city consisted of two crossed anchors intersected vertically by a sceptre (Pl. 394) up to the time when it was abandoned in favour of a woman's head seen in profile wearing a traditional Russian head-dress known as a *Kokoshnik* (Fig. 398). The Moscow mark took the form of a Saint George and the Dragon (Fig. 396) until they also adopted the *Kokoshnik,* as we have come to call the woman's head. The precise year when this change took place cannot be given with any certainty, as most of the available reference books, dealing very summarily with Russian hall-marks in any case, stop short, tantalizingly, just before this period is reached. Bäcksbacka is the most helpful in his recent book on St. Petersburg hall-marks—he reproduces an unbroken series of marks, one or more for each year, running consecutively from 1742 up to and including the one for 1896, which is shown with the crossed anchors and sceptre. There the series stops abruptly. A note is included to the effect that the St. Petersburg mark at about 1900 was the *Kokoshnik*. The reason he has not reproduced the intervening anchor marks must surely be that they do not exist, and that the *Kokoshnik* was adopted either later in 1896 or in the following year. Further, we do know that the Eggs for 1899 bear the *Kokoshnik,* and that most of the Eggs took about two or three years to complete and were marked while still in an early rough state.

On this evidence it seems that 1896 may be taken as a working approximation to the year when the *Kokoshnik* was adopted in place of the crossed anchors in St. Petersburg.

It is not unreasonable to assume that Moscow changed from the St. George and Dragon to the *Kokoshnik* in the same year, although it must be remembered that there is no specific evidence to confirm this. Very often, in addition to the *Kokoshnik*, one or two tiny letters are just decipherable close to it; these are the initials of the Inspector at the Hall (see Pl. 403).

There seems to be no rule about which direction the *Kokoshnik* should face.

RUSSIAN GOLD AND SILVER STANDARDS

The Russian gold standards in general use at this time were reckoned in *zolotniks* in the same way as ours are expressed in carats. The gold alloy of 96 parts, contains in Fabergé's objects, either 56 or 72 *zolotniks* of pure gold, just as our alloy of 24 parts, or carats, contains a certain proportion of pure gold, 9, 18 or 22 parts being the most common. It is useful to remember that the 96 parts of the Russian alloy correspond to the 24 parts of the English alloy —a ratio of four to one. Hence, if the Russian gold standards (56 and 72 *zolotniks*, for instance) are divided by 4, the results given represent the English standard equivalents (14 and 18 carats respectively).

The Russian standards for silver are also indicated by the number of *zolotniks* of pure silver out of 96 *zolotniks* of alloy. The most frequently found proportions are 84 and 88, although it is not altogether uncommon to find objects stamped 91. The English 'sterling' standard requires that at least 925 parts out of a total of 1000 parts of silver alloy be pure silver. By proportional calculation it thus becomes clear that while the Russian standards 84 and 88 are below the English standard for sterling silver, the standard 91 is above.

MAKERS' MARKS

Most, but by no means all, Fabergé objects bear some sort of mark of the House. The first obvious exceptions to this rule are the carvings in stone; a mark, even if practical, would almost always disturb the surface beauty of such pieces, and when a signature of some sort is found, for example, on the under-surface of a stone animal, this is tantamount to a proclamation that this carving is not by Fabergé at all, but one of the commonly found German copies usually lacking any personality whatsoever. The collector must, however, be on his guard against hard-and-fast rules. I remember a most attractive neph-rite frog which bore a signature engraved in bold letters on the contour of the stomach—the Frog was clearly Fabergé of the highest order and the signature was equally clearly a fake. Again, I have examined several authentic animal carvings, which are fully signed under the base or foot. The stone figures are generally engraved with the name Fabergé underneath, and on this flat surface the signatures do not appear out of place and are undoubtedly genuine. The flowers are usually unsigned, but sometimes carry a signature engraved on the gold stalk or even beneath the rock-crystal pot.

The form of the signature stamped or engraved on an object usually reveals its origin of manufacture; those pieces made in St. Petersburg simply bear the name Fabergé in Russian characters, thus: 'ФАБЕРЖЕ', without any initial, usually followed, or preceded, by the workmaster's initials. Very often, either the workmaster's initials or the name of the firm are left out. Objects made in St. Petersburg are sometimes marked К.Ф. Most workmasters' initials appear in Roman letters but some are stamped in Russian characters, for example 'I.P.' for Julius Rappoport.

When pieces were made specifically for the European market, the name usually appears thus: 'FABERGE' or C. FABERGE in Roman capitals or C.F. in initials.

The pieces made in Moscow are marked with the signature К. ФАБЕРЖЕ beneath an Imperial double-headed eagle, or, as in St. Petersburg, they too are simply stamped with the initials К.Ф.

LXXXIV. Rocaille Egg
Presented to Barbara Kelch by her husband
Dated 1902
In a private collection in the United States
Full description in the catalogue of specially commissioned Easter Eggs

It may be taken as a rule that no workmaster's initials appear on Moscow-made objects, although exceptions are to be found—the brooch shown on Pl. 200 is one such exception. The double-headed eagle is not found on pieces made in St. Petersburg, although again, as if to prove this rule, the present writer has found a pair of objects bearing each the usual St. Petersburg signature, the initials of the workmaster Julius Rappoport and, surprisingly, a boldly stamped Imperial Eagle; these are illustrated on Pls. 71 and 72 and take the form of silver-gilt stands supporting two Chinese porcelain dishes. The presence of the double-headed eagle in this instance may indicate that Rappoport was commissioned to make these mounts for the Moscow shop and stamped them accordingly. The combined appearance of the full Moscow mark with the initials of the workmaster Fedor Rückert on silver items is explained by the fact that this craftsman, working in Moscow, had his own extensive workshops and identity.

Collectors of Fabergé objects have long been puzzled by the absence of the Imperial Eagle on St. Petersburg pieces and its invariable presence on those from Moscow. This rule has become, in effect, a watertight method of discovering the origin of any article, and it would appear that there must have been some very good reason for it. I must record my deep sense of gratitude to Andrea Marchetti, at one time the manager of the Moscow silver workshop, for giving me the simple answer. 'You see', he said, 'in Moscow it was the firm who made the piece, and of course the firm, as a Royal Warrant holder, was entitled to the use of the Imperial Cypher; but in St. Petersburg you will notice that each piece is signed by the particular workmaster responsible for its manufacture, so really it was not the firm's production at all, but the original work of the man whose signature it bore—and that man, whether it was Perchin, Wigström, or any other, was not entitled to the Royal Cypher—and that is why you never find it on St. Petersburg pieces.'

It was all so simple after all, and so reasonable too!

Fabergé had branches in Odessa and Kiev, and although no objects of fantasy were ever made in either of these cities, a good deal of jewellery was produced in the small workshops which were set up in both places—about twenty-five men in Odessa and ten in Kiev. These pieces of jewellery were generally stamped К.Ф.

Silver articles made expressly for export to Great Britain after the year 1910 were all of an especially high grade (91 as opposed to the more usual 84 or

88). This was the result of a test case which Fabergé brought against the Worshipful Company of Goldsmiths in that year.

Fabergé's of St. Petersburg was in the habit of sending registered parcels containing pieces intended for sale here to Fabergé's of London; one of these parcels was intercepted by His Majesty's Customs in 1908 and passed on to the Goldsmiths' Company who decided that the enamelled cigarette-cases and other pieces they found had either to be hall-marked or sent back to Russia. In 1910 Fabergé brought his action which attempted to exempt his pieces largely on the legalistic grounds of their being 'jewellery' rather than 'plate'. The plea failed, and the firm was obliged from then on to send their wares for assaying and hall-marking while still in the rough prior to enamelling. They were further obliged to experiment with a purer silver—one which would be acceptable to the jealous and parochial goldsmiths in London: this problem was never solved satisfactorily by Fabergé, and those objects made for England which were enamelled on the higher grade (91) silver, were usually inferior to those enamelled on the lower grade (88). Owing to the lower firing point of the purer (and softer) metal, it was not possible to bring the furnace up to the high temperature essential for really fine translucent enamelling.

It will be noticed that, more often than not, part of a Fabergé mark is stamped upside down. There does not appear to be any consistency at all about this—it is merely one further evidence of the very casual way in which this whole business of marking precious metals was conducted in Russia.

On occasions, too, the signature of the House is not stamped at all, but engraved; this does not necessarily indicate a faked work, as there are many examples of pieces, the purity of whose origins are entirely beyond question, which are signed in this way. The most striking example I can recall is the Imperial Easter Egg for 1913 in rock crystal and containing a basket of spring flowers.

Marks are often very faint indeed owing to their having been stamped before the piece was finished. If a mark is a very distinct and sharp one, it does not render it necessarily suspect, although it is true that a forger, unless he were extremely subtle, would probably go out of his way to make a very clear mark.

Sometimes an article will be found stamped with foreign control marks, usually English or French (or occasionally even both), giving thereby some indication as to its possible history. The cigarette-case on Pl. 78 is punched with an Austrian control mark.

Very occasionally, a piece turns up bearing the signature A. ФАБЕРЖЕ or А.Ф. in addition to the usual workmaster's initials; such pieces were designed by Agathon Fabergé, the younger brother of Carl, who died at the early age of thirty-three (see Pl. 191).

There existed in Russia a system of 'Co-operatives' or '*Artels*' of jewellers working independently and making objects for Fabergé and other firms such as Ovtchinnikov and Khlebnikov. There were certainly four of these Co-operatives, whose number included some of the finest craftsmen and even one or two of Fabergé's workmasters. They had their own mark which was often stamped next to the name of the firm to whom the piece had been sold. The mark of the Third Co-operative, to give an example, appears thus:

$$\boxed{3^{\text{ЯА}}}$$

Immediately after the Revolution, Fabergé's premises were taken over by an organization known as the Leningradskoe Yuvelirnoe Tovarishchestvo (Leningrad Jewellery Brotherhood). This Brotherhood, or Trade Union, inherited a number of completed and unfinished Fabergé objects, and these, together with pieces by other contemporary goldsmiths and silversmiths, they stamped with their own mark Л.Ю.Т. (L.U.T.). This mark is shown on Pl. 405.

The Brotherhood is still flourishing in the Soviet Union.

Finally, too much homage should not be paid to marks; so often one finds that a comparatively modest object in silver is ostentatiously stamped in several places, while some superb masterpiece of untold value is not marked at all. Carl Fabergé's own attitude to these matters is the one that, in the final analysis, should be adopted by collectors; it is the most artistically desirable and incidentally the safest!

CHAPTER XI

The Designers, Craftsmen and Managers

THE ST. PETERSBURG HOUSE

THE DESIGNERS

Carl Fabergé was himself the principal source of ideas as well as the final judge of whether a design was to be carried out or not. Agathon, his young brother, died after only some twelve years in the firm, but his enthusiasm, discrimination and skill as an artist and designer played a vital part in forming the style known as 'Fabergé'. Later on, Carl Fabergé's sons, Eugène, Agathon, Alexander, and Nicholas, also worked as designers.

François Birbaum, a Swiss, was Fabergé's head designer; a brilliant artist, his range was not confined to any one branch of his craft, interesting himself in gold work, enamelling, stone carving and jewellery. He died in 1947 in Aigle, Switzerland, where he had settled down as a painter and pastellist.

Alexander Ivashov and *Zosim Kritzky,* both Russians, designed objects of fantasy and silver.

Oscar May, a St. Petersburg German, and *Hugo Oeberg,* a Moscow Swede, designed objects of fantasy and jewellery. *Alina Zwerschinskaya,* Holmström's daughter, and *Alma Pihl* were jewellery designers.

Eugène Jacobson, a Balt, designed silver articles.

On occasions an artist not working for the House would be commissioned for a specific article; for example Alexandre Benois designed an elaborate clock embellished with cherubs for Alexander III, and Scheftel, a German, was commissioned by Fabergé to design a neo-Gothic *garniture de table* for the Kelch family.

Jan Lieberg-Nyberg, a Lett, principally designed silver articles; was later transferred to the Moscow branch.

The Designers, Craftsmen and Managers

THE MODELLERS

The carvings in stone of animals, birds and small figures were carried out from original wax models.

Boris Froedman-Cluzel, a St. Petersburg Swede, now working at the Art Academy in Cairo, as professor of sculpture.

Gratchov, a Russian.

Grünberg-Salkaln, a Lett.

Eugenia Ilinskaya-Andreoletti, a Russian Italian, a specialist in animal carvings, now in Paris.

Kurtz, a Balt.

Strich, a Russian Jew, who worked after the Revolution in Tel Aviv and Haifa.

Timus, a Balt.

George Malychev, a Russian who also modelled the miniature statues which formed the surprise in some of the Imperial Eggs. He died in Russia.

MINIATURE PAINTERS

Vassily Zuiev (court miniaturist). Remained in Russia after the Revolution.

Krijitski, a Russian.

de Benckendorff, a Balt, watercolourist and court painter.

Blaznov, a Russian.

I. Geftler, a St. Petersburg German.

Prachov, a Russian who specialized in painting ikons.

Serge Solomko, a Russian watercolourist.

Horace Wallick, an Englishman.

Wegner, a Russian of German origin.

Zehngraf, of German origin, excelled in portrait work.

WORKMASTERS

Erik August Kollin. Born 1836, died 1901. A Swedish Finn from Pojo, he was apprenticed in Ekenäs, then in St. Petersburg where he worked first for Holmström before opening his own workshop in 1870. His speciality was gold filigree work, carving and engraving, and the creation of gold objects generally.

Kollin's workshops made the gold replicas of the treasures found during the excavations at Kerch in the Crimea. When he opened his workshop in 1870, he had arranged to work exclusively for Carl Fabergé, who took over control of the House in the same year. His mark is E.K.

The Designers, Craftsmen and Managers

Michael Evlampievich Perchin. Born 1860, died 1903. Of peasant stock, he was born in Petrozavodsk. Self taught at first, he later became apprenticed to various goldsmiths in a small way of business. In 1886 he opened his own shop, working exclusively for Fabergé, under whose guidance his extraordinary talent developed. His workshop made the Imperial Easter Eggs, with the exception of the first two or three, until his death, when his chief assistant, Henrik Wigström, took over. Despite the great number of pieces of all types made by Perchin, the superb quality of the craftsmanship was never varied. The signature ФАБЕРЖЕ with no workmaster's initials sometimes indicates that the object so marked was made in the principal workshop (Perchin's, afterwards Wigström's).

His mark is М.П.

Henrik Wigström. Born 1862, died about 1930. A Swedish Finn from Ekenäs, Wigström was Perchin's chief assistant when he set up his workshop in 1886; after Perchin's death in 1903, he took over control and his initials became the mark of the shop. The responsibility for making the Imperial Eggs passed on to Wigström after the death of his old chief and friend. He was one of the finest craftsmen of all times. The figures in stone were assembled at Wigström's.

His mark is H.W.

Julius Alexandrovitch Rappoport. Born 1864, died 1916. Rappoport, a German Jew, was trained in Berlin under Scheff. He settled in St. Petersburg in 1883 and established his workshop for the manufacture of silver articles. From that time on he became Fabergé's principal silversmith, specializing in large silver pieces for the table as well as purely decorative objects. When most of the workmasters moved to the new large premises in Morskaya Street, Rappoport remained where he was in his commodious workshop in the factory quarter of St. Petersburg at the Ekaterininski Canal, 65.

His mark is I.P.

August Wilhelm Holmström. Born 1829, died 1903. A Swedish Finn born in Helsingfors, Holmström served his apprenticeship in St. Petersburg, where in 1857 he purchased the workshop of a craftsman named Hammerström. From that time he worked for Fabergé as chief jeweller for the firm; on his death his adopted son Albert Holmström inherited the workshop and continued along the lines laid down by his father. Albert (born 1876, died 1925 in Helsinki) was assisted by his nephew Oskar Pihl Jr. Ryynänen, a Finn, was chief workmaster, and Feodorov and Vladimir Nikolaev, both Russians, were workmasters at Holmström's.

His mark is A.H.

Alfred Thielemann. Born in St. Petersburg, of German parents, this crafts-man controlled the second main workshop for the manufacture of jewellery. Karl Rudolph Thielemann, his son, took over control when he died between 1908 and 1910. Thielemann did not make any objects of fantasy, and pieces of this nature stamped with the initials A.T. are generally by Alexander Tillander, workmaster to the firm of Hahn in St. Petersburg. A. Tobinkov in St. Peters-burg also marked his objects A.T. He worked for Nichols and Plincke, and made silver pieces.

Thielemann's mark is A.T.

August Fredrik Hollming. Born 1854, died 1915. A Finn born in Loppis; came from Tavastehus to St. Petersburg and was apprenticed there in 1876 and became workmaster about four years later. He specialized in gold work and enamelled and stone objects. Enamelled brooches and other items of jewellery are sometimes found, bearing Hollming's initials. After he died the shop was, for a short period, taken over by his son Väinö, who was assisted by a Finn named Hanhinen. A star between the two initials of Hollming's name serves to differentiate it from that of Holmström.

His mark is A✶H.

Johan Viktor Aarne, a Finn born in 1863 in Viipuri, apprenticed in St. Peters-burg, he became workmaster in Tampere, Finland in 1891, then the same year returned to Russia to join Fabergé. He made gold and enamel objects of the first quality; died in Viipuri, where he owned the principal jewellery and silver firm in the town, having left St. Petersburg.

His mark is B A or occasionally, J.V.A.

Karl Gustav Hjalmar Armfelt, a Swedish Finn who took over from Victor Aarne. Was born in Hangö, apprenticed by 1895 with Paul Fredrik Sohlman in St. Petersburg. With Fabergé until 1916, then settled down in Tavastehus.

His mark is Я.A.

Anders Johan Nevalainen, a Finn born in 1858 in Pielisjärvi. Apprenticed in St. Petersburg in 1876; workmaster for Fabergé from 1885. Made small articles in gold and silver in Holmström's workshop. He sometimes made pieces for the Moscow branch in the same way as Rappoport did, and his initials then appear together with the usual Moscow mark.

His mark is A.N.

Gabriel Niukkanen, a Finn who made cigarette-cases and small articles in gold and silver.

His mark is G.N.

Philip Theodore Ringe, a German from St. Petersburg, made jewellery and objects of fantasy and cigarette-cases. Workshop taken over after his death by his widow, Anna M. Ringe, with help of Soloviev and Michelsson at 12 Morskaya Street.

His mark is T.R.

Vladimir Soloviev, a Russian who took over from Ringe after his death; he specialized in small enamelled silver pieces. His initials are often found under an enamelled surface.

His mark is B.C.

Anders Michelsson, a Swedish Finn born 1839 in Pyttis, took over Ringe's workshop jointly with Soloviev.

His mark is A.M.

G. Lundell, a Swedish Finn living in St. Petersburg, made cigarette-cases. Later became chief workmaster in Odessa.

His occasional mark is Г.Л.

Fedor Afanassiev, a Russian who made small objects of fantasy, usually enamelled.

His mark is Ф.А.

Edward Wilhelm Schramm, a German from St. Petersburg who made cigarette-cases and small jewelled articles.

His mark is E.S.

Wilhelm Reimer, a Balt, born in Pernau, who made jewels and gold objects. Died about 1898.

His mark is W.R.

Andrej Gorianov, carried on Reimer's workshop after his death.

His mark is А.Г.

LXXXV. Painted triptych Ikon, the silver-gilt frames in rococo taste enriched with rose-diamonds, enamelled opalescent pink over *guilloché* fields. On the left door, the painted likeness of St. Alexander Nevsky, and on the right, that of St. Mary Magdalen. The central panel represents the Finding of the True Cross by Constantine, Emperor of Byzantium and his mother Helena. The following inscription is engraved in Russian on the side of the Ikon: To Leonid Koltcheff, Prebendary and Archpriest, Confessor to Her Majesty in pious rememberance from Xenia and Olga. 1866–1916. The dates refer to the 50 years service of Father Koltcheff as Court Priest to the Royal Family

Signed: M.II.   Silver mark: Crossed anchors   Height 8¾".
Width (open): 8".   *In a private collection*   Depth (closed): 1½".

The Designers, Craftsmen and Managers

Stephan Wäkevä, a Finn born 1833 in Säckjärvi. Became workmaster in 1856. Made large silver pieces as well as table ware; after his death, his son Alexander carried on the business.

His mark is S.W.

Friedrich Rutsch, a German from Heidelberg, was a maker of chains, snaps and other accessories. Did not work exclusively for Fabergé.

After his death, he was followed by *Gerassimov.*

Epifanov-Zahudalin, a Russian, was an engraver on gold and silver; he had no mark.

Robert Pestou, a German of French Huguenot origin, was a stone engraver of outstanding skill; he had no mark.

Karl Woerffel, a German from St. Petersburg, who originally owned the large workshops by the Obvodny Canal, where stone articles of all types from animal carvings to large bowls and *tazze* were produced. When this business failed, Fabergé took over the shops, putting Woerffel in control. After Woerffel's death his countryman Alexander Meier took over the management. Working in stone, neither of these craftsmen had a mark. Before Woerffel worked exclusively under Fabergé's guidance, he made many pieces combining the use of silver with stone in a rather ungainly German manner, groups of Niebelungen toiling under the weight of nephrite bowls, and so on.

Kremlev and *Derbyshev* were Russian lapidaries of quite exceptional skill whose delicate touch is seen in many of the animal and flower studies. They had no marks.

Svetchnikov, a Russian, specialized in animal carvings.

Alexander Petrov, a Russian, was the chief enameller; the perfection of countless Fabergé objects depended upon the profound feeling he had for his material, his intuitive flair and endless patience. His son Nicholas took over when his father died. Some of the finest Norwegian and Swiss enamellers studied with Petrov. Working in enamel, he had no mark.

Vassily Boitzov, also a Russian, was the other great Fabergé enameller. Surprisingly, Bäcksbacka gives B.Б. as Boitzov's mark.

Käki and *Kämärä,* who succeeded him, both Finns, made the fitted wood boxes that contained the objects of fantasy and the jewels; these were as beautifully made, in their way, as the articles themselves and were generally of polished ivory-coloured holly wood, although birch and cedar wood boxes are quite frequently found containing early pieces. They also made the leather and velvet jewel-cases and boxes covered with grey *moiré* silk.

Otto Saikkonen, a Finn, and *Alfred Maripou,* an Estonian, who succeeded him, made the oak cases for the larger objects. On the administrative side, Fabergé was much assisted by *Paul Blomerius,* of Swedish origin, who had a talent for languages and a shrewd appreciation of the benefits of foreign trade.

THE MOSCOW BRANCH. 1887–1918

DESIGNERS

Michel Ivanov, a Russian.
Baron de Klodt, a Balt.
Ivan Kostrioukov, a Russian.
Fedor Kozlov, a Russian.
Jan Lieberg-Nyberg, a Lett.
Navozov, a Russian.
Sheverdyaev, a Russian.

MODELLERS

Luigi Buzzi, an Italian.
Baron de Klodt, brother of the designer.
Helena Shishkina, Sokolov and *Sokolovsky* were Russians.

WORKSHOP MANAGERS

Michael Tchepournov, a Russian, controlled the extensive silver workshops and was himself a fine craftsman.
No mark.

Knut Oskar Pihl, a Swedish Finn, born 1860 in Pojo, died 1897, was the manager of the jewellery shops; he was assisted by another Swedish Finn, Oskar Sewon, and succeeded on his death by a Pole named *Mitkievitch.* He was trained with August Holmström in St. Petersburg and married his daughter. His son Oskar Woldemar Pihl became chief assistant workmaster at Holmström's in 1913, and is at present chief designer at Tillander's in Helsinki.
Pihl's occasional mark is O.P.

Gustav Jahr, a Balt, was in charge of the workshops where objects of fantasy were made.

No mark.

Fedor Rückert, a Moscow German, enamelled silver in the traditional Russian seventeenth-century manner. Did not work exclusively for Fabergé.

His mark is Ф.Р.

BRANCH MANAGERS

Allan Bowe, assisted by his brothers *Arthur* and *Charles Bowe.* When Bowe's partnership with Fabergé was dissolved in 1906, *Otto Jarke* became manager. *Andrea Marchetti,* an expert in silver and gems, followed, then Alexander Fabergé took over until the Branch was closed down in 1918.

THE ODESSA BRANCH. 1890–1918

WORKSHOP MANAGERS

Brockmann, a St. Petersburg German, was chief workshop manager, followed by *G. Lundell,* then *Niukkanen,* then *Filippov. Vladimir Nikolaev* was also for a time in charge of the twenty-five or so men who worked there on small items of jewellery and silver.

BRANCH MANAGERS

Allan Gibson, a Moscow Englishman, and *Ivan Antony,* a Balt, followed by *George Piggott,* a Moscow Englishman, then *Vladimir Drougov, Georg Kral,* of Czech origin, and on his death, *Zinoviev,* a Russian, became the last manager.

THE KIEV BRANCH. 1905–1910

Balachov, a Russian, was the designer attached to this branch.

The small workshop for the production of jewellery consisted of about ten men.

The manager was *Vladimir Drougov,* an expert in precious stones; he managed at Odessa when the Kiev branch closed down.

THE LONDON BRANCH. 1903–1915

R. A. Pinks, of Irish descent, was the designer. *Frank Lutiger,* a Swiss, and *Alfred Pocock,* an Englishman, were modellers.

The Designers, Craftsmen and Managers

Arthur Bowe (brother of Allan Bowe) was manager until 1906 when new premises were opened under joint management of *Nicholas Fabergé* and *H. C. Bainbridge*.

The outstanding difference between the St. Petersburg House and the Moscow and Branch Houses was administrative. In St. Petersburg the workmasters each ran their own shops, taking on and paying their own craftsmen, whereas in Moscow, Odessa and Kiev, Fabergé employed the craftsmen himself, putting them under the control of managers. This is why I have referred to workshop managers in the Moscow House as opposed to the workmasters at St. Petersburg.

Just how fundamental was this difference is seen in the way the St. Petersburg workmaster was given the personal credit for the creation of each object which he was allowed to sign with his own initials, in marked contrast to the impersonal way in which the Moscow pieces were, with rare and early exceptions, all grouped together under the firm's name. Allan Bowe, who was Fabergé's partner in the Moscow business, had a remarkable flair for organization as well as an extremely wide knowledge of his craft.

INITIALS OF UNKNOWN WORKMASTERS

The initials A.R. have been found on objects bearing Fabergé's signature. Mr. Bainbridge refers to a light blue enamelled ink-pot marked K. Fabergé without the usual double-headed eagle of the Moscow House, and the initials A.R. In addition to this, Mr. Henry Hill has given me details of a silver double ash tray marked in precisely the same way. The initials are possibly those of a workmaster in either Odessa or Kiev whose name we do not know; if he had worked in Moscow a double-headed eagle would have appeared over the name Fabergé. The initials И.П. (I.P.) have been found together with the usual Moscow House mark on a silver carafe stamped with the St. George and Dragon hall mark used prior to 1896 (see plate 397); the identity of this craftsman is not known. Mr. Bertram Hill and the late Captain Harold Spink have examined a silver tea-set similarly marked, but bearing the initials E.W.—another unknown early Moscow workmaster. The initials I.C.A. which are stamped on the desk set on Pl. 179 are also unknown.

Beilin, Bock and Britzin (see p. 129) worked at Fabergé's before establishing their own firms.

128

FABERGÉ'S WORKMASTERS
AND THEIR MARKS

ERIK AUGUST KOLLIN	E.K.
MICHAEL EVLAMPIEVICH PERCHIN	M.П.
HENRIK WIGSTRÖM	H.W.
JULIUS ALEXANDROVITCH RAPPOPORT	I.P.
AUGUST WILHELM HOLMSTRÖM	A.H.
ALFRED THIELEMANN	A.T.
AUGUST FREDRIK HOLLMING	A✶H.
JOHAN VIKTOR AARNE	B.A.
KARL GUSTAV HJALMAR ARMFELT	Я.A.
ANDERS JOHAN NEVALAINEN	A.N.
GABRIEL NIUKKANEN	G.N.
PHILIP THEODORE RINGE	T.R.
VLADIMIR SOLOVIEV	B.C.
ANDERS MICHELSSON	A.M.
G. LUNDELL	Г.Л.
FEDOR AFANASSIEV	Ф.A.
EDWARD WILHELM SCHRAMM	E.S.
WILHELM REIMER	W.R.
ANDREJ GORIANOV	A.Г.
STEPHAN WÄKEVÄ	S.W.
KNUT OSKAR PIHL	O.P.
FEDOR RÜCKERT	Ф.P.

FABERGÉ'S COMPETITORS

There were many goldsmiths and jewellers apart from Fabergé carrying on successful businesses in Russia, and especially in St. Petersburg, before the Revolution.

Fabergé was by far the most original and enterprising in this field and his influence profoundly affected the work of his contemporaries.

The most notable of these firms were Beilin, Bock, Bolin, Britzin, Butz, Denissov, Gratchov, Guériat, Hahn, Khlebnikov, Köchli, Kortmann, Lorié, Marshak, Morozov, Ovtchinnikov, and Rimmer.

Other firms specializing in carved stone animals recognizably different in character from Fabergé's were Denissov-Duralsky and A. I. Sumin.

CHAPTER XII

Conclusions

After half a century has passed, it should be possible to consider the place that Fabergé is entitled to occupy in the art history of his time, for, without question he belongs to that small company of inspired decorative artists who seem to have given a recognizable signature to a particular epoch.

It is difficult to avoid the conclusion that much of the Fabergé oeuvre, and the Easter Eggs in particular, appear as mutely beseeching advocates for a perpetuation of the dynasty.

Whether we recognize it or not, there lies in us all a certain sympathy for the great Egyptian Kings who made such elaborate efforts to take their possessions with them on the soul's journey to eternity. A faint echo of this hopeless cry for preservation is generally discernible at the end of any vigorous movement in art.

The gorgeous trifles that we have been examining in some detail, accoutrements of a pampered society, emerge, in one sense, as the pathetic symbols of a world whose standards and way of life generally are destined soon to be swept away. I say in one sense because these *objets de luxe* always retain a distinct identity of their own, which artistically is their saving grace, by reason of the rigid discipline exercised by Fabergé himself. It was perhaps the world's last chance of showing what could be done in this field.

Even so, much of the Russian goldsmith's work can be justly labelled *fin-de-siècle,* although some of the reproach is removed from this when we stop to consider in what distinguished company he finds himself; the writings of Swinburne and Maeterlinck, the illustrations of Beardsley and the music of Richard Strauss are all *fin-de-siècle,* but none of them, I take it, entirely without merit.

The real trouble does not lie here, the real trouble is concerned with man's

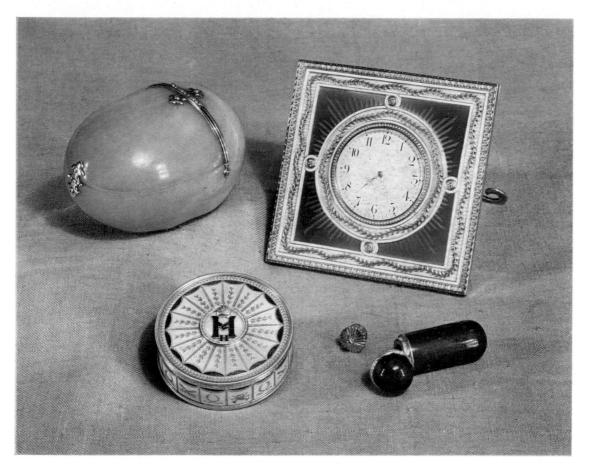

LXXXVI. *Top Left*: Table Box carved as a gourd in bowenite with gold mounts. Length: $4\frac{1}{8}''$. *Right*: Red gold strut Clock enamelled pale translucent blue and opalescent white with green gold acanthus and laurel decorations. $4\frac{1}{4}''$ square. *Front Left*: Imperial gold Presentation Box enamelled opalescent oyster with motifs expressed with gold *paillons* and translucent strawberry, the hinged cover with the crowned cypher of Nicholas II. Diameter: $2\frac{1}{2}''$, height: $\frac{13}{16}''$. Gold mark: 72. These three items signed M.П. *Front Right*: Scent *flacon* with red and green gold laurel mount, enamelled translucent strawberry over a floral *guillochage*. Length: $2\frac{1}{8}''$.
Signed: H.W.
The Presentation Box in the collection of the Duke of Alba.
The other objects in the collection of Messrs. Wartski

quest for the ideal. A preoccupation with the perfect, the belief that you must be producing the very *ne plus ultra* in your chosen medium, is itself an admission of sterility. You are saying in effect that yours is to be the work of art to end all works of art. A desire to replace nature instead of the more seemly operation of trying to represent or express her is an abject confession that the traditional striving of the artist has been abandoned. It is the hall-mark of an art that is sick.

To the perfectionist, all evidence of personal endeavour, any clue as to how the work was produced, becomes objectionable. The way in which Vermeer patted away all the brush-strokes in some of his painting illustrates this point very well. Those last Greek sculptures of athletes, tired and somehow meaningless under the weight of too much modelling and stroking, fail to stimulate us now precisely because they are too good to live. Voltaire put the matter tersely: 'Le mieux est l'ennemi du bien.'

A striking example of the perfectionist busy at his vile work in our own time is provided by most of the purveyors of coloured films; the nearer they approach perfect naturalism, the further they retreat from any work of real artistic value. The actors are no longer characters in a drama, they become instead gesticulating waxworks in whom we find it difficult to believe.

The reason for this attitude is usually an urgent feeling that the only effective way of avoiding complete obliteration in the memory of others is to commit to posterity, in as monumental, permanent and faithful a form as possible, the artist's complete personal credo, so that it may be proof against the *débâcle* which is generally assumed, with reason, to be near at hand.

Master craftsman though he was, Fabergé, happily, had too many problems to overcome in his work ever to fall completely into this particular pit, although he may sometimes have stumbled dangerously near the brink. His practice of treating each individual project as a distinct and special challenge was in itself an insurance against this disaster. The perfection of his technique was not allowed to become automatic.

While it is not claimed that Fabergé consciously checked every angle and measurement of his Easter Eggs more carefully because he felt that the Revolution was just round the corner, it must be pointed out that a normal intelligence could detect around him unmistakable signs of *malaise* without very much difficulty. Strikes were not altogether unknown even in the comparatively model conditions in Morskaya Street. The stormy history of the ill-fated

Romanovs was in itself a stern reminder that conditions of near starvation, even when they are combined with suffocating superstition and ignorance, will inevitably produce political extremists with their own grim methods of surmounting difficulties.

The tragic scenes at Hodynka Field outside Moscow when, after the Coronation of Nicholas II, the traditional distribution of gifts and roubles was so bungled that about a thousand people lost their lives in the ensuing stampede, were in a sense a fitting opening for a reign in which intrigue and obscurantism became the order of the day, making it possible in 1902 for a sadistic reactionary such as Plehve as Minister of the Interior to wield almost unlimited power. Student and peasant risings and government-inspired pogroms were frequent occurrences, and revolution was in the air. Fabergé would have been an extremely dull person, and he was far from this, not to have realized that the radical breezes blowing in from the West boded no good for the traditional Russia he knew and loved, and this thought may subconsciously have influenced his style. As it turned out, Alexander Tillander was actually killed by his own workers when the Revolution broke.

A great deal of prejudice has to be overcome before the work of this modern goldsmith is to be fairly judged. Many people find it impossible to believe that enamelled gold boxes were being made as recently as 1916 of a quality and a beauty that bear comparison with the very finest examples of eighteenth-century France. Collectors are too often apt to take on trust what they read, instead of accepting with good grace the evidence of their eyes.

Much of what Fabergé attempted, he attained perfectly. His lively mind was an unending source of inspiration to his workpeople, and within the range he set himself he may be truly called *Maître*.

Chronological Table of Events

1814 Gustav Fabergé born in Pernau on 30th February.

1842 Firm established by Gustav in Bolshaya Morskaya Street in St. Petersburg.

1846 Peter Carl Fabergé born in St. Petersburg on 30th May. Baptized in the Protestant Church.

1860 Gustav retires to Dresden leaving business under management of Zaiontchkovsky.

1861 Carl Fabergé confirmed in the Kreuzkirche in Dresden.

1862 Agathon, Carl's brother, born in Dresden.

1870 Fabergé takes control of firm at age of twenty-four.
New ground-floor premises taken opposite original basement, now closed.

1872 Fabergé marries Augusta Julia Jacobs.

1874 Eugène, Fabergé's eldest son, born. (Died in Paris, 1960.)

1876 Birth of his second son, Agathon. (Died in Helsinki, 1951.)

1877 Birth of his third son, Alexander. (Died in Paris, 1952.)

1881 Alexander II assassinated on 13th March.
Accession of his son Alexander III.

1882 Fabergé's younger brother Agathon arrives from Dresden to join firm at age of twenty.
The House exhibits for first time at Pan-Russian Exhibition in Moscow, and wins Gold Medal.
Death of Peter Hiskias Pendin.

1884 First Imperial Easter Egg presented to the Empress.
Birth of Fabergé's fourth son, Nicholas. (Died in Paris, 1939.)
Tsar grants his Royal Warrant to the House of Fabergé in 1884 or 1885.

1885 House awarded Gold Medal at Nuremberg Fine Art Exhibition for gold replicas of Scythian Treasure.

1886 Michael Perchin joins the firm.

1887 Allan Bowe becomes partner and Moscow Branch founded.

1888 Special Diploma received at Northern Exhibition in Copenhagen; the House was *hors concours,* being represented on the jury.

1890 St. Petersburg premises doubled in size. Branch opened in Odessa.
Pamiat Azova launched. Tsarevitch Nicholas sent on educational journey to Greece, Egypt, India, Indo-China and Japan.

1891 First stone of terminus of Trans-Siberian Railway laid by Tsarevitch.

1893 Death of Gustav Fabergé in Dresden on his seventy-ninth birthday.
'Art Nouveau' movement launched in Europe.

1894 Death of Alexander III on 1st November.
Marriage of Nicholas II on 7th December.
Eugène Fabergé joins the firm.

1895 Death of Fabergé's brother Agathon at age of thirty-three.

1896 Coronation of Nicholas II.
House awarded State Emblem at Pan-Russian Exhibition at Nijny-Novgorod.
The *Kokoshnik* was almost certainly adopted as State mark for gold and silver throughout Russia in 1896.

1897 *Hors concours* at Northern Exhibition in Stockholm, Eugène Fabergé a member of jury.
Granted Royal Warrant by Court of Sweden and Norway.
Death of Oskar Pihl.

1898 Premises bought at 24 Morskaya Street and reconstruction started.

1900 Removal to Morskaya Street.
Imperial Eggs exhibited for first time at Paris 'Exposition Internationale Universelle'. Carl Fabergé, member of jury, acclaimed *Maître* and decorated with Légion d'Honneur.

1901 Death of Eric Kollin.

1903 Arthur Bowe sent from Moscow to London to start up business for Fabergé from Berners Hotel.
Death of Michael Perchin; workshop taken over by his chief assistant, Henrik Wigström.
Death of August Holmström, succeeded by his son Albert.

1904 Outbreak of Russo-Japanese war.
Birth of Tsarevitch.
Fabergé invited to visit King Chulalongkorn of Siam.

London branch removes to Portman House, Duke Street, Grosvenor Square.

Objects by Fabergé exhibited for first time in England by Lady Paget at an Albert Hall bazaar in aid of Royal Hospital for Children.

1905 Nicholas II leaves the capital after shots fired at Winter Palace.

Kiev branch founded with Vladimir Drougov as manager.

1906 Partnership with Allan Bowe dissolved. Otto Jarke becomes manager of Moscow branch.

London branch removes to 48 Dover Street under Nicholas Fabergé and H. C. Bainbridge.

Beginning of business connection with Siam, India and China.

1907 Artists working at Sandringham finish models for stone animal carvings. Baron Foelkersam's *Inventaire de l'Argenterie* published, in which he writes: 'This firm (Fabergé's), which is one of the best and most famous in the world, is renowned above all for its *objets d'art*.

'Articles made in Fabergé's workshops are known for their technical excellence, especially as regards enamelling, stone polishing and engraving.'

1908 Carl Fabergé arrives in London from St. Petersburg to see Dover Street premises on 29th January, and leaves hurriedly the same day for Paris when informed that he would be expected to seek audience with Queen Alexandra.

1910 Kiev branch closed down; considered unnecessary in view of existence of older Odessa branch.

Fabergé brings his unsuccessful test case against the Worshipful Company of Goldsmiths on 7th, 8th, 9th and 10th November.

1911 London branch moves to 173 New Bond Street.

Nicholas II commissions Fabergé to carve miniature stone figures of Empress's Cossack Bodyguard.

1913 Tercentenary of Romanov rule brings about revival of Russian Mediaevalism in applied arts known as 'Old Russian Style'.

1914 Outbreak of world war.

Agathon Fabergé overhauls and catalogues Imperial Crown Jewels.

1915 Bond Street shop closes down. Death of August Hollming.

1916 Death of Julius Rappoport.

1917 Russian Revolution.

The House closes for short period at beginning of Revolution.

1918 Firm finally closed down by Bolsheviks.

Carl Fabergé escapes in September via Riga, Berlin, Frankfurt and Homburg to Wiesbaden as a courier attached to a foreign Embassy.

1920 Arrives at Lausanne in June.

Dies on 24th September at the Hotel Bellevue, La Rosiaz.

1921 Agathon resumes work on Crown Jewels under Soviet orders, from Autumn 1921 until Spring 1923.

1925 Death of Carl Fabergé's widow at Cannes on 27th January.

1927 Madame Bontiron donates a nephrite *bratina* by Fabergé to the Musée des Arts Décoratifs in Paris.

1928 Agathon Fabergé escapes from Russia.

1929 Eugène brings his father's remains from Lausanne Crematorium to Cannes, and buries them in the grave with his mother.

Sets up tombstone in black Swedish porphyry bearing this inscription:

CHARLES FABERGÉ

joaillier de la Cour de Russie

né 18 mai 1846 à St. Petersbourg

décédé 24 septembre 1920 à Lausanne

AUGUSTA FABERGÉ,

née JACOBS

née 25 decembre 1851 (vieux style) à Tsarskoé Selo

décédée 27 janvier 1925 (nouveau style) à Cannes.

FABERGÉ FAMILY TREE

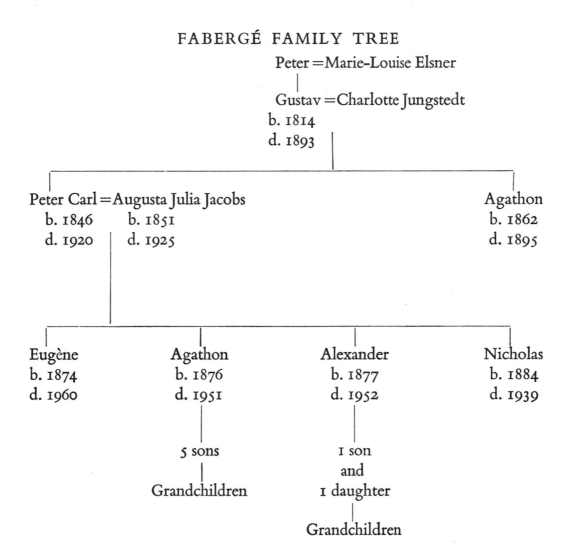

Peter = Marie-Louise Elsner

Gustav = Charlotte Jungstedt
b. 1814
d. 1893

Peter Carl = Augusta Julia Jacobs
b. 1846   b. 1851
d. 1920   d. 1925

Agathon
b. 1862
d. 1895

Eugène
b. 1874
d. 1960

Agathon
b. 1876
d. 1951

5 sons

Grandchildren

Alexander
b. 1877
d. 1952

1 son
and
1 daughter

Grandchildren

Nicholas
b. 1884
d. 1939

Appendix A

This is a translation of part of the Jury's report on the International Exhibition held in Paris in 1900:

We inspected with pleasure the work shown by Mr. Fabergé, the jeweller and goldsmith who, as a member of the Jury, was *hors concours*. He showed us several interesting examples of the goldsmiths' art, including a candelabrum in the manner of Louis XVI, and a large ornamental piece decorated in the modern style in which the use of nephrite, bronze [sic] and silver was praiseworthy.

But what was particularly charming was his collection of precious objects in gold and enamel, made to satisfy the national tradition for giving presents at Easter time—the great and the humble, the rich and the poor alike. The collection of Easter Eggs on loan from the Imperial Treasure was quite exquisite. These pieces, which so transcend their class, are worthy to be regarded as goldsmithery rather than jewellery. Their delicate settings, secret openings, carving and enamelling were quite remarkable.

Appendix B

The following is a translation of part of the Foreword of a catalogue, evidently the second, issued by the Moscow branch of the firm in 1899:

The publication of this, our second price list, is due to the steadily increasing number of enquiries for our products which we are receiving from the Russian provinces. As it is impossible to give a sufficiently clear picture of the varied character of our production by mere correspondence, and as we wish to satisfy our correspondents from other towns, we have undertaken this second edition with illustrations and approximate prices. In this way we hope to enter into closer contact with those of our clients who, because they live in the provinces, have no opportunity of visiting our premises personally and of seeing for themselves our rich selection of goods.

We do not intend to include in the present price list the whole enormous variety of objects which could only be seen personally. The limited space of a price list does not allow us to dwell on detail. We have only been able to present here the most important items and these only in typical designs. Moreover, we beg to draw the attention of the public to two facts which, amongst others, account for some of the discrepancies between what is shown in the price list and our actual selection of goods:

1. Our production is subject to frequent changes depending on the whims and dictates of fashion, as a result of which new designs are put on the market every day.

2. Many of the best designs cannot be included here, because they would thus be liable to imitation by our competitors.

Our goods are made in our own factory of the very best quality materials. The finest artists working exclusively for our firm supply us with a rare variety of designs which can compete successfully with the most superb examples produced by our foreign competitors in this field. Regarding quantity we beg to point to the really vast selection of all kinds of goods made in silver, gold and diamonds in all shapes and designs including the most recent ones. As to the quality of our products, it will be sufficient to acquaint our customers with the following four principles which have always guided us during the many years of our business:

1. It is our strict rule not to supply any goods of poor quality under any circumstances; in other words, every object, be its value no more than one rouble, is made carefully and solidly.

2. It has always been our endeavour—and our clients can see this for themselves—to offer to the public the greatest possible number of entirely new forms and designs. Goods which have gone out of fashion will not remain in our shop: once a year they are collected and melted down.

3. We try to produce our goods in such a way that the value of each object purchased from us fully corresponds with the sum paid for it, i.e. we sell our goods as cheaply as their careful execution permits.

4. Thanks to our considerable capital resources, we are always able to make and hold at the disposal of our clients a large quantity of the most varied and valuable articles.

PRICES:

5. Under no circumstances do we tolerate the possibility of any objects equal in quality to our own being sold elsewhere at a lower price than that fixed by us, for which reason our own prices are always moderate and correspond to the quality of the stones and the workmanship which went into the production of the article; at the same time, we beg to point out that goods made of best quality material will naturally be more expensive than those made of materials of inferior quality.

The range of models and designs fully corresponds to the range of prices. Taking into account both the needs of the higher classes of society as well as the interests of the middle class, we provide both the luxury and expensive goods to satisfy the most refined taste as well as the inexpensive goods within the reach of the not so well-to-do.

HOW TO ORDER

Information and Explanation. All information and explanation concerning our products will be supplied by us immediately upon request.

Orders, Claims and Payments on Account. Our factory is so equipped that we are able to execute all orders given to us. Orders are executed with the same careful attention whether they are of small importance or large and complex. Repairs of gold, diamond and silver articles are carried out carefully and without delay.

We also accept old diamond jewels for remodelling according to the most recent designs. The same applies to all kinds of repairs.

In case at the time of receipt of an order any one of the articles ordered is temporarily sold out, our clients are immediately notified and the approximate time of delivery stated. If nothing to the contrary has been stipulated in the order, the part of the order which is immediately available will be despatched at the same time as this information.

In order to avoid misunderstandings, we would ask our clients to describe the goods required as accurately as possible and to state the approximate price.

We should also be glad if in the interest of a speedy and accurate delivery of the goods required, the client would state his name and address as clearly as possible.

It would further be much appreciated if our clients would kindly enclose with their orders or instructions the amount corresponding to the value of the required goods plus postage, or, in order to avoid the expense entailed by the remittance of the money, instruct us to send the goods against C.O.D.

When ordering goods to be specially made, we require our clients to be good enough to send us one third of the value of the order on account.

Carriage and Insurance charges for goods sent to the provinces are put on the buyer's account.

Exchange and Return of Goods. We are always willing to exchange or accept the return of goods purchased from us with the exception of the following cases:

1. When the article shows traces of having been worn.

2. When so much time has elapsed since the purchase that the object in question has gone out of fashion.

3. When the object has been made to order or altered upon the instructions of the client.

4. When the goods are returned C.O.D.

Address for Correspondence: Moscow. Kuznietski Most, d.

Kupetsheskavo Obshtchestva, 4.

Telegraphic Address: Moscow, Fabergé.

Telephone No. 1173.

Appendix C

Contents of a letter received on the 31st of March, 1951, from Mr. Gudmund Boesen, curator of the Royal Collection at Rosenborg Castle in Copenhagen, concerning the Egg illustrated on Pls. 309 and 310.

The Egg was given by Queen Marie of Denmark (born Princess of Hesse, 1767–1852) to her daughter Princess Wilhelmine Marie, who married a Duke of Schleswig-Holstein Glücksburg; after her death in 1891, according to her will, it came into the possession of King Christian IX of Denmark (the father of Queen Alexandra of England and the Empress Marie Feodorovna of Russia). Since 1900 it has been in the Royal Collection at Rosenborg; it had already been exhibited in Copenhagen for a time, however, in 1879 at the great Industrial Exhibition.

According to a family tradition first referred to by the Princess Wilhelmine Marie, the Egg was originally presented by a Duchess Charlotte of Orleans (three Duchesses of Orleans with the name Charlotte died in 1722, 1744 and 1761 respectively) to Caroline, Queen of England (wife of George II, married in 1705, and died in 1737)—hence the monogram of two Cs beneath a crown which appears on the ring contained in the Egg. Queen Caroline, according to this tradition, gave it to her daughter Mary (1723–72), who married the Landgrave Frederick of Hesse, grandfather of Queen Marie of Denmark, previously mentioned. If this tradition is historically trustworthy, the date of the Egg may be put at the first third of the eighteenth century, which seems quite reasonable.

It is, however, interesting to learn that a similar Egg existed in Denmark at that time, a fact which makes the traditional date even more likely. An inventory dated 1743 of the property of the late Queen Anne Sophie of Denmark lists 'A gold Egg with a small gold enamelled hen inside. Within the hen, a signet [sic] with a royal crown set with 40 brilliants, 6 rose-cut diamonds and 6 pearls, and with a cornelian on which is engraved a posy.'

Sometimes I think that this must be our Egg, even if there are differences in the description, and that tradition is wrong. But at least the date seems to be confirmed. There are no marks, either on the Egg itself or on any of the contents.

Appendix D

[Details supplementary to those given in captions to the plates bearing the same numbers]

COLOUR PLATES

VIII. Rectangular gold musical box with chamfered corners featuring enamel-painted panels of six palaces owned by the Youssoupoff family in pale opalescent sepia. The lid shows the Archangelskoe Palace, and the front panel, the residence on the Moika Canal in St. Petersburg where Rasputin was put to death by Felix Youssoupoff, one of the two sons whose initials appear on this box. The pictures on the lid and bottom are painted in enamel over a sun-ray pattern; the others are painted over a background of parallel lines. The borders are enamelled with opalescent beads and translucent emerald leaves on *sablé* paths. The initials of Felix and Zénaïde and their two sons, Nicholas and Felix, are painted beneath Imperial crowns at the four corner panels. The diamond thumb-piece is composed of the numerals XXV.

This box was presented to the Prince and Princess Youssoupoff on their twenty-fifth wedding anniversary.

Signed: H.W.   Gold mark: 72 $3\frac{1}{2}'' \times 2\frac{5}{8}'' \times 1\frac{3}{4}''$

In a private collection in the United States

XIII. *Left to right:* Engraved yellow gold box enamelled translucent royal blue on an engraved field, the hinged lid mounted with a carved green gold foliate bezel, a border of half pearls and a miniature painting after Greuze within a frame of brilliant diamonds.

Signed: M.Π.   Gold mark: 72 $1\frac{9}{16}'' \times 1\frac{1}{4}'' \times 1\frac{3}{16}''$

Bowenite hinged box with red and green gold laurel mount set with rose diamond thumb-piece.

Signed: Φ.A. $2'' \times 1\frac{1}{2}'' \times \frac{7}{8}''$

Rock crystal and yellow gold heart-shaped box, the sides enamelled opalescent oyster on a diapered ground and the crystal panels in the base and cover edged by rose diamonds.

Signed: H.W.   Gold mark: 72 $1\frac{9}{16}'' \times 1\frac{9}{16}'' \times \frac{9}{16}''$

Rhodonite casket mounted in yellow gold and enamelled translucent emerald and opaque white, with a rose diamond thumb-piece.

Signed: H.W.   Gold mark: 72 $2\frac{3}{8}'' \times 1\frac{1}{2}'' \times 1\frac{7}{16}''$

In a private collection in England

XVI. Group of objects from the collection formed by Madame Elisabeth Balletta of the Imperial Michel Theatre.

A large baroque pearl, profusely set with rose diamonds as a swan with an obsidian beak, and cabochon ruby eyes.

No marks. Length: $2\frac{3}{8}''$

Red gold note-case with carved green gold laurel borders enamelled with stripes in opaque white and pale pink. The front surmounted by an opalescent white enamelled plaque applied with the Imperial Eagle in rose diamonds within a half pearl border suspended from a swag motif in coloured golds and pearls. Fitted with a gold fluted propelling pencil with a moonstone knop.

No marks. Height: $2\frac{7}{8}''$. Width: $1\frac{13}{16}''$

Gold mounted fan, the sticks enamelled translucent coral with a dark sepia plant design against a *guilloché* field and set with brilliant and rose diamonds. The antique French painted fan itself is mounted on pierced mother-of-pearl sticks inlaid with gold.

Signed: A.H. Length: $13\frac{3}{4}''$

Octagonal gold *bonbonnière* enamelled translucent mustard on an engraved sun-ray ground, the hinged lid and flange set with borders of rose diamonds and bearing an oval painted miniature of a young girl after Greuze within a rose diamond border.

Signed: M.Π. Width: $1\frac{7}{16}''$. Height: $1\frac{13}{16}''$

Superb replica of the Peter the Great Statue by Falconet in golds of colour supported on a carved emerald.

Signed: M.Π. Length: $2''$. Height: $1\frac{3}{4}''$

Engraved gold box with sides decorated in Louis XV *basse-taille* technique with sapphire blue floral swags, and lid trellised with a pattern of rose diamonds against a blue enamelled background and displaying the intertwined initials of Madame Balletta for whom this handsome box was designed by the Grand Duke Alexander, whose initials and anchor cypher appear on the bottom.

Signed: H.W. $4'' \times 2\frac{3}{4}'' \times 1''$

Hexagonal gold *bonbonnière* enamelled opalescent white on a wave patterned engraved ground, the hinged lid formed of a single carved opal bordered by rose diamonds.

Signed: M.Π. Width: $1\frac{3}{8}''$. Height: $\frac{7}{8}''$

In a private collection in the United States

XX. Miniature-frame in engraved red gold, enamelled opalescent white and surmounted by the Imperial Crown. An oval miniature painting of Marie Feodorovna, signed by I. Geftler, is set within a rose diamond border.

Signed: H.W. Height: $2\frac{5}{16}''$

Imperial Presentation Box in dull green gold enamelled translucent pale rose on sunray and wave-pattern *guilloché* ground and embellished with carved *rocaille* scrolls set with diamonds, the lid centred by the diamond-set cypher of Nicholas II within an oval diamond border.

Signed: M.П. $4'' \times 2\frac{5}{8}'' \times 1\frac{1}{2}''$

Circular red and green gold-mounted *bonbonnière* enamelled opalescent white on an engraved field.

Signed: К. ФАБЕРЖЕ Diameter: $1\frac{3}{4}''$

Gold cigarette-box enamelled translucent royal blue on an engraved scallop-patterned field with borders enamelled opaque white and translucent red and green with opalescent white beads on gold *sablé* paths. Rose diamond thumb-piece.

Signed: H.W. Gold mark: 72 $3\frac{3}{4}'' \times 2\frac{1}{2}'' \times \frac{11}{16}''$

In a private collection in the United States

XXI. Red and green gold hand-seal enamelled translucent pale mauve on a *guilloché* background with a moonstone finial and a white chalcedony sealing stone engraved with the initials of Queen Victoria of Spain, the original owner.

Signed: H.W. Length: $4\frac{1}{4}''$

Silver gum-pot enamelled translucent pale green on a *guilloché* field, the brush set with a cabochon garnet finial.

Signed: B.A. Height: $3''$

Circular gold *bonbonnière* of exceptional quality enamelled opalescent pale flame with painted enamel warm sepia motifs, bordered by gold *sablé* paths with opaque white enamelled beads, and red and green translucent enamelled floral and ribbon decorations.

Signed: H.W. Gold mark: 72 Diameter: $2\frac{3}{16}''$

In a private collection in the United States

XXII. Cigarette-case enamelled translucent 'love-bird' green on a *guilloché* pattern of swags with red and green gold mounts with a wavy flange in the eighteenth century manner and a moonstone push-piece. $3\frac{3}{4}'' \times 2\frac{1}{2}'' \times \frac{3}{4}''$

Fluted aventurine quartz hand-seal with matching gold mount and translucent pale green enamelled silver collar within red and green gold laurel bands, set with a cornelian sealing stone.

Signed: M.П. Height: $2\frac{3}{8}''$

Red gold cigarette-case enamelled opalescent white on a wavy engraved ground, elaborately decorated with coloured *paillons* following the technique of Jean Coteau and carried out in the manner of Salembier and set with a brilliant diamond push-piece, and a half pearl border.

Signed: M.П. $4'' \times 2\frac{3}{8}'' \times \frac{13}{16}''$

In a private collection in the United States

XXIII. Yellow and red gold mounted hand-seal, enamelled translucent pink on a *guilloché* ground and set with rose diamonds and half pearls, and surmounted by a fluted bowenite globular knop.

Signed: ФАБЕРЖЕ Height: $2\frac{11}{16}''$

Two-toned silver-gilt-mounted opalescent chalcedony strut clock with a sun-ray patterned panel enamelled translucent strawberry and backed with ivory.

Signed: M.Π.   Silver mark: crossed anchors $4\frac{1}{4}''$ square

Red and green gold-mounted cigarette-case enamelled translucent pale apricot on a scalloped ground, set with rose diamonds and a cabochon ruby push-piece.

Signed: M.Π. $3'' \times 1\frac{13}{16}'' \times \frac{13}{16}''$

In the Collection of Mrs. Dennis Hamilton Kyle

XXVII. Standing double-sided miniature-frame in the form of a fire-screen with superbly chased floral swags and trophies in five colours of gold. The framework, enamelled opaque white *champlevé*, is set with two oriental pearl finials; the rectangular frame itself is enamelled opalescent white on one side against a scalloped ground with an oval photograph of Nicholas II within a half-pearl border. The reverse, enamelled opalescent pale rose, holds a photograph of the Tsarina similarly framed.

Signed: H.W.   Gold mark: 72   Height: $7''$. Width: $3\frac{3}{4}''$

In a private collection in the United States

XXVIII. Standing clock carved from a block of Siberian nephrite, the numerals represented in enamel by pink roses and green leaves, the hands set with rose diamonds.

Signed: H.W.   Gold mark: 72   Height: $3''$

In the Collection of Mrs. India Minshall

XXIX. Red and green gold strut clock with border of carved acanthus leaf, enamelled translucent pink on an engraved striped background further embellished with floral swags, the dial set within a ring of half pearls and fitted with gold hands. Ivory backed.

Signed: H.W. $5\frac{3}{8}'' \times 3\frac{1}{4}''$

Four-colour gold double marriage cup, the four facets of the fluted stems each of a different shade of gold and the bowls similarly varied and engraved; the cups are taken apart by means of a bayonet fitting.

Signed: M.Π.   Height together: $3\frac{9}{16}''$

Carved rock crystal semi-circular box, the gold bezel enamelled opaque white and set with a square-cut ruby at either corner and the thumb-piece composed of a triangular ruby and rose diamond cluster, the hinged lid engraved with a swag design.

Signed: ФАБЕРЖЕ $2\frac{1}{2}'' \times 1\frac{1}{4}'' \times \frac{7}{8}''$

Siberian nephrite watering-can with gold handle and rose, enamelled translucent strawberry on an engraved ground with rose diamond mounts. Originally from the Balletta Collection.

Height: $1\frac{1}{2}''$. Length: $4\frac{1}{8}''$

Oval scent bottle enamelled translucent pale blue on an engraved ground with a hinged lid surmounted by a half pearl, mounted with a red gold bezel with a green gold laurel collar and fitted with a fluted gold stopper.

Signed: M.Π.   Height: $1\frac{7}{8}''$

Red gold sealing-wax holder enamelled with opaque white stripes and mounted with chased green gold meander patterned bands.

Signed: M.Π.   Length: $3\frac{7}{8}''$

In a private collection in the United States

XXX. Group of objects from the Royal Collection at Sandringham.

Raspberries in rhodonite with nephrite and small green translucent enamel leaves and red gold stem in a rock crystal pot.   Height: $6\frac{1}{4}''$

Box in engraved yellow gold enamelled pale opalescent white and sepia, decorated with white opaque enamel beads and translucent emerald green and strawberry enamel conventionalized borders. The lid is enriched by a wreathed painting of Falconet's statue of Peter the Great in St. Petersburg; a similar painting of the Peter and Paul Fortress appears on the bottom of the box.

Signed: H.W.   Gold mark: 72.   Diameter: $2\frac{5}{8}''$. Height: $1''$

Box in engraved yellow gold enamelled translucent pale pink and opaque white, decorated with green gold chiselled swags and set with rose diamonds and a moss-agate lid within a pearl border.

Signed: H.W.   Gold mark: 72. $1\frac{3}{8}'' \times 1'' \times 1''$

This box also bears the English control mark and the initials C.F.

Bowenite cup with dull yellow gold fluted handle set with a gold rouble (1756) enamelled translucent strawberry, and two cabochon sapphires.

Signed: E.K.   Gold mark: crossed anchors.   Height: $2\frac{1}{16}''$

Dull grey metal automatic elephant with cabochon ruby eyes and ivory tusks; a Mahout enamelled opaque white with an elephant-hook sits on a yellow gold rug enamelled translucent green and set with rose diamonds. One of the diamond collets may be moved aside and a gold key inserted to wind the clockwork mechanism, and when a tiny lever under the stomach is pressed, the elephant walks slowly along swinging its head and tail. This toy was given by his family to His Majesty King George V on Christmas Day 1929.

No marks. In original case.   Length: $1\frac{7}{8}''$

Box in engraved red gold enamelled translucent royal blue, decorated with green gold carved mounts and a basket of flowers in rose diamonds, cabochon rubies and emeralds on the lid.

Signed: M.Π.   Diameter: $1\frac{3}{8}''$. Height: $\frac{13}{16}''$

Nephrite letter-opener surmounted by a white chalcedony elephant set with sapphires, rose diamonds and cabochon ruby eyes, on a yellow gold mount enamelled translucent strawberry and opaque white.

Signed: M.Π.   Gold mark: crossed anchors.   Length: $5\frac{1}{2}''$

Nephrite letter-opener with red gold handle enamelled with translucent strawberry and opalescent white stripes, set with a carved green gold mount.

No marks.   Length: $5\frac{1}{8}''$

XXXI. *Left:* Moss agate brooch set with rose diamonds and mounted in gold and silver. Length: $1\frac{1}{16}''$

Centre: Yellow gold ring of a chequered pattern set alternately with half pearls and enamelled translucent pale blue on fluted rectangular panels.

Signed: B.A.   Gold mark: crossed anchors   Width: $\frac{1}{4}''$

Right: Gold brooch in rococo taste enamelled translucent *bleu de roi* on a sun-ray background and set with a brilliant diamond. Height: $1\frac{5}{8}''$

In the Collection of Mrs. Kenneth Snowman

XXXII. *Left:* Cornelian and carved red and green gold swivel seal.

Signed: M.II.   Height: $2\frac{1}{8}''$. Width: $1\frac{3}{4}''$

Right: Nephrite and carved red and green gold Imperial swivel seal.

Signed: H.W.   Height: $1\frac{5}{8}''$. Width: $1\frac{3}{8}''$

In a private collection in the United States

XXXIV. *Left to right:* Nephrite elephant with cabochon ruby eyes and diamonds set in tip of trunk. Length: $2\frac{1}{2}''$

Grey Kalgan jasper elephant with rose diamond eyes. Length: $1\frac{1}{8}''$

Figured cornelian goldfish in the Chinese style. Length: $2\frac{3}{16}''$

Amazonite figure of the 'three wise monkeys' combined in a single *netsuké* carving. Height: $1\frac{3}{16}''$

Aventurine quartz pig with rose diamond eyes. Length: $1\frac{5}{8}''$

In the Collection of Mr. and Mrs. Kenneth Snowman

XXXVII. Mandrill in dark grey and violet agate with rose diamond eyes. Height: $1\frac{15}{16}''$

Elephant in bowenite with cabochon Siamese ruby eyes. Trunk to tail length: $2\frac{3}{8}''$

Chimpanzee in striated agate with olivine eyes. Height: $2\frac{1}{8}''$

Hare in bowenite set with ruby eyes. Height: $1\frac{5}{8}''$

Gibbon in bowenite with garnet eyes. Height: $1\frac{1}{2}''$

Hippopotamus in blue agate with rose diamond eyes. Length: $1''$

Litter of four piglets, two in aventurine quartz and two in striated agate, connected by a gold crossed mount stamped M.II. $1\frac{7}{8}'' \times 1\frac{1}{2}''$

Pig in aventurine quartz with rose diamond eyes. Length: $1\frac{1}{16}''$

In the Collection of Major R. Macdonald-Buchanan, C.V.O., M.B.E., M.C.

XXXIX. Ibis in varicoloured agate with carved gold legs and bill, set with rose diamond eyes, and supported on an ebony base. Height: $2\frac{3}{4}''$

In a private collection in the United States

XL. Crouching frog carved in jadeite with gold-set rose diamond eyes. Height: $3\frac{9}{16}''$

Originally from the Collections of Lady De Grey (Marchioness of Ripon) and Lady Juliet Duff.

In a private collection in the United States

Appendix D

XLII. Group of animal carvings from the Royal Collection at Sandringham.

Top: Aventurine quartz shire horse with cabochon sapphire eyes. A portrait model of Sandringham's champion 'Field Marshal'. Length: 7″. Height: 6″

Left to right: Varicoloured agate field mouse with cabochon sapphire eyes, platinum whiskers and gold strands of straw. Height: $2\frac{1}{2}$″

Varicoloured agate duck of a downy texture, with rose diamond eyes and yellow gold legs. Height: $1\frac{1}{8}$″

Obsidian cock with speckled white agate feathers, purpurine comb, rose diamond eyes and red gold legs stamped H.W. 72. Height: 2″

Dark grey and white stone poodle (possibly a pebble) with yellow-stained cabochon chalcedony eyes. Length: $3\frac{1}{8}$″

Purpurine pig. Length: 2″

Varicoloured agate grass snake with rose diamond eyes. Length: $2\frac{1}{4}$″

Butter-coloured stained chalcedony duckling with rose diamond eyes foiled green, and red gold legs stamped H.W. 72. Height: $2\frac{1}{4}$″

Nephrite frog with cinnamon diamond eyes set in yellow gold, and rose diamond teeth. Length: $2\frac{1}{8}$″

White chalcedony goose with head and feathers in obsidian and beak in stained quartzite, rose diamond eyes and red gold legs stamped H.W. 72. Length: $2\frac{7}{8}$″

Crocidolite pheasant with rose diamond eyes and red gold legs stamped H.W. 56. Length: $2\frac{7}{8}$″

Labradorite magpie with translucent quartzite body, rose diamond eyes and red gold legs. Length: 2″

Cornelian duck with cabochon ruby eyes and red gold legs stamped H.W. 72. Height: $1\frac{5}{16}$″

Striated agate dachshund with rose diamond eyes. Length: 3″

XLIV. Parrot carved from a single white opal and perched in a miniature yellow gold cage. The bird is set with cabochon Siam ruby eyes and has red gold talons; the opal is itself a remarkable specimen showing many vivid tones of green, yellow and blue, as well as a bright flame colour in the feathers at the back. The cage has a removable gold wire netting and a drawer; there are two feeding bowls, one filled with gold seed.

Cage signed: M.П. Height of cage: 3″. Diameter: $1\frac{9}{16}$″ Height of parrot: $1\frac{5}{16}$″

In a private collection in the United States

XLV. *Left:* A portrait model of the house boy (Dvornik) who used to sweep out Fabergé's St. Petersburg premises. The face in aventurine quartz, with sapphire eyes, shirt in lapis lazuli, breeches in grey Kalgan jasper, waistcoat in obsidian, white translucent quartz apron and black Siberian jasper boots and cap, to which is applied a pierced gold badge giving the address of the firm 24 Morskaya, beneath the word Dvornik in Russian characters. He holds a gold broom. Height: 5″

Centre: Policeman (Gorodovoi) in Caucasian obsidian, aventurine quartz, jasper, gold, silver and enamel and moonstone eyes. 251 is applied in gold on the cap. Height: 6″

Right: Ukrainian peasant (Hohol) in aventurine quartz, lapis lazuli, white quartz, coffee jasper cloak, hair and moustache, cabochon sapphire eyes, black jasper hat and boots and purpurine belt, collar and front of shirt decorated with opaque enamel, and holding a gold pipe.   Height: $5\frac{3}{8}''$

All these figures are engraved ФАБЕРЖЕ under the right boot.
In the Collection of Sir William Seeds, K.C.M.G.

XLVI. Gipsy woman with aventurine quartz face and hands, nephrite skirt, purpurine headdress, black Siberian jasper hair and shoes, mottled green stone shirt and an extremely effective Paisley shawl in figured red-brown Ural marble. The eyes are brilliant diamonds, the ear-rings gold and the coins silver.

This carving is a portrait model of Vara Panina, the celebrated gipsy, the extraordinary range and beauty of whose voice kept audiences entranced nightly at Moscow's Tzigane restaurant Yar in spite of her extreme ugliness. A victim of her unrequited love for a member of the Imperial Guard, she took poison and died on the stage in front of him singing 'My heart is breaking'.   Height: $7''$
In a private collection in the United States

XLVII. *Left:* Carpenter (Plotnik) with aventurine quartz face and arms, purpurine shirt, lapis lazuli breeches, white quartz apron, brown jasper hair and beard, black Siberian jasper boots, cabochon sapphire eyes, testing a silver axe and with mountings in gold stamped 72, and axe stamped H.W. 91.   Height: $5''$

Centre: Labourer (Zemlekop) in purpurine, lapis lazuli, black and brown jasper, aventurine quartz face and hands, tawny aventurine coat, quartzite socks, cabochon sapphire eyes and holding a silver-gilt shovel.   Height: $4\frac{1}{2}''$

Right: Peasant (Mujik) playing a silver-gilt balalaika stamped H.W. ФАБЕРЖЕ, 88. Face and hands in aventurine quartz, cabochon sapphire eyes, hair and moustache in stained cornelian. Grey Kalgan jasper blouse, lapis lazuli breeches, socks in quartzite, boots in stained granular quartzite, bench in banded brown chalcedony.   Height: $4\frac{1}{2}''$

The two standing figures are engraved ФАБЕРЖЕ under the right foot.
In the Collection of Sir William Seeds, K.C.M.G.

XLIX. Scent bottle in the form of a carved female head supported on a classical pedestal. The head in dull yellow topaz forms the stopper which is ringed by rose diamonds at its base. The bottle in red gold is enamelled translucent pale green and is decorated with dull green gold mounts.
Signed: H.W.   *From the Collection of the late Marquess of Portago*   Height: $3\frac{3}{4}''$

Buttercup in red gold enamelled translucent yellow with carved nephrite leaves in a rock crystal pot.   *In the Collection of Robert Strauss, Esq.*   Height: $5\frac{3}{4}''$

Ant-eater carved in striated agate and set with rose diamond eyes.
In the Collection of Mrs. Arthur Sutherland   Length: $3''$

Appendix D

LVII. A circular *bonbonnière* enamelled translucent pale blue on a *moiré* ground and mounted in red gold with carved green gold acanthus leaves and swags. The lid features, under the glass cover, two articulated painted ivory figures of a boy and a girl dressed in Swedish peasant costume applied to an oxidized black background. When the box is agitated the two figures assume naturalistic and amusing dance positions. This superb box is fully signed by Fabergé and bears the initials of the chief workmaster, Henrik Wigström.   Diameter: $2\frac{9}{16}''$. Height of box: $\frac{11}{16}''$

In a private collection

LXII. Group of flowers in rock crystal pots.
From left to right:

Daphne, flower in opalescent white and translucent red enamel with rose diamond centres set in gold collets, stalk in dull red gold, leaves in nephrite.   Height: $4\frac{1}{4}''$

Flowering currant, berries in purpurine, aventurine quartz and white chalcedony, dull red gold stalk and nephrite leaves.   Height: $5\frac{1}{2}''$

Spray of cornflowers in translucent enamel with rose diamond centres and yellow gold stalk and leaves, oats in red gold, and Chinese forget-me-nots in turquoise with rose diamond centres and yellow gold stalk and leaves.   Height: $10''$

Violets in translucent enamel with gold leaves enamelled green and brown, with a dull red gold stalk.   Height: $4\frac{1}{2}''$

Alpine strawberries in translucent enamel with a pearl and diamond flower, dull red gold stalk and nephrite leaves.   Height: $4\frac{1}{4}''$

In the Collection of Alexander Schaffer, Esq.

LXVI. *Left:* Spray of Gentian (Exacum) planted in a pale jadeite tubular tub filled with blackened metal simulating soil, supported upon a cloudy grey agate platform. The flowers painted in pale pink and white opaque enamel and centred each by a rose diamond, the calyx in thin translucent pale green enamel, allowing the yellow gold to be seen at the edges, the stalks in meticulously engraved dull green gold, and the leaves in carved nephrite.

Signed: H.W.   Gold mark: 72   Height: $6\frac{1}{2}''$

Centre: Seven separate sprays of Anemone in gold thinly enamelled in naturalistic shades with carved nephrite leaves and dull green gold stalks, in a rock crystal jar with a gold base enamelled opalescent oyster on a *guilloché* background and translucent strawberry, and standing on four fluted bun feet.

Signed: ФАБЕРЖЕ   Height: $7\frac{3}{8}''$

Right: Sun Plant (Portulaca) in gold in a rock crystal pot, the three flowers thinly coated on both sides with translucent yellow enamel and centred by a brilliant diamond, the stalks, leaves and buds in lightly engraved dull green gold.

Signed: H.W.   Height: $7\frac{1}{4}''$

In the Collection of Robert Strauss, Esq.

Appendix D

MONOCHROME PLATES

44 and 45. The following is a translation of the postcard illustrated on these Plates.

A strange coincidence! I was just going to write to you when I received your letter of the first of November. I have already been here two months, where everything is wonderful, good and cheap. Full pension for 20 marks. The Grand Duke Cyril Constantinovitch also lives here with his family and the wealthy director of the Triangle rubber factory.

Oh yes—they are all without any money! And the future is not reassuring. I also wrote to my son to bring goods here where there is an enormous demand, but have not had any reply. I am living here on marks, as in Italy or France it would be $3\frac{1}{2}$ times more expensive, and in Switzerland 6 times. How are you getting on there? Have you got enough fuel and food? There is no news from Agathon or Alex.

With kind regards to your wife

from

C. Fabergé.

52. Louis XVI French snuff-box in engraved red gold, enamelled translucent scarlet, decorated with opaque white, translucent green and scarlet enamel. The lid is set with a painted enamel panel.

Signed by Joseph Etienne Blerzy and dated 1777 (Paris) $3\frac{1}{4}'' \times 2\frac{3}{8}'' \times 1\frac{5}{16}''$

In a private collection in the United States

58. 'Tiffany glass' jar mounted in oxidised silver and set with pearls. A striking example of 'Art Nouveau' by Fabergé.

Signed: B.A.   *In the Collection of Robert Strauss, Esq.*   Height: $4\frac{1}{8}''$

59. Silver-gilt strut clock enamelled translucent grey-blue set with three painted miniature portraits of Nicholas II, Alexandra Feodorovna and their son, the Tsarevitch.

$7'' \times 4\frac{5}{8}''$

Both these typically Edwardian pieces are signed M.II. and none of the miniatures is signed.

In the Wernher Collection, Luton Hoo

60. Green gold *minaudière* in an 'Art Nouveau' design, with compartments for powder and rouge on one side, and a clip for notes on the other, divided by a mirror backed by an ivory writing-panel. The four thumb-pieces are set with cabochon sapphires as is the top of a gold pencil which slides down the back of the case. The surface is decorated with an elaborate pattern of lily of the valley leaves in green gold, two of

which are torn, relieved by flowers in brilliant diamonds set in silver against a background of red-tinted gold.

Signed: К. ФАБЕРЖЕ. $3\frac{1}{16}'' \times 2\frac{1}{8}'' \times \frac{9}{16}''$

In the Collection of Lady Cox

61. Silver miniature-frame enamelled translucent crimson with silver mounts gilded red and green, containing miniature portrait of Nicholas I. $3\frac{5}{8}'' \times 3''$

In the Wernher Collection, Luton Hoo

73, 74 and 75. Triptych ikon in the Byzantine style in silver-gilt, richly set with emeralds, rubies, sapphires and pearls. Presented by the Nobility of St. Petersburg to Nicholas II and his wife on November 3rd, 1895, the occasion of the birth of their first child, the Grand Duchess Olga, and portrays their respective patron saints, Nicholas, Alexandra and Olga, painted on silver in natural colours against a dark brown background. The outside is panelled with Russian birch finished in ivory, and is designed to represent a church steeple. The framework is very finely chased and set with emeralds, rubies and sapphires.

Signed: М.П. Height: $10\frac{1}{4}''$

In the Collection of Alexander Schaffer, Esq.

91. A bowenite frame with a red gold mount decorated with a green gold acanthus leaf pattern, containing a translucent warm sepia enamel painting of Durham Cathedral on an engraved gold background.

Signed: H.W. $6\frac{3}{16}'' \times 4\frac{5}{8}''$

Yellow gold *bonbonnière* enamelled with translucent warm sepia paintings of Windsor and Balmoral Castles, each encircled by opaque white enamel beads and a pattern of painted enamel roses and translucent green enamel leaves set with rose diamonds.

Signed: H. W. Gold mark: 72. Diameter: $2\frac{1}{4}''$

Both objects in the Royal Collection at Sandringham

117. Cigarette-case in engraved red gold, enamelled translucent pale primrose, and decorated with a carved green gold laurel leaf mount and a cabochon sapphire push-piece.

Signed: К. ФАБЕРЖЕ. $2\frac{5}{16}'' \times 1\frac{1}{2}'' \times \frac{1}{2}''$

In the Collection of Peter Otway Smithers, Esq., M.P.

118. Engraved silver box for stamps, enamelled translucent rose and opaque white.

Signed: H.W. $1\frac{7}{8}'' \times 1\frac{1}{16}'' \times \frac{9}{16}''$

In the Collection of Miss F. E. Morrice

119. Engraved red gold box with bevelled rock crystal panels top and bottom.

Signed: М.П. $1\frac{9}{10}'' \times \frac{4}{5}'' \times \frac{4}{5}''$

In the Collection of Michael H. Crichton, Esq., O.B.E.

120. Rock crystal cigarette-case with a yellow gold mount enamelled translucent royal blue with a green gold leaf *paillon* visible through the layers of enamel. Push-piece set with a brilliant diamond.

Signed: ФАБЕРЖЕ. $3\frac{1}{4}'' \times 2'' \times \frac{9}{16}''$

In the Collection of Mrs. Leland Hayward

121. Cigarette-case in engraved silver enamelled translucent grey, with red gold mounts and a rose diamond thumb-piece. This case was made for the English market and bears the control mark and date letter indicating that it was allowed into Great Britain in 1910–11.

Signed: H.W. and FABERGE and C. F. in Latin characters. $3\frac{1}{2}'' \times 2'' \times \frac{7}{16}''$

In the Collection of Peter Otway Smithers, Esq., M.P.

122. *Bonbonnière* in engraved green gold enamelled translucent golden-brown, surmounted by a gold rouble within a rose diamond border, with a rose diamond thumb-piece.

Signed: M.П.   Gold marks: 72 and crossed anchors.   Diameter: $1\frac{7}{8}''$. Height: $\frac{7}{8}''$

In a private collection in England

128. *Left:* Red-brown cornelian pumpkin-shaped box, the removable segment with a yellow gold mount enamelled opaque white and set with rose diamonds.

Signed: ФАБЕРЖЕ.   Gold marks: 72 and crossed anchors.   Diameter: $2\frac{3}{16}''$

Height: $\frac{7}{8}''$

Centre: Engraved smoky topaz-quartz bottle in the form of a lyre, with red gold mounts and set with rose diamonds, the top enamelled translucent pink and surmounted by a pearl finial.

Signed: M.П.   Gold mark: crossed anchors.   Height: $2\frac{9}{16}''$

Right: Shaped nephrite box set with rose diamonds and a cabochon ruby in yellow gold.

Signed: M.П.   Gold mark: crossed anchors.   Length: $1\frac{7}{16}''$. Height: $\frac{7}{8}''$

In the Royal Collection at Sandringham

137. Presentation Table Box in engraved red gold enamelled translucent bottle-green and opaque white, with formal inlaid borders of carved yellow gold husks and berries against a background of translucent strawberry enamel, and set with wreaths and rosettes in rose diamonds. The lid, which is hinged, is surmounted by a large Imperial Eagle in brilliant and rose diamonds, framing miniature portraits of Nicholas II and Alexandra Feodorovna, to whom this splendid box was given on the 300th Anniversary of the Romanov accession in 1913.

Signed: К. ФАБЕРЖЕ. $4\frac{1}{8}'' \times 3\frac{1}{16}'' \times 1\frac{1}{4}''$

In the Wernher Collection, Luton Hoo

146. *Left:* Bell-push in pale green bowenite with carved red and green gold mounts, set with rose diamonds and a pink stained chalcedony push. $2'' \times 2'' \times 1\frac{7}{8}''$

Centre: Seal in red and green gold enamelled translucent green and strawberry and opaque white, surmounted by a white onyx ball, and set with an engraved cornelian for sealing. Height: $1\frac{7}{8}''$

Right: Clock in engraved rock crystal with red gold mounts set with four cabochon rubies; the dial encircled by a carved gold wreath enamelled translucent green with rose diamond ties. Given by Alexandra Feodorovna to Queen Victoria, this clock had its permanent place on the desk of H.M. King George V.

These three objects are signed by Perchin. Height: $4\frac{7}{8}''$

In the Royal Collection at Sandringham

147. Engraved tubular silver cigarette-case enamelled translucent pale blue with red gold mounts, set with two rings of brilliant diamonds, stained pink chalcedony ends and diamond thumb-piece. A match compartment is fitted at one end, and the other when opened reveals an amber cigarette-holder with a matching enamel and diamond mount.

Signed: H.W. Case: $3\frac{5}{8}'' \times 1\frac{3}{4}'' \times 1\frac{3}{8}''$

In the Collection of Her Grace the Duchess of Leeds

150. Picture frame composed of fluted yellow gold half-columns enamelled opalescent white with translucent pale pink enamelled ties, and adorned with finely chiselled *quatre-couleur* gold floral mounts set with moonstones. The frame is surmounted by the crowned initial E in rose diamonds, applied to a translucent pink enamelled plaque, and is supported on two inverted cone-shaped feet. Formerly in the possession of the Grand Duchess Elizabeth Feodorovna, sister of Alexandra Feodorovna.

Signed: M.Π. Height: $12''$

In the Collection of Mrs. Ferrier

164. Three hand seals:

Left: carved rhodonite in the form of a hooded figure in the 'Art Nouveau' style.

Height: $2\frac{13}{16}''$

Centre: gold and nephrite set with rose diamonds and cabochon rubies in an oriental inlaid design.

Signed: A ⚹ H. Gold mark: crossed anchors. Height: $3''$

Right: aquamarine hexagonally carved with facets and mounted with a gold snake with a cabochon ruby set in its head.

Signed: E.K. Gold mark: crossed anchors. Height: $2\frac{3}{4}''$

In the Collection of Messrs. Wartski

168. *Above:* Sealing-wax holder in engraved red gold, enamelled translucent pale peach and opalescent white, with apple-green dots, sepia foliate motifs and steel-coloured dashes, with carved green gold mounts and a cornelian seal.

Signed: M.П.   Length: $5\frac{11}{16}''$

Below: Sealing-wax holder in engraved red gold, enamelled with translucent green and opalescent white stripes, with green gold carved mounts, and set with pearls and a white onyx seal.

Signed: ФАБЕРЖЕ.   Length: $4\frac{1}{4}''$

Both in the Wernher Collection, Luton Hoo

171. Double bell-push in bowenite, the concave top enamelled opalescent rose on a radiating pattern, and decorated with carved coloured gold flower scrolls set with a demantoid garnet looping round the moonstone buttons, supported on four fluted bun feet.

Signed: M.П.   *In the Collection of Messrs. Wartski*   Length: $2\frac{13}{16}''$

172. Bell-push in engraved red gold, enamelled opalescent white with carved green gold mounts, and cabochon garnet push, supported on three bun feet. Formerly in the Collection of the Dowager Marchioness of Milford-Haven, sister of the last Tsarina.

Signed: M.П.   Gold mark: crossed anchors.   Diameter: $2\frac{1}{8}''$. Height: $1\frac{1}{2}''$

In the Collection of Lady Brabourne

181. Lorgnette in engraved yellow gold, enamelled translucent pale rose, with carved gold scroll mounts in the style of Louis XV.

Signed: M.П.   Length: $6\frac{3}{4}''$

Nephrite letter-opener with engraved gold handle enamelled translucent orange-red, rimmed with rose diamonds.

No marks.   Length: $8\frac{1}{8}''$

Pill-tube in engraved red gold, enamelled translucent pale leaf-green and opalescent white with carved green gold mounts.

No marks.   Length: $2''$

In the Wernher Collection, Luton Hoo

185. Silver and hardstone chess-set, the pieces of one side formed of tawny aventurine quartz mounted in silver and set on circular silver feet, the other side of grey Kalgan jasper similarly mounted, the board with nephrite squares alternating with pale apricot serpentine with silver frame mount moulded with acanthus and laurel borders, a bun foot at each corner, the sides inscribed in Russian:

'To warmly beloved and dear Commander General Adjutant Alexei Nikolaievitch Kouropatkin in memory of Manchuria 1904–1905 from those devoted and grateful to him.'

Signed: Я.А.   Board: $25''$ square

In the Collection of Dr. J. G. Wurfbain

188. Octagonal nephrite box with yellow gold mounts enriched with opaque white enamel and set with a ruby and rose diamond thumb-piece. The lid is mounted with a warm sepia enamel miniature painting of an English church by a river.

Signed: H.W.   English Control Mark. $2\frac{3}{4}'' \times 2\frac{3}{4}'' \times 1\frac{1}{8}''$

Nephrite jar and cover in the form of a pear with red gold mounts and green gold finial set with rose diamonds.

Signed: M.Π.   Height: $2''$

Rectangular purpurine box with yellow gold bezel decorated with a fine opaque white enamel line and a carved laurel border.

Signed: H.W.   Gold marks: 72 and English Control. $2\frac{3}{4}'' \times 1\frac{1}{4}'' \times \frac{3}{4}''$

Rock crystal box in the form of an egg with yellow gold clasp and hinge set with rose diamonds.

Signed: M.Π.   Length: $2\frac{3}{16}''$

Square purpurine box with red gold mounts enamelled opaque white and translucent green.

Signed: H.W.   Gold marks: 72 and English Control. $1\frac{3}{4}''$ square $\times \frac{3}{4}''$

Red gold notebook with green gold carved mounts enamelled translucent pink on a *guilloché* ground with red gold pencil set with a Mecca-stone knop.

Signed: H.W. $4'' \times 2\frac{7}{8}''$

Smoky topaz heart-shaped box with yellow gold mount and set with rose diamonds and a cabochon ruby thumb-piece.

Signed: M.Π.   Length: $1\frac{3}{4}''$

Nephrite box in the form of an egg with rose diamond and cabochon ruby clasp and hinge set in red and yellow golds.

No marks.   Length: $1\frac{7}{8}''$

White onyx bell-push with red gold mounts and nephrite frog with rose diamond eyes, on a yellow gold rug enamelled opaque white and translucent red, forming the push.

Signed: M.Π. $2\frac{1}{16}'' \times 1\frac{1}{2}'' \times 1\frac{1}{2}''$

In the Royal Collection at Sandringham

189. Obsidian pen-holder mounted in yellow gold, and set with rose diamonds and a carved gold snake.

Signed: T.R.   Gold mark: crossed anchors.   Length: $6\frac{5}{16}''$

In the Collection of Messrs. Wartski

190. Scent bottle in engraved yellow gold, enamelled translucent green and set with rose diamonds and a cabochon ruby.

Signed: H.W.   Height: $2\frac{1}{8}''$

In the Collection of Peter Otway Smithers, Esq., M.P.

191. Scent bottle in engraved red gold, enamelled translucent sky blue with red and green gold swags, and set with rose diamonds. Designed by Agathon Fabergé.
Signed: A.Ф. and M.П.   Height: $2\frac{1}{4}''$

In the Collection of Messrs. Wartski

192. Set of brushes and chalk-holders, four of each, intended for use in the game of *Préférence*. Engraved red gold, enamelled translucent mustard, with green gold carved mounts and dull red gold monograms made up of the initials M. and L. Designed for the Lanskoi family.   Diameter of brushes: $2\frac{3}{8}''$
Signed: M.П.   Gold mark: crossed anchors.   Length of chalk-holders: $2\frac{1}{4}''$

In the Collection of Messrs. Wartski

193. Translucent mauve enamelled silver strut-clock with carved red and green gold mounts and a half-pearl bezel round the dial.
Signed: H.W. $5'' \times 3\frac{5}{8}''$
    White onyx triple bell-push with red and green carved gold mounts, enamelled translucent peach and opaque white and set with rose diamonds and three Mecca-stone pushes.
No marks.   Length: $4\frac{3}{16}''$
    Red gold miniature frame enamelled opalescent pale blue and decorated with four-colour gold floral mounts set with four cabochon rubies and a pearl bezel. Backed with mother-of-pearl.
Signed: B.A.   Height: $2\frac{5}{8}''$
    Bowenite double bell-push with red and green gold mounts, translucent rose enamel and cabochon garnet and moonstone pushes.
Signed: M.П.   Gold mark: crossed anchors.   Length: $3\frac{7}{16}''$
    Nephrite miniature-frame set with rose diamonds, cabochon rubies and *quatre-couleur* gold floral swags. Backed with mother-of-pearl.
Signed: B.A.   Height: $2\frac{1}{4}''$
    Bowenite letter-opener with a red gold mount enamelled translucent strawberry and opaque white with two flowers in white, yellow and green enamels.
Signed: M.П.   Length: $5\frac{15}{16}''$
    Red gold pencil in the form of a paper-knife enamelled translucent pale blue with two green and red gold carved wreath mounts.
No marks.   Length: $3\frac{3}{4}''$

In the Collection of Her Majesty Queen Elizabeth the Queen Mother

194. Parasol handle in bowenite, with engraved red gold collar enamelled translucent cinnamon, set with two rings of rose diamonds and mounted with a carved green gold snake with a cabochon ruby set in the head.
No marks.   Height: $2\frac{3}{8}''$

In the Collection of Villiers David, Esq.

195. Parasol handle in engraved yellow gold, enamelled translucent pink, strawberry, green and opaque white, with motifs painted in dark grey, with carved green gold mounts, and set with rose diamonds and a brilliant diamond in the top which unscrews to disclose a compartment for powder.

Signed: M.Π.   Gold mark: crossed anchors.   Length: $3\frac{1}{8}''$
In the Walters Art Gallery, Baltimore

196. Rock crystal parasol handle, finished mat and mounted with two engraved gold collars, rimmed with rose diamonds, and enamelled opalescent white with sepia painted festoons.

Signed: M.Π.   Length: $8''$
In the Collection of the Marchioness of Milford Haven

200. Engraved green gold brooch enamelled translucent lavender with a floral spray in red gold with rose diamonds set in silver collets.

Signed: O.P.   Diameter: $1\frac{1}{8}''$

201. Pink topaz and rose diamond cluster brooch set in yellow gold and silver.

No marks.   Length: $\frac{15}{16}''$
Both in the Collection of Mrs. E. Tomlin

202. Bow brooch set with rose diamonds and a pearl centre in platinum.

Signed: A.H.   Length: $2\frac{1}{2}''$
In the Collection of Mrs. Julius Strauss

203. Mauve enamel, brilliant and rose diamond brooch mounted in yellow gold and silver.

Signed: O.P.   Gold mark: St. George and Dragon.   Diameter: $1''$
In the Collection of Bryan Ledbrook, Esq.

204. Fine Siberian amethyst, cut cabochon and set with brilliant diamonds in platinum, as a brooch.

No marks.   Length: $1\frac{5}{8}''$
In the Collection of Madame Tamara Karsavina

205. Green gold Iris brooch enamelled translucent mauve with dull green gold leaf and red gold engraved stalk and a rose diamond framework set in silver.

Signed: К.Ф. $1\frac{3}{8}'' \times 1''$
In the Collection of Mrs. G. H. Kenyon

206. Bracelet of engraved green gold leaves set with brilliant diamonds and five rubies in red gold collets. An early Moscow piece.

Signed: К.Ф.   Gold mark: St. George and Dragon.   Length: $7\frac{1}{2}''$
From the Collection of Miss Woollcombe-Boyce

207. Pinky-blue mecca stone, brilliant and rose diamond pendant in the form of a bell, mounted in yellow gold and silver.

Signed: A.T. Length: $2\frac{3}{8}''$

In the Collection of Bryan Ledbrook, Esq.

208. Imperial gold ring set with brilliant and rose diamonds with the crowned cypher of Alexander III set against an opaque turquoise enamel background. Formerly in the Collection of H. C. Bainbridge, Fabergé's representative in London, and traditionally believed to have been the Tsar's personal ring made by Fabergé. Length: $1\frac{1}{16}''$

In the Collection of Mrs. Robert Allan

209. Red gold locket pendant enamelled translucent pale pink and set in silver with rose diamonds and two whole pearls.

Signed: A ∗ H Length: $1\frac{7}{8}''$

In the Collection of Bryan Ledbrook, Esq.

210. Brooch pendant in engraved and tinted green gold, with the initial A enamelled translucent strawberry against a background of painted blue, green and white enamels and set with sapphires and a pearl drop. Designed for Mrs. Allan Bowe.

No marks. $1\frac{3}{4}'' \times 2\frac{9}{16}''$

In the Collection of Mrs. E. Tomlin, the daughter of Allan Bowe

211. Tie-pin in yellow gold in the form of an Imperial Eagle enamelled opaque royal blue and set with a brilliant diamond, the crown set with rose diamonds.

Signed: A.H. Height of Eagle: $\frac{11}{16}''$

From the Collection of the late Richard Bradshaw, Esq.

212. Gold pectoral cross set with moonstones, rose diamonds and coloured gem stones. Original Fabergé photograph.

In the Collection of Alexander Schaffer, Esq.

215. Group of gem-set Easter Eggs in enamel, gold, platinum and various stones.

Some signed: К.Ф.

In the Collection of Mrs. Emanuel Snowman

217. Yellow gold bangle, a replica by Fabergé of a jewel from the Scythian Treasure. The delicacy of the carving is exceptional.

No marks. $2\frac{7}{8}''$ across

In the Collection of Mrs. Arthur Sutherland

218. Group of gem-set Easter Eggs in enamel, gold and various stones.

Some signed: К.Ф.

In the Collection of Mrs. A. Kenneth Snowman

230. *Left to right:* Dark grey agate toucan with varicoloured agate bill and rose diamond eyes on a silver-gilt perch with a white onyx base. Height: 2″

Rock crystal guillemot, satin finished with cabochon ruby eyes. Height: $2\frac{3}{4}$″

Grey chalcedony baby penguin with rose diamond eyes and red gold feet signed H.W. and stamped 72. Height: $2\frac{1}{8}$″

Dark grey and brown agate hen with rose diamond eyes and red gold feet.

Length: $1\frac{3}{16}$″

Browny-red agate cockerel with rose diamond eyes and red gold feet. Length: $\frac{7}{8}$″

Pale agate hen with cabochon ruby eyes and red gold feet. Length: 1″

Swallow in obsidian and inlaid white chalcedony with rose diamond eyes and red gold feet. Length: $2\frac{5}{8}$″

Snail in parti-coloured cream and brown agate. Length: $\frac{3}{4}$″

In the Royal Collection at Sandringham

231. Striated agate baby penguin with rose diamond eyes and gold chased feet. Signed: M.Π. Height: $1\frac{3}{4}$″

In the Collection of the Viscount Rosslyn

248. Trumpeting elephant in nephrite with rose diamond eyes.

Height: $5\frac{5}{8}$″. Length leg to leg: $3\frac{3}{8}$″

Nephrite elephant with almond-shaped eyes set with brilliant diamonds in yellow gold. Length: $4\frac{1}{4}$″

Nephrite conventionalized sparrow with rose-diamond eyes.

Length, tail to beak: $1\frac{7}{16}$″. Width: $1\frac{3}{4}$″

In the Collection of Her Majesty Queen Elizabeth the Queen Mother

263. Chelsea Pensioner with aventurine quartz face and hands, purpurine coat, black Siberian jasper hat and boots, gun-metal cuffs, translucent brown enamelled stick, enamelled medals, gold buttons and cabochon sapphire eyes.

Height: $4\frac{3}{4}$″

In the Royal Collection at Sandringham

264. Russian peasant girl with pale jasper face and hands, purpurine dress, white stone sleeves and petticoat, stained yellow jasper slippers worn over pale brown jasper boots, sapphire eyes, on a nephrite base. Signed: C. Fabergé. Height: $6\frac{1}{4}$″

Made about 1910 for Lord Revelstoke
In the Collection of R. Thornton Wilson, Esq.
Photograph by courtesy of the Metropolitan Museum of Art, New York.

Appendix D

265. Coachman with aventurine quartz face, reddish jasper beard, lapis lazuli coat, purpurine belt, nephrite skirt, brown jasper boots, mottled jasper gloves, nephrite cap with fur in obsidian, gold riding stick and sapphire eyes.
Signed: C. Fabergé. Height: $5\frac{1}{2}''$

In the Collection of Alexander Schaffer, Esq.

266. Natural stone carving of an officer of the Imperial Horse Guards. The greatcoat in grey jasper with purpurine epaulets, the feet obsidian, the hands and belt white jade, the face aventurine quartz, the moustache, eyebrows and hair, brown jasper; sapphire eyes, and the helmet, sword, buckle, buttons, spurs and fittings in gold.
Signed: H.W. Height: $7\frac{1}{2}''$

In the Collection of Alexander Schaffer, Esq.

269. *Left:* Golden topaz-quartz carving of a pug dog with large cabochon jewelled eyes and a gold collar and pendant. Height: $1\frac{9}{16}''$
   Centre: Russian peasant woman composed of natural hard stones. Height: $2\frac{3}{16}''$
   Right: Chrysoprase carving of a dog. Height: $1\frac{3}{16}''$

In the Collection of the Armoury Museum in the Kremlin, Moscow

273. Obsidian cock with purpurine comb, jasper wattles and pink gold feet.
Signed: H.W. Height: $3\frac{7}{8}''$
   Dark red speckled jasper croaking frog with tourmaline eyes. Height: $2''$
   Obsidian turkey with lapis-lazuli head, purpurine comb and pink gold feet.
Signed: H.W. Height: $3\frac{13}{16}''$
   Bowenite frog with cabochon garnet eyes and rose diamond teeth set in yellow gold, designed as a box with a red gold lid enamelled opaque black and set with rose diamonds.
Signed: M.Π. Length: $2\frac{5}{8}''$
   Snail in chalcedony showing many shades of grey, green, mauve and brown.
Length: $4''$
   Varicoloured agate sturgeon with rose diamond eyes. Length: $2\frac{5}{8}''$
   Speckled brown jasper dab with rose diamond eyes. Length: $2\frac{3}{4}''$
   Group of rabbits in cornelian, bowenite and lapis lazuli with cabochon ruby eyes and another tiny oviform example in the same stone with rose diamond eyes. Lengths: 2 to $\frac{3}{4}''$
   Nephrite chameleon with brilliant diamond eyes set in yellow gold. Length: $2\frac{5}{16}''$

In the Royal Collection at Sandringham

274. Dark sherry agate negro's head with rose diamond eyes set in yellow gold, hollowed out as a bowl with a yellow and red gold rim. When held up to the light the stone imparts an attractive golden glow.
Signed: M.Π.   Gold mark: crossed anchors.
Length: $2\frac{3}{16}''$; Breadth: $1\frac{7}{8}''$; Depth: $1\frac{3}{8}''$

In the Author's Collection

275. Nephrite Freedom Box enriched by festoons and mounts in red and green gold and standing on three ball feet. The fluted cover is surmounted by a dull yellow gold Imperial Eagle polished in parts.

Signed: M.Π.   Gold mark: crossed anchors.   Height: $8\frac{3}{4}''$

In the Wernher Collection, Luton Hoo

276. Full size circular table in palisander wood by Fabergé, decorated in the classical manner with carved silver mounts and nephrite plaques; the top is composed of a single piece of nephrite 24″ across and the lower circular tray is carved from a smaller piece. No further details known.

Wartski photograph.

277. Jadeite *Magot* with gold cuffs and belt enamelled opalescent white, the latter studded with rubies and rose diamonds. Ruby and rose diamond eyes and a carved ruby tongue. The head and hands are so balanced that the slightest movement sets them in motion.

Signed: M.Π.   Height: 12″

In a private collection

278. *Kovsh* carved from an exceptionally large and fine piece of nephrite with yellow and green gold carved mounts enamelled translucent strawberry and set with rose diamonds.

Signed: H.W.   Gold mark: 72.   Overall length: 12″

Engraved yellow gold cigarette-case enamelled a translucent maize colour and set with a diamond crown and push-piece.

Signed: A.H.   Gold mark: crossed anchors. $3\frac{3}{4}'' \times 2\frac{3}{8}'' \times \frac{5}{8}''$

Both these objects from the Collection of the late M. Maurice Sandoz
Photographed together to indicate their relative sizes

280. Terrestrial globe in engraved rock crystal, supported on a dull green silver-gilt stand with polished red gold carved mounts. This early piece illustrates how Fabergé was feeling his way towards the effects he later achieved with golds of differing shades.

Signed: E.K.   Height: $3\frac{7}{8}''$

In the Royal Collection at Sandringham

281. Miniature grand piano in nephrite decorated with carved gold swags and bearing the name C. Fabergé painted on opalescent white enamel.

Marks not known.   Approximate height: $1\frac{1}{2}''$

Original Fabergé photograph

284. Silver replica of the Tsarevitch's paddle-steamer. The enamelled inscription above the wheel translated, reads: 'For the Heir Tsarevitch Alexis Nicolaivitch from the Volga Shipbuilders'. The double-headed eagle and the year 1913 in relief appear within this inscription, and the enamelled flags display the crowned Imperial initials.

Appendix D

The steamer, which is gold-mounted, contains a musical mechanism which plays 'God save the Tsar' and 'Sailing down the Volga'.

The last seven windows below aft are part of a small drawer containing dry batteries which light tiny bulbs throughout the ship when a button is pressed.

Signed: H.W.   Length: 28″; Width: $4\frac{5}{8}$″

Height from bottom of hull to top of funnel: $4\frac{1}{2}$″

In the Collection of the Hammer Galleries

285. Spray of cornflowers in enamel, diamonds and gold, with ears of corn in gold, in a rock crystal vase.   Height: $7\frac{15}{16}$″

Rock crystal hand seal with dull yellow gold mount set with rose diamonds and a cabochon ruby.

Signed: E.K.   Gold mark: crossed anchors.   Length: $2\frac{5}{8}$″

Miniature Louis XV roll-top desk in yellow and red golds enamelled translucent pale mauve and opalescent white; the interior is lined with engraved mother-of-pearl and divided into pigeon holes. A small gold key locks this delightful piece.

Signed: ФАБЕРЖЕ   Height: $4\frac{3}{8}$″

In the Collection of Her Majesty Queen Elizabeth the Queen Mother

301. Small enamelled pansy with diamond centre, nephrite leaves in a rock crystal pot.   Height: $4\frac{1}{4}$″

Pink and white enamelled wild rose with red gold stamens and set with a brilliant diamond, with a green gold stalk and nephrite leaves in a rock crystal pot.   Height: $5\frac{3}{4}$″

Five field daisies enamelled opaque white with bronze-foiled rose diamond centres on green gold stalks, nephrite leaves in a silver flower-pot enamelled opaque terra cotta.

Signed: H.W.   Height: $3\frac{1}{16}$″

In the Royal Collection at Sandringham

302. Flowering cranberry with cornelian and chalcedony berries and nephrite leaves; red gold stalk in a rock crystal jar.   Height: $4\frac{5}{8}$″

Pansy enamelled opaque violet with brilliant diamond centre, nephrite leaves, green gold stalk in a rock crystal pot.   Height: 6″

Small raspberry plant in rhodonite with nephrite leaves and red gold stalk, in a rock crystal jar.   Height: $3\frac{9}{16}$″

In the Royal Collection at Sandringham

303. Two chrysanthemum plants thinly enamelled pale yellow and pink on green gold with nephrite leaves, in a rock crystal vase.

Signed: H.W.   Height: $9\frac{7}{8}$″

Lilies of the valley in pearls and rose diamonds on green gold stalk with nephrite leaves in a rock crystal jar.   Height: $5\frac{7}{16}$″

Quartzite mock-orange with olivine centres on a red gold stalk with nephrite leaves in a rock crystal jar.   Height: $5\frac{9}{16}''$

Yellow gold rose and bud enamelled opaque pink with green translucent enamelled leaves and rose diamond dew-drops, in a rock crystal vase.   Height: $3\frac{7}{16}''$

In the Royal Collection at Sandringham

309. An old French Ivory Easter Egg containing a smaller gold egg, a hen enamelled gold with brown spots and set with diamond eyes, a crown set with 40 diamonds and six pearls, based on a cornelian intaglio showing an eagle flying over a town and the inscription 'Il Defend'.

310. Here the gold egg is seen with one end unscrewed showing a naturalistically enamelled yolk and white; this is actually a lid which opens on a hinge to reveal the hen within. When the smaller cap at the other end of this egg is unscrewed, a small sponge is to be found. The diamond ring seen here forms two of the crown's six arches, and the principal stone covers a crowned monogram consisting of two 'C's.

Length of ivory egg: $2\frac{1}{2}''$
Length of gold egg: $2''$

In the Royal Collection at Rosenborg, Copenhagen
By kind permission of His Majesty the King of Denmark

Reference to another similar egg had been unearthed in a sale catalogue of Augusta Sibylla, Duchess of Baden-Baden, dated 8th May 1775, by Francis Watson of the Wallace Collection; it is described as follows:

'Un œuf d'or d'un artifice singulier; il contient un jaune d'œuf émaillé d'où l'on peut faire sortir une poulette renfermant dans sa poitrine une couronne; au fond de la couronne se voit le portrait du feu le sérénissime margrave époux de la sérénissime Augusta Sibylla.' 350 fl.

Bibliography

Album de l'Exposition rétrospective d'objets d'art de 1904, à St. Petersbourg. Adrien Prachoff. St. Petersburg. 1907.

Inventaire de l'Argenterie. Edition du Ministère de la Maison de sa Majesté l'Empereur. Baron A. E. Foelkersam. St. Petersburg. 1907.

Staruie Ghodie (Times Past, a magazine of the arts). Petrograd. March. 1915.

Stolitza Y Usadba (Town and Country), 'The Journal of Elegant Living'. Petrograd. 1st April, 1916.

Les Joyaux du Trésor de Russie. Commissariat National des Finances. Moscow. 1924–1926.

Das Grüne Gewölbe zu Dresden. Jean Louis Sponsel. Leipzig. 1925–1932.

The Life and Tragedy of Alexandra Feodorovna, Empress of Russia. Baroness Sophie Buxhoeveden. Longmans, Green and Co. 1928.

Gold Alloys. George E. Gee. Crosby Lockwood and Son. 1929.

Peter Carl Fabergé, His Life and Work. Henry Charles Bainbridge. B. T. Batsford Ltd. 1949.

Les Automates. Alfred Chapuis and Edmond Droz. Éditions du Griffon. Neuchatel. 1949.

A History of Russia. Sir Bernard Pares, K.B.E. New and Revised Edition. Jonathan Cape. 1949.

St. Petersburg Jewellers, Goldsmiths and Silversmiths 1714–1870. L. Bäcksbacka. Konstsalongens Förlag, Helsinki. 1952.

Index

Note: Animals, birds, reptiles etc. are all entered under 'Animals' and not named separately unless for a particular point of interest.

169

Index

Bonbonnières, 60, 145, 146, 152, 154, 155, Pls. 88, 89, 91, 95, 122, 143, Col. Pls. XVI, XX, XXI, LVII.

Bottle, topaz lyre-shaped, 155, Pl. 128; *see* Scent-bottles

Boucher-painted eggshells, 74

Boutiron, Madame, 136

Bowe, Allan, 127, 128, 134, 135, Pls. 16, 17, 18; Mrs. Allan, 161

Bowe, Arthur, 127, 128, 134

Bowe, Charles, 127, Pl. 31

Bowen, G. T., 58

Bowenite, 57, 58; some uses of: in barometer, Pl. 152; in bell-pushes, 156–9, Pls. 146, 171, 172, 177, 188, 193; box, 144, Col. Pl. XIII; cup, with rouble inset, 148, Col. Pl. XXX; elephants, frogs and other animals, 149, 163, Pl. 273, Col. Pl. XXXVII; frame, 154, Pl. 91; garniture de bureau, Pl. 187; letter-opener, 159, Pl. 193; parasol handle, 159, Pl. 194; rabbits, 163, Pls. 104, 105, 273; vase for miniature tree, Pl. 292

Bowls: carved nephrite, Pl. 76; stone, generally, 70; Chinese, on Fabergé stands, Pls. 71, 72; coin set in, 53

Boxes: various descriptions, 77, 144–8, 154, 155, 158, 164; silk lid-lining, Pl. 406; box-making firms, *see* Käki, Kämärä; favoured materials for, 60, 61; gold-mounted stone, 70; agate, Pl. 160; to Grand Duke Alexander's design, Col. Pl. XVI; aventurine, Col. Pl. XII; bowenite, Col. Pl. XIII; carved topaz, Pls. 67, 70, 82, 83; Chinese jade, converted into powder box, Pl. 66; cigar, cigarette, *see* Cigar boxes, Cigarette boxes, cornelian pumpkin-shaped, Pl. 128; Coronation, Col. Pl. I; with dancing figures (articulated), Col. Pl. LVII; enamel, *see* 'various descriptions', above, and for types, Pls. 47, 118, Col. Pls. IV, VII, IX, XII, XIII, XIV, XXX; *see also* Bonbonnières, Cigar and Cigarette boxes; in French classic style, Pl.

47; green presentation, Col. Pl. V; groups of, Col. Pls. XIII, XX; Imperial presentation, Col. Pl. XX; with movable puppets (Opera box), Col. Pls. LX–LXI; nephrite, Pls. 128, 188; nephrite freedom, Pl. 275; nephrite with Nicholas II miniature, Pl. 130; *see also* Cigar boxes; 'Opera box', Col. Pls. LX–LXI; pink presentation, Col. Pl. II; powder, pink enamelled, Col. Pl. VII; powder, circular enamelled, Col. Pl. XIV; compact, *see* 'Chinese jade' above; presentation table, with portraits, Pl. 137; purpurine, Pl. 188; rhodonite, Col. Pl. XIII; rock crystal, Pls. 113, 114, 188, Col. Pl. XIII; rock crystal and gold, Pl. 119; rock crystal semi-circular, Col. Pl. XXIX; shell, Pls. 69, 70, 160; silver and enamel, for stamps, Pl. 118; snuff, *see* Snuff-boxes; Sweetmeat, *see* Bonbonnières; turquoise, Pls. 80, 81; various, Col. Pl. XXX; white porcelain, Pl. 95; yellow enamel with Imperial cypher, Col. Pl. IV; Youssoupoff, Col. Pl. VIII; box-lid animal heads, Pls. 261, 262

Bracelet, 160, Pl. 206

Brass *Kovshi*, 53

Bratini, 52

Britzin firm, 129

Brockmann (workshop manager), 127

Brooches, 160, Col. Pl. XXXI; amethyst, Pls. 204, 221; diamond, enamel gold, 117, Pl. 200; diamond rose, Imperial treasure, Pl. 56; gold, 149, Col. Pl. XXXI; gold, translucent lavender enamel, Pl. 200; gold and mauve enamel, Pl. 203; Iris, green gold and diamond, Pl. 205; moss agate, 149, Col. Pl. XXXI; pearl and platinum bow, Pl. 202; topaz (pink), Pl. 201; brooch pendant, 161, Pl. 210

Brushes, chalk-holders (Préférence game), 159, Pl. 192

Buckle, enamel and silver, Pls. 223, 225

Index

Opaque and translucent enamelling, 54, 73

Opera box, with movable puppets, Col. Pls. LX, LXI

Opera glasses, Pl. 158

Orletz, *see* Rhodonite

Ovtchinnikov firm, 119, 129

Oxidized silver, 52

Paddle-steamer, silver replica, 164–5, Pl. 284

Paget, Lady, arranges 1904 London Fabergé exhibition, 135

Paillons (under enamel surface), 54

Palisander wood, 59; bell-push, Pl. 107; cigarette-case, Pls. 110–112; with nephrite for full-size table, 164, Pl. 276

Palladium, added to gold, 51

Pamiat Azova cruiser (Azova Egg), 82, 134

Panagias, enamelled, 65

Pan-Russian Exhibition of 1882, 35

Panina, Vara (gipsy model), 151, Col. Pl. XLVI

Pansy, with five Imperial children, Pl. 298; described, 73

Paper-knives, 62

Parasol handles, 63; silver-gilt for, 53; bowenite, 159, Pl. 194; rock crystal, 160, Pl. 196; yellow gold, 160, Pl. 195

Paris 1900 International Exhibition, 35–6

Parrot in cage (opal), Col. Pl. XLIV

Paul I, Tsar, 87

Pazaurek, Professor, 45

Peacock clock, James Cox's, 75, Pls. 311, 312

Pearls, *see notably* Pls. 202 (brooch); 209 (locket); 210 (with sapphires, pendant); 57 (necklace); *see* captions generally for pearls, half-pearls

Pectoral cross, gold, moonstones, etc., 161, Pl. 212

Peking, mechanical clocks for (Cox), 75

Pencils, pens, pen-holders, pen-trays, 62, 145, 153, 159, Pls. 60, 189, 193

Pendants, Pls. 210, 214

Pendin, Peter Hiskias, 32–3, 133

Perchin, Michael, 35, 50, 56, 79, 117, 122, 129, 133, 134; for Eggs designed by, *see* Marks: Perchin

Pestou, Robert, 125

Peter the Great statue, replica, 145, Col. Pl. XVI

'Petit feu', 54

Petouchov, discoverer of purpurine manufacture, 59

Petrov, Alexander and Nicholas (workmasters), 125

Photograph frames, 62–3; *see also* Frames, Picture frame

Picardy, 31, 48

Picture frame, opalescent white enamelled, 156, Pl. 150

Pigott, George (workshop manager), 127, Pl. 32

Pihl, Alma (designer), 120, Pl. 39

Pihl, Knut Oskar (workshop manager), 126, 129, 134

Pihl, Oskar Woldemar (workmaster), 126

Pihl, Oskar (junior), 122

Pill-tubes, 157, Pl. 181

Pinks, R. A. (designer), 127

Pitti Palace 'cartoon' stone figures, 70

Platinum, working of, 52

Plehve Ministry, 132

Plique à jour enamelling, 55

Pocock, Alfred (modeller), 127, Pl. 28

Poklewski-Koziell, S. and A., 37

Poliarnaya Svesda (yacht), 85; *see* Eggs: Danish Palaces

Polishing of enamel, 54, 56

Powder-boxes, enamelled, Col. Pls. VII, XIV; compact, *see* Box; Chinese jade

Prachov (miniature and ikon painter), 107, 121

Purpurine, 26, 59, 150, 158, Pl. 188, Col. Pls. XXXVIII, XLII

Quartz, 57, 58; *see* Stones; bonbonnières, Pl. 143

Queen Victoria caricature, Pl. 260

Index